Reinhold Rost

Essays Analytical Critical, and Philological on Subjects Connected with Sanskrit Literature by the Late H. H. Wilson

Reinhold Rost

Essays Analytical Critical, and Philological on Subjects Connected with Sanskrit Literature by the Late H. H. Wilson

ISBN/EAN: 9783741180736

Manufactured in Europe, USA, Canada, Australia, Japa

Cover: Foto ©Andreas Hilbeck / pixelio.de

Manufactured and distributed by brebook publishing software (www.brebook.com)

Reinhold Rost

Essays Analytical Critical, and Philological on Subjects Connected with Sanskrit Literature by the Late H. H. Wilson

WORKS

BY

THE LATE

HORACE HAYMAN WILSON,
M.A., F.R.S.,

MEMBER OF THE ROYAL ASIATIC SOCIETY, OF THE ASIATIC SOCIETIES OF
CALCUTTA AND PARIS, AND OF THE ORIENTAL SOCIETY OF GERMANY;
FOREIGN MEMBER OF THE NATIONAL INSTITUTE OF FRANCE;
MEMBER OF THE IMPERIAL ACADEMIES OF ST. PETERSBURGH AND VIENNA,
AND OF THE ROYAL ACADEMIES OF MUNICH AND BERLIN;
PH. D. BRESLAU; M. D. MARBURG, ETC.;
AND BODEN PROFESSOR OF SANSKRIT IN THE UNIVERSITY OF OXFORD.

VOL. IV.

LONDON:
TRÜBNER & CO., 60, PATERNOSTER ROW.
1864.

ESSAYS

ANALYTICAL, CRITICAL AND PHILOLOGICAL

ON SUBJECTS CONNECTED WITH

SANSKRIT LITERATURE.

BY THE LATE

H. H. WILSON, M.A., F.R.S.,

BODEN PROFESSOR OF SANSKRIT IN THE UNIVERSITY OF OXFORD,
ETC., ETC.

COLLECTED AND EDITED BY

DR. REINHOLD ROST.

IN THREE VOLUMES.

VOL. II.

LONDON:
TRÜBNER & CO., 60, PATERNOSTER ROW.
1864.

CONTENTS OF VOL. II.

		Page
	Table of Contents	v–vi
VI.	*Analytical Account of the Panchatantra*	1– 80
	Introductory Remarks	1
	Book I	5
	Book II	28
	Book III	33
	Book IV	44
	Book V	46
VII.	*Hindu Fiction*	81–159
	Review of L. Deslongchamps' Essai sur les Fables Indiennes	81
	Review of Prof. H. Brockhaus' edition of the Kathásaritságara, Book I–V	109
	Analysis of Book VI–XVIII	128
VIII.	*Extracts from the Daśakumáracharita*	160–289
	Introductory chapters	160
	Chapter I, History of Rájaváhana . . .	164
	— II, — — Apaháravarmá . .	189
	— III, — — Upaháravarmá . .	210
	— IV, — — Arthapála	221
	— V, — — Pramati	233
	— VI, History of Mitragupta	242
	Story of Dhúmini	248

CONTENTS.

	Page
Story of Gomini	250
— — Nimbavati	254
— — Nitambavati	256
Chapter VII, History of Mantragupta	266
— VIII, History of Visruta	270
IX. On the Art of War as known to the Hindus	290—309
X. Translation of the Meghaduta	310—400

VI.

ANALYTICAL ACCOUNT

OF THE

PANCHA TANTRA,

ILLUSTRATED WITH OCCASIONAL TRANSLATIONS.

Read June 5, 1824.
From the Transactions of the R. Asiatic Society, Vol. I, No. 3, (1825) p. 155—201.

"As the active world is inferior to the rational soul, so Fiction gives to mankind what History denies, and in some measure satisfies the mind with shadows, when it cannot enjoy the substance."—LORD BACON.

WHAT the profound observer, quoted above, pronounced generally of fiction, is peculiarly pertinent, when applied to the Hindus. The history of their progress, in the arts of civilized life, is so clouded with mythology, and overcast by time, that our efforts to penetrate the obscurity have been hitherto of little avail. As the mind, therefore, has little substantial gratification to expect from this branch of intellectual enjoyment, it may be permitted to indulge in the shadows, that are abundantly presented, and dwell with more interest, than the subject would otherwise excite, on the copious materials afforded by the mass of Hindu fable within its reach.

The elucidation, which such an inquiry promises to afford of the past manners of the Hindus, before they were metamorphosed, and degraded by the influence of foreign subjugation, constitutes an advantage of more than imaginary value. We see what they were more distinctly than through the medium of any general description; and can trust to their own pictures of themselves more confidently than to any crude and imperfect exhibitions, delineated from present experience, or circumscribed research. In this point of view, therefore, Hindu fable becomes a valuable accession to real knowledge, and serviceably supplies that want of sober history, which all Oriental inquirers have such perpetual occasion to lament.

It is not only with respect to themselves, however, that the fictions of the Hindus are calculated to add to our stock of knowledge: and the influence, which they have exercised on the state of manners in Europe, will only be duly appreciated, when we shall be better acquainted with the extent of the obligations we owe them. By whatever channel they may have been conveyed to the West, the Oriental origin of most of the tales, which first roused the inventive faculties of our ancestors, is universally admitted; but the advocates of the Gothic or Arabic origin of romance agree in referring its birth-place to the East.

It is now too late to inquire, whether we are to

consider Persia as the birth-place of fictitious narrative: for, if such narrative was cultivated there, it must have been clad in the Pehlevi language; and both body and dress are irrecoverably lost. We must, therefore, be content to admit the claims of the Hindus, amongst whom we may trace the original of much that has interested, and amused, our forefathers and ourselves.

The oldest collection of fables and tales, of the class here intended, is the work that passes by the title of the Fables of Bidpai, or Pilpay. The history of this work is too well known to require any elucidation. Mr. Wilkins, and Sir William Jones, brought to light its original, from amongst the hidden stores of Sanskrit literature; and Mr. Colebrooke gave the text itself of the Hitopadeśa to the public. The learning and industry of the Baron de Sacy have finally traced the work through all its stages; and there are few subjects of investigation, the history of which has been more successfully ascertained than the Bibliographical adventures of the solutary instructions of *Vishńuśarmá*, or *Fables of Pilpay*.

Although the stories of the Hitopadeśa are undoubtedly identical with most of those, which are found in all the forms of Pilpay's fables, yet it has been clearly shown by Mr. Colebrooke, that it is not the source from which its successors have been directly derived. It is, in fact, itself but a scion of the same parent stock, and in common with the rest, originates, as it indeed admits, from an older collection, the *Pancha Tantra*. The text of this work is not very rare in India, and it were therefore to have been wished, that it had been selected for translation, in preference to the Hitopadeśa; but the opportunity has passed. The identity of the two works, for the greater part, renders the translation of both a work of supererogation: and, fully as the topic has been developed, it is likely that a main defect will long continue to mutilate it, at the very outset. The deficiency has, in some measure, been supplied by the sketch, given by Mr. Colebrooke, of the contents of the Pancha Tantra; but, as his chief object was only to substantiate the greater affinity between it and the Kalila wa Damna, than between the Arabic work and the Hitopadeśa, he has not prosecuted its details farther than was sufficient to effect his purpose. In the want, therefore, of a full analysis, and in the little likelihood that exists, of a translation of the entire work being now published, it has been presumed that a more minute account of the Pancha Tantra, than has yet been given to the world, will not be an unacceptable communication to the Royal Asiatic Society of London.

In offering a detail of the contents of the Pancha Tantra, it was of course desirable to collate them with those of the Hitopadeśa, and Kalila wa Damna, which has been accordingly effected; and to relieve the dryness of analytical detail, as well as to convey an idea of the merits of the composition, it has been thought advisable to introduce translations of a number of the stories. Some affinities have also been pointed out between the narratives of the Pancha Tantra, and those met with in popular works in Europe; but the want of access to books has necessarily limited this part of the inquiry. Some illustrations of national or literary peculiarities have also been occasionally, but sparingly, added; lest the paper should be rendered too voluminous, and under the impression that many members of the Society are better able to appreciate the extent to which such illustrations may be needed, and better qualified to supply them.

The *Pancha Tantra* is so called from its being divided into five *Tantras*, or sections, and is referred to under that name in the Hitopadeśa. It is better known, however, in common speech, by the denomination of *Panchopákhyána*, which may be rendered the "Five (collections of) Stories:" and under this appellation the work may be met with in most parts of India.

The ensuing analysis is founded upon an examination of three copies of the work; one of which was procured in Calcutta, the others in Benares. These copies agree in all essential points, although they present, abundantly, the variations to be expected in compilations of such a character; where stanzas, and even stories, are often omitted or inserted at the pleasure of the transcriber.

The invocation, with which, like all Hindu works, the Pancha Tantra commences, differs very importantly from that of the Hitopadeśa. In the latter work, it is addressed to Śiva, in the former to Saraswatí. One manuscript, indeed, calls upon all the Hindu Pantheon, on Brahmá, Rudra, Kumára, Hari, Indra,

Yama, &c. &c., the elements, the planets, the Munis, Rishis, and all the other objects of Hindu reverence, to be propitious to the reader; but this is a solitary reading, and a probable interpolation. The homage to Saraswati is followed by a tribute of respect to the authors of ethical compositions, of whom are named Manu, Váchaspati, Uśanas (Śukra), Paráśara, Vyása, and Chánakya.[1] It is then stated, that Vishńu Śarmá, having extracted the essence of all the most celebrated works of this class, composed the *Níti*[2] *Śástra*, in five Tantras, or chapters. We are then introduced to the

---

[1] Authors of very different character. The first is the Legislator, whose code has been rendered into English by Sir William Jones. The works of Váchaspati, the teacher of the Gods, and of Śukra, the preceptor of the (daityas) Titans, have not, it is believed, been found on earth.[*] Paráśara, the father of Vyása, is the reputed author of an institute of laws, and the chief interlocutor of the Vishńu-Puráńa. To Chánakya is ascribed a treatise on (Níti) regal polity, which is cited by authors of some antiquity, as Dańdí, in the Daśa Kumára [p. 183.] Chánakya was the minister of Chandragupta, and the chief agent in his elevation to the throne of Magadha. [Lassen, Ind. Alt., II, 199 ff.]

[2] Sir Wm. Jones translated the term Níti by Ethics, and he has been followed by all Sanskrit scholars, in the interpretation. This is not, however, the precise import of the term. As applied to a class of writings, or division of science, it would be, more correctly, polity, the art of regal administration, both in peace and war, including the moral, as well as political, obligations of a sovereign. [Benfey, Pantschatantra. Leipzig: 1859. I, p. XV.]

[*] Váchaspati is the same with Vrihaspati, as Uśanas is identified with Śukra. Institutes of law, ascribed to Vrihaspati and to Uśanas, are extant.—H.T.C.

frame work of the whole, the education of the King's sons by Vishńu-Śarmá; on which occasion the apologues were composed. This is introduced in the Hitopadeśa, but with some variations; and, as it affords an example of the concurrences and disagreements of the two collections, I shall give it at length from the Pancha Tantra.

"There is a city in the Southern country, named Mahilāropyam, the king of which, learned, munificent, distinguished among princes and scholars, was named Amara Śakti. He had three sons, youths of no capacity, nor diligence: Vasu Śakti, Bhadra Śakti[1], and Ananta Śakti. Observing them averse from study, the king called his counsellors, and said to them, "you are aware that my sons are little inclined to application, and incapable of reflection. When I contemplate them, my kingdom is full of thorns, and yields me no pleasure. It is said by the wise, 'Better is a son unborn; better is a dead son, than one who is a fool. The first may cause affliction for a little while, but a fool, as long as life endures.' Again 'of what use is a cow who has no milk with her calf; of what use is a son who has neither knowledge, nor virtue? Better it is, that a wife be barren, that she bear daughters or dead children, and that the family become extinct, than that a son, endowed with your form, wealth, and family-credit, should want understanding.' If, therefore, by any means, their minds can be roused, do you

---

[1] In some copies, Ugra-śakti.—H.T.C[olebrooke].

declare it." On this, a counsellor replied, "Prince, the study of grammar alone is the work of twelve years, how then is a knowledge of Dharma, Artha, Káma, and Moksha[1], to be speedily conveyed?" Another counsellor, named Sumati, observed, "Prince, the powers of man are limited by his transitory existence; but to acquire a knowledge of language alone, demands much time. It is better that we think of some means of communicating the substance of each science, in a compendious form; as it is said, 'The Śabda Śástra (Philology) is a boundless ocean: life is short, and the difficulties are many; the essence, therefore, is to be taken, as the swan extracts the milk from the water.'[2] There is a Brahman, named Vishńu Śarmá, celebrated for his perfect acquisition of the sciences. To him entrust your sons, and he will render them well informed." On hearing this, the king sent for Vishńu Śarmá, and addressed him, "Venerable Brahman, confer a favour upon me, by instructing these princes in polite literature, and rendering them superior to the youths, their companions; in recompense of which, I promise you lands of large extent." Vishńu Śarmá

---

[1] The four objects or occupations of human life: Duty, Wealth, Desire, and Final Liberation.

[2] This is a popular notion among the Hindus, originating, probably, in the colour of the bird. (Or rather, because the bird seems, as the Hindus apprehend, to extract his food, by suction, from solution in water; wherefore a bird of this genus is considered to be an emblem of discrimination, as being capable of separating milk from water.—H.T.C.)

replied, "Hear, O king, my words. I am not a retailer of knowledge for lands and wealth; but if I do not instruct your sons in the Níti Sástra, I will forego my own name. There is no need to say more. I do not utter this vaunt through any desire of wealth; for wealth is useless to any one whose passions are mortified, and subdued: I wish but to gratify you, and to do the will of Saraswatí. Let it be written, therefore, that if, in six months from this day, I do not make the princes more proficient than many people, in various branches of knowledge, it shall not be allowed to me, a Brahman, to point out the way of God." The king, highly gratified by this assurance, delivered his sons to him, and retired; and Vishńu Śarmá, taking the princes with him, repaired to his own house; where, for their instruction, he composed these five chapters: Mitra bheda, dissension of friends; Mitra prápti, acquisition of friends; Kákolúkíya, inveterate enmity; Labdha praśamana, loss of advantage; Aparíkshita káritwa, inconsiderateness. Reading these, the princes were, in six months, highly accomplished; and the five Tantras became famous throughout the world. Whosoever reads this work, acquires the whole Niti Sástra, and will never be overthrown by Indra himself."

The commencement of the Pancha Tantra, which is thus given, differs materially, in some respects, from the Hitopadeśa, of which the Mitralábha, or acquisition of friends, constitutes the first, and the Mitra bheda, or dissension of friends, the second book. The arrangement of the Pancha Tantra is, no doubt, the original, as the same is observed in the Kalila wa Damna of 'Abdallah Mokaffah, exclusive of the avowedly additional prolegomena. It may here also be observed, that in the large collection of stories, made by Somadeva in the eleventh century, and usually known as the *Vrihat Kathá*, we have a chapter appropriated to the same stories, that occur in this section of the Pancha Tantra, following nearly the same order. I shall, therefore, refer occasionally to this series also in my remarks; and shall here state, that it begins in the same manner as the Pancha Tantra, and its Arabic translation, with the journey of the merchant, and his abandonment of his ox, Sanjívaka, in the forests, on the borders of the Yamuná.

Many varieties of minor importance occur in this part of the story, not only as related in the Hitopadeśa, but as told in different copies of the Pancha Tantra. They are, however, of no consequence. It is only worth while to observe, that most copies of the latter agree in naming Mahiláropya as not only the residence of Amara Sakti, but as the city whence the merchant departs. One manuscript has a laboured description of the splendour and strength of the town. Now, in general, in both the Pancha Tantra and the Hitopadeśa, the places named are real[1]; and there seems every

---

[1] So Agnolo Firenzuola, the Florentine translator, has laid the scenes of the several narratives in various real localities, transferred to Italy.

reason, therefore, to conclude, that Mahiláropya was a city, in the south of India, of some celebrity, when these stories were first composed. We need not be much at a loss for its identification, as the name approaches sufficiently to Mahilapur, Meliapur, or St. Thomé; where our own records indicate a city of some consequence, in the beginning of the Christian era, as the scene of the labours and martyrdom of St. Thomas, occurrences very far from invalidated by any arguments, yet adduced against the truth of the tradition. The Hitopadeśa changes the residence of the King to Páṭaliputra, on the Ganges; and although it leaves the merchant's residence in the south, it alters the name to Suvarńavatí, that is, the "Golden." Hamilton calls St. Thomé, Mailapúr, "The City of the Peacock," and the import of Mayil, in the Tamul language, is a Peacock, whilst púr is the ordinary Sanskrit addition, signifying town. There is no good authority, however, for supposing this to be the original designation of Meliapúr, and it may be only a vernacular modification of the name, whilst Mahiláropya furnishes a much nearer approximation to the Maliarpha of Ptolemy, which has been hitherto supposed the same with Meliapúr, or St. Thomé.*

---

* [Lassen, Ind. Alt., III. 204, places Maliarpha much further north, near Masolipattana. It has also been shewn by Babington (Lassen, l. l., I, 165) that the original name of Meliapúr was Mahámalayapora, with which it would be more hazardous to identify Mahiláropya than with Maliarpha.—According to the popular etymology, Meliapúr more probably means Jasmine-town

The name of the ox that falls, and is left behind, is in all the books, Sanjívaka, whence the Arabic Shanzebeh; those of the jackals, Karataka and Damanaka, altered to Kalíla and Damna. The lion is uniformly termed in the Sanskrit Pingalaka; the Arabic leaves him unnamed.

The first story, in all the Hindu books, is "the monkey and the timber." It is the second in the Arabic. The story of "the man, who could not avoid his destiny," related by the merchant's servant, is an addition; being, however, grafted upon a verse, in the original, which inculcates the irresistible force of fate. "What fate protects, is safe, though it be unwatched; and that which is guarded with the greatest precaution if destiny defend it not, will surely be destroyed. One who is left without a guardian in a forest shall escape with life; whilst another perishes in the house, and in spite of every care."*

There is a very great variety in the different manuscripts, in the passages that follow. The Hitopadeśa has also the story of "the Dog and the Ass," which is not found in the Pancha Tantra, Kalíla wa Damna, or Vrihat Kathá: the next story, in all these three, being "the Fox and Drum," which the Hitopadeśa omits.

The Hitopadeśa has again the story of "the Cat and

(mayiléi) than peacock-town (mayil). See Graul, Reise in Ostindien. Leipzig: 1856. Vol. III, p. 355 and Winslow's Tamil Dictionary s. v. mayilei.]

* [Panchatantra I, p. 24. Benfey, l. l., I, § 28.]

the Lion," in which it differs from all the rest; whilst the Pancha Tantra has the story of "Dantila, a merchant of Varddhamána," which does not occur in the Arabic.** The merchant incurs the displeasure of the sweeper of the palace, who, in revenge, mutters insinuations against his character, for the king to overhear. When questioned further, he pretends not to know what he has uttered, and to have talked in his sleep: the insinuations, however, produce their effect. When the merchant has discovered the cause of his disgrace, and reconciled the menial Gorambha, the latter takes an opportunity of venting an insinuation against the king himself, so wholly absurd, that the prince is convinced, his servant prattles unmeaningly, and he acknowledges the merchant's innocence. The object of this story is to shew, that the meanest individuals, about the person of a prince, are not to be offended with impunity.

The story of "the goblin Ghantákarna," is peculiar to the Hitopadeśa. That of "Kandarpaketu," agrees in the general course, although not in the first part, with the adventures of "Deva Śarmá," in the Pancha Tantra, which latter is precisely followed in the story of the Násik, or religious man, in the Kalíla wa Damna; and Tahíd, in the Anvári Soheilí. One of the incidents of this story has attracted extraordinary admiration, if we may judge by the endlessly varied copies, and

---

** (Benfey, I. I., § 40—41. H. Kurz ad "Esopus, von B. Waldis" Leipzig: 1862, B. I. fab. 69.)

modifications of it, which have appeared in the East, and in the West: the loss of her nose by the confidante and its supposed recovery by the intriguante, for whom she had been substituted, affording a miraculous proof of the wife's innocence, imposing upon her husband, has been retold in a vast number of ways. It is repeated, with different degrees of modification, in the "Roman and Turkish Tales," in the "Decameron" of Boccacio [VII, 8.], the "Novelle" of Malespini [140.], the "Cent nouvelles Nouvelles,"[38.], the "Cheveux Coupés," a fabliau, by Guérin,* in the "Contes" of La Fontaine [I, 31.], in the "Women pleased," of Beaumont and Fletcher [Act III, Sc. 4.], and in "The Guardian" of Massinger.** The story itself, as told in the Hitopadeśa, has been versified by Hoppner; and, as narrated in the Anvári Soheili, it has been rendered into English verse, by Atkinson.***

The next story, in the Pancha Tantra, is omitted in all the works, derived from this original. It is, however, a well known story, being the same as Malek and Shírín in the Persian Tales, and the Labourer and Flying Car in the additional stories from the Arabian Nights.† It is also narrated, with some variation, in the Vrihat Kathá [Tar. 12]. The Muhammedan con-

---

* [ap. Legrand d'Aussy, Fabliaux. Paris: 1829, Vol. II, p. 340.]
** [ed. of 1813, Vol. IV, p. 185.]
*** [Benfey, l. l., I. p. 110–47. F. H. von der Hagen, Gesammtabenteuer. Vol. II, p. XLVIII ff.]
† [transl. by J. Scott. 1800, p. 1 ff.]

trivance of a box, and the personification of Muhammed, are rather clumsy substitutes for the fiction of the original, in which the adventurer, in love with a princess, personates Vishńu, and rides on a wooden representation of Garuda guided by a pin, and moving by magic, the prototype of the flying steed of Magellan; " the wondrous horse of brass, on which the Tartar king did ride," and other self-moving machines of celebrity, in oriental and chivalric romance.*

The story of "the Gopi and her two lovers" is here peculiar to the Hitopadeśa; but it is familiar to European story-telling. It is the third of the three fabliaux, De la Mauvaise Femme,** and occurs in Le Roman des Sept Sages,*** and the Novelle of Bandello [II, 11], Boccacio [VII, 6], Sansovino [III, 10], and other similar collections.

The next story of "The Two Crows," is common to all the collections; as is that, interwoven with it, of "The Crane, or Swan, killed by the Crab."† This portion of the original has been made great use of by the author of the Buhár Dánish, who has compiled his story of "The Mouse and Prince of Ghilán" almost wholly of extracts from the Pancha Tantra. This portion of the latter work contains a quotation of some

---

* [Benfey, l.l., I, p. 159–63. Gesammtabenteuer, I, p. CXXXV ff.]
** [Legrand d'Aussy, IV, p. 189–91.]
*** [ed. Keller, p. CL. Cf. Benfey, l. l., I, p. 163—97.]
† [Benfey, l. l., I, p. 167—79. B. Waldis' Esopus II, 26, and note.]

interest in the literary history of the Hindus. It is a passage from the astronomical writings of Varáhamihira, and occurs, without variation, in the two best manuscripts of the original. This citation is justly considered, by Mr. Colebrooke, as a proof of the astronomer's priority to the composition of the Pancha Tantra, and a satisfactory corroboration of other arguments, favourable to his existence, at the time usually assigned to him, in the fifth century of the Christian era.[1]

A striking proof occurs here, also, of the more exact correspondence between the Pancha Tantra and Kalíla wa Damna, than between the latter and Hitopadeśa. In the story of "The Two Crows," the interwoven story in both the former works is that of "The Crane, or Swan, killed by the Crab;" and it is not till the apologue of the Crows is closed, that the "Lion led into a Snare by the Hare" occurs. In the Hitopadeśa the first is omitted, and the second put in its place; and instead of a Hare, the beguiler of the forest monarch is an old Stag. The story of "The Crab and (Vaka) Crane," is not found in the Hitopadeśa earlier than the last section, or Sandhi, to which several of the fables, belonging to this part of the Pancha Tantra, are transferred.

The next story, "The Flea, the Bug, and the King," is omitted from the Hitopadeśa. It occurs in the Kalíla wa Damna, but not exactly in the same order.

---

[1] As. Res. IX. 361, and Hindu Algebra, Introd. Also Preface Sanskrit Dictionary, xiv. [Benfey, I. I., II, 392—96.]

The adventures of the Jackal, who falls into the dyer's vat, are not given in the Arabic version. They are told in the Hitopadeśa, but in a different section, that of Vigraha, or war [ed. Schlegel et Lassen, p. 91]. They are also copied in the Bahár Dánish.

The next story of "The Lion with his three Ministers (the Tiger, Crow, and Jackal), and the Camel," whom they ensnare and destroy, holds the same place in the Pancha Tantra, and Kalíla wa Damna. It is briefly told in the Hitopadeśa, but in the Sandhi section, or Chapter on Peace [p. 121].

The ensuing story of the Títtibha occurs in all the three works in the same place; but there is a great difference in its internal arrangements. In the Hitopadeśa [p. 72], it includes no other apologue whatever; in the Kalíla wa Damna only one, "The Tortoise and the Geese"; in the Pancha Tantra it comprehends five: "The Tortoise and the Geese"; "The three Fishes"; "The Elephant, destroyed by the Sparrow, the Woodpecker, the Fly, and the Frog"; "The Swan, creeping Plant, and Fowler"; and "The Ram killed by the Lion". In the Kalíla wa Damna the first, as observed, occurs in the same place, the second somewhat earlier, and the other three are omitted.[1]

In the Hitopadeśa the two first occur in the fourth section [p. 110]; the other three are wanting.

The story of the Títtibha, or Títawé, is one of the

---

[1] They appear to have been wanting in Mr. Sotheby's copy of the Pancha Tantra.—H.T.C.

decisive proofs of the Indian origin of these fables. The personified ocean, or Varuṅa, and Garuḍa, the bird of Vishṅu, are inadequately represented by the Vakíl al Bahr and the Anka, the king and lord of the feathered race. But the name of the bird is alone sufficient. The Titawé, although it is found in the Arabic lexicons, and is said to be a species of the Katá,[1] has very little appearance of an Arabic term; nor can it be resolved to any satisfactory root. It is, therefore, probably only a transcript of the Sanskrit Títtibha, Bengali Títib, and Hindu Títhrí: the names, throughout India, for a kind of Sandpiper,[2] very numerous on the sandy banks and shores of rivers. The strutting gait of this bird is supposed, universally, to indicate his inordinate conceit; and thence the appropriate selection of him, in the story, as defying the sea. This characteristic is so commonly attributed to the Títtibha,

---

[1] The Katá is described as a bird frequenting watery places. Golius and Meninski explain (كطا) Katá, avis columbae similis magnitudine et formâ, quae gregatim volat; et e longinquo aquam petere novit, vocem, kattá, edens, unde illi nomen. [See also S. de Sacy, Chrest. arabe, (2ⁿᵈ edit.) II, 368 ff.] There are said also to be two kinds, one much larger than the other. Burckhardt, in his Travels in Syria, calls the Katá a species of partridge, and mentions their being met with in the mountains of Belba, Kerek, Djebel, and Thera, in such flocks, that the Arab boys often kill two or three at a time, by throwing a stik at them. The Títtibha is encountered in numerous flocks, but is in size unlike either a pigeon or a partridge, and is a very different bird.

[2] The Tatíhrá or Tatíhri (Sansk. Tittibha) is a Jarana, the Parra Goensis of Gmelin, or Tringa Goensis of Latham. See Am. Dict. p. 125, and Hunter's Hind. Dict. t. 514.— H.T.C.

that it is proverbially said to sleep on its back, with
its legs upwards, to prevent the sky from falling.*

This section of the Hitopadesa, or Mitra Bheda,
contains no more apologues, but closes with that of
The Birds and Sea, and the engagement between the
Lion and the Bull, and the death of the latter. In the
Pancha Tantra, the Kalila wa Damna, and Vrihat
Kathá, the Jackals converse together, during the
contest, and narrate several stories. The first, in the
former work, is that of the Lion tricked out of the
Camel's flesh by the Jackal, which is not related in
any of the rest, being very like that of The Lion, his
Ministers, and the Camel, noticed above.**

A small cluster of stories occurs in the Pancha
Tantra, which are all omitted in the other works.
They are peculiarly Hindu; and, as novelties affording
some relief to the dry detail hitherto pursued, we shall
translate them.***

"In Ayodhyá, the capital of Kosala,¹ reigned a
monarch of great splendour and power, named Puru-
shottama. On one occasion, the Governor of the
Forests came and announced to him, that the woodland
chiefs were all in a state of rebellion, instigated and

---

* [A Hindustani proverb says: *talihri se asmán thámá jáegá?*
i. e. will the sky be supported by the sandpiper?]

** [Benfey, l. l., I, p. 251.]

*** [Benfey, l. l., I, p. 258 ff. II, p. 142—48.]

¹ The province of Oude and its capital, the modern Faizábád,
is usually identified with the ancient city In popular belief.
[Lassen, Ind. Alt., I, 129.]

headed by Vindhyaka, the Rájá of the Vindhya[1] hills. The king sent his chief minister Balabhadra, to quell the rebels.

"When Balabhadra was gone, there came to the capital, at the close of the rains, a Śramańaka,[2] or mendicant of the Bauddha religion, who, by his skill in divination, his knowledge of hours, omens, aspects, and ascensions, his dexterity in solving numbers, answering questions, and detecting things covertly concealed,[3] and his proficiency in all similar branches of knowledge, acquired such fame and influence, that it might be said he had purchased the country, and it was his own. The report of his reputation at last reached the king, who sent for him, and treating him with great civility, asked him whether it was true, that sages could tell the destinies of others. The mendicant replied, Your Majesty will know by the result. They then entered into conversation, in which he so entertained the king, that his daily society became indispensible.

"One day he absented himself from court; and on

---

[1] The authority of the Kośala monarch appears to have extended much beyond the limits of the modern province of Oude: an inscription found at Ratnapur in the Chatis-ghar district, dated Śaliváhana 781, or A.D. 859, states that province to be dependent upon the sovereign of Kośala. [Journal R. As. Soc., Vol. IV, p. 5 ff.]

[2] From subsequent passages, however, it appears that the usual confusion of Bauddha and Jaina occurs in the Pancha Tantra; and that, in fact, the latter alone is intended, whichever be named.

[3] [Benfey. l. l., II. p. 440, Note 600.]

the next, when he made his appearance, he accounted for his absence by stating that he had been upon a visit to Paradise; and that the deities had sent by him their compliments to the king. The king was simple enough to believe him, and was filled with astonishment and delight. His admiration of this marvellous faculty so engrossed his thoughts, that the duties of his state, and the pleasures of his palace, were equally neglected.

"Things were in this condition, when the valiant Balabhadra, having reduced the forest chieftains to obedience, returned. To his surprise, he found the king in a close conference with a naked mendicant, instead of being, as usual, surrounded by his ministers. Having ascertained from the latter, the pretensions of the ascetic, he approached the monarch, and inquired, if what he had heard of the mendicant's celestial visit, was truth. The king assured him that it was, and the ascetic offered to satisfy the general's apparent scepticism, by departing for Swarga in his presence. With this intent, the king and his courtiers accompanied the Sramańaka to his cell, which he entered, and closed the door. After some delay, Balabhadra inquired of the king when they were to see the mendicant again. He answered, 'have patience; the sage upon these occasions quits his earthly body, and assumes an ethereal person, with which alone he can approach Indra's heaven.' 'If this is the case,' replied Balabhadra, 'bring wood and fire, and let us burn his cell.' 'Why so,' asked the king. 'So please your Majesty,' answered the general, 'by consuming the earthly body of the ascetic, we shall prevent his re-assuming it, and then your Majesty will always have an angelical personage in your company. A case of this kind is well known.

"In Rájagriha dwelt a Bráhman named Deva Śarmá. He had no children, a subject of bitter affliction to his wife, who could not look upon a neighbour's infant without tears. At last her husband desired her to desist from farther lamentation, as by the efficacy of some mystic words he had secured her having a son of eminent beauty, and auspicious destiny. Highly delighted with this prophecy (indications of the fulfilment of which soon began to appear), the Bráhman's wife anticipated eagerly the period of her delivery. What therefore was her surprise, and the horror of her attendants, when the offspring, so anxiously sighed for, and impatiently expected proved to be a snake! The assistants exclaimed, Let the monster be destroyed. But the parent, with maternal affection, interfered to preserve her progeny, and carefully protected and reared the snake.

"After a time, the nuptial festivals of a neighbour's son awoke the envy of Deva Śarmá's wife and she reproached her husband for not having thought of a suitable match for their child. He replied, I would do so, if I could get admittance to Pátála, and present my supplications to Vásuki[1]. I do not think any other so

---

[1] The serpent monarch of Pátála, the region under the earth, inhabited by the Nágas, or snakes.

great a fool, as to wed his daughter to a son like thine.
Finding, however, his wife was sadly distressed, he
proposed, in order to divert her thoughts, that they
should travel; and equipping themselves plentifully
for their journey, they set out. After some months,
they arrived at a city, named Bhaṭṭanagara, where
they were hospitably received and entertained, on the
night of their arrival, by an acquaintance. In the
morning the Bráhman's friend asked him why he had
come, and whither he was going. The Bráhman told
him he was in search of a wife for his son; on which
the other offered him his own daughter, a girl of great
beauty, and insisted on his taking her away with him.
Accordingly, Deva Śarmá returned to his own city
with his destined daughter-in-law. When the people
of the city saw her, they opened their eyes in admiration of her grace and loveliness, and asked her
attendants, how they could think of sacrificing such
a jewel of a girl to a serpent. Their words filled her
servants with distress, and they were urgent with the
damsel to effect her escape. She refused, saying, It
must not be; there are three things, which are final
from the first: The command of a king, the vow of an
ascetic, and the gift of a maiden. That too which is
previously resolved by destiny, cannot fail to be, as it
happened to Pushpaka, and the Gods.

"The maiden's attendants now asked her, who Pushpaka was, and she thus proceeded:

"Pushpaka was the favourite parrot of Indra, a bird
of wonderful beauty, extraordinary abilities, and pro-

digious learning. One day he was perched on Indra's hand, and was repeating the hymns of the Vedas, when Yama arrived. The parrot immediately flew away abruptly. The Deities afterwards asked him why he had withdrawn; he replied, how could he face the destroyer of life. The Deities, in order to remove his fears, assured him that they would protect him; and, prevailing on him to accompany them, they returned to Yama, and begged him, at their intercession, to abstain from ever taking away the life of the parrot. Yama replied, that he knew nothing about the matter, and referred them to Kála (Time), to whom they accordingly repaired. Time referred them to Death, who, he said, was at hand: and they hastened to prefer their suit to him. They no sooner encountered the grisly terror, than the parrot fell dead. Exceedingly distressed and perplexed by this accident, they returned to Yama, and inquired of him what it meant; he replied, that Fate had fixed the parrot's life, and that no care on their parts would have been of any avail.

"Therefore, I say, whatever is foredoomed by destiny cannot fail to come to pass.

"In this manner she resisted their persuasions, and the marriage took place. She performed her duties diligently, feeding her serpent-husband during the day with milk, and keeping him in her chamber at night, in a spacious basket. One night she was alarmed by the appearance of a man in her chamber, and jumping up in terror, she ran to the door to make her escape.

The person called to her to stop, and dismiss her fears, as he was her husband; and, to assure her, reassumed his ophitic form, and crawled into the basket, whence immediately after, he again issued, in all the bloom and vigour of human adolescence, and glittering with gold and gems.

"In the morning, Deva Śarma, who had observed what was going forward, approached the basket, before his son was risen, and seizing the deserted skin of the snake, threw it into the fire; in consequence of which the youth was constrained to adhere to his natural figure, and continued ever after to constitute the pride of his parents, and the happiness of his family."

"The king of Ayodhyá, having heard this narrative from Balabhadra, hesitated no longer to follow his advice. The mendicant's cell was therefore immediately set on fire, and he perished in the flames."

The next story in the Pancha Tantra, and Kalíla wa Damna, is that of The Monkeys and Fire-fly; and the moral is stated precisely to the same effect in both, that it is absurd to try to bend a stubborn tree, or prove a sword upon a stone.

The story of Dharma Buddhi and Dushta Buddhi[*], the honest man and the rogue, as narrated in the Pancha Tantra, is faithfully followed in the Arabic, with the exception of an interwoven story, omitted in the latter. It is the story of the Vaka, or Crane, who tempted the Ichneumon to destroy the Snake, and

---

[*] (Benfey, l. l., I, p. 275—79.)

was afterwards destroyed by the same. The story occurs in the Sandhi section of the Hitopadeśa [p. 111].

The witty story of The Rats who eat iron, and the Hawks that carry off children, is the next in the Pancha Tantra, and Kalila wa Damna*. It is the last of the section in the latter; but we have a few more stories in the former work, as the story of The Two Parrots who learned respectively harsh and gentle phraseology, according to their natural dispositions, to prove that merits and defects are innate.

The next story agrees, in name, with the last in the Kalila wa Damna, being that of The King's Son and his Companions: the resemblance, however, proceeds no farther, the incidents being quite different, although some, if not all, of those in the Arabic tale, are to be found in other Sanskrit works. In the Pancha Tantra, a Prince, a Minister's, and a Merchant's Son, pass their days together in the woods and groves, hunting, riding on horses, or elephants, driving cars, and practising archery. Their fathers reproach them for their neglect of their several duties; and, in resentment, they determine to leave their home. They go to Rohanáchala, (Adam's Peak in Ceylon)**, where they find each a gem of great price; and to preserve it, on their way back, through the forests, where lay the Phellis, or Villages, of the Bhillas, they swallow the

---

* [Benfey, l. l., I, p. 283 f. H. Kurz ad B. Waldis' Esopus, Vol. II, p. 142. (B. III, fab. 96).]

** [Benfey, l. l., II, p. 447, Note 652.]

gems, and then convey them home in safety, although they narrowly escape being ripped open by the Palliputi, or chief of the foresters.

The Prince acquires a sovereignty of his own, and leaving to his two friends the direction of affairs, amuses himself in his palace, after his own fashion. He has a pet Monkey, as it is said "Parrots, Pheasants, Pigeons, Monkeys, and their like, are naturally the especial favourites of Kings." This Monkey he sets to watch him, as he sleeps in a pavillion, in his garden. A troublesome bee settles on the Prince's face, in spite of the Monkey's pains to drive him off, till the latter, highly incensed, snatches up his master's sword, and, making a blow at the bee, cuts off the Rájá's head.

This apologue, therefore, is a very old acquaintance, the moral is the same: a sensible foe is preferable to a foolish friend[1]. The death of Sanjívaka, the grief of the Lion, and the councils of the Jackals, close this, the first and longest division of the Pancha Tantra, in the same manner as the corresponding sections of the Kalíla wa Damna, Hitopadeśa, and Vṛihat Kathá. This first section, according to the original enumeration, comprehends thirty-one stories[2].

---

[1] The form familiar to us is the story of the Gardener, the Bear, and the Fly, in which it occurs in the Anvári Soheili, and Ayár Dánish. [Benfey, l. l., I, p. 292 ff. II, p. 538. B. Waldis II, 99, & note, Vol. II, 112.]

[2] In Mr. Sotheby's copy, only twenty-six.—H.T.C.

SECTION SECOND.

THE ACQUISITION OF FRIENDS.

The *Mitra Prápti*[1], or acquisition of friends, is the same as the Mitra Lábha of the Hitopadesa, with the difference only of transposition. It is the same also as the seventh chapter of the Kalíla wa Damna: the sixth being a probable addition of the translator, who, in his idea of poetical justice, has put Damna upon his trial, and condemned him to death; occurrences not hinted at in the Hindu work. Neither have we the few narratives that occur in his section; nor are the moral remarks, or the judicial proceedings, of a Hindu complexion.

The Mitra Prápti opens, like the Mitra Lábha, with the description of the scene of action, placed by both in the South, with this variety, that the one states it to lie on the banks of the Godávari, and the other, that it was not very far from the city Pramadáropyam. The Crow, or Raven, Laghupatanaka, opens the business in all the copies. The fowler is very minutely described in the Pancha Tantra, as an inhabitant of the city, living by bird-catching, of an uncouth figure, with splay feet, and clumsy hands; round as a ball; sturdy, though advanced in years; clad in red

---

[1] It is also read Samprápti, which has the same import.

garments, with his hair bound into a knot on his head, carrying a net and staff, and followed by dogs: in short, he looked like Destiny with the fatal noose; like the personification of Sin; like the heart of iniquity; like the monitor of the wicked; like the friend of Death." This description is reduced to "like fate," in the Hitopadeśa; and in the Arabic, to "ill looks, and the net and the staff."

The Hitopadeśa [p. 10] is singular in the story told by Chitragriva, of "The Traveller and the Tiger," to dissuade the Pigeons from descending on the grain. The Pancha Tantra, again, is alone in the story, told by the same to recommend unanimity, of "the Bhárunda*," a bird with two necks, one refusing to part with a share of nectar, the other swallowed poison, and the bird died.

The other circumstances of this story are continued, alike in all, to the formation of the friendship between the Rat, and the Crow; but the discussion is much more protracted, and contains much more matter, peculiarly Hindu, in the Pancha Tantra, than in either of the other works. The Rat replies to the Crow's protestations, "I have no faith in your oaths; as it is said, 'Put no faith in a foe, who even has vowed friendship to you: Vṛitra was killed by Indra, in spite of his reiterated oaths[1].' Again, 'An enemy of the Gods is

---

* [Benfey, l. l., II, p. 525 suggests the form *bherunda*. See also I, 309 & 538, and Loiseleur Deslongchamps, Essai sur les Fables indiennes. Paris: 1838, p. 45.]

[1] The story is narrated in several of the Puráńas, and is al-

not to be destroyed until he places trust in them. The embryo of Diti was destroyed by Indra, only when she ceased to fear him*."

In another passage we have allusions to some traditions, which are but little known.—

"He that observes, 'I might say, I abound with amiable qualities, and no one can be inclined to do me harm,' speaks that which is ridiculous. It is related that the valuable life of Páṅini (the grammarian) was destroyed by a lion; and an elephant demolished the sage Jaimini, though he composed the Mímánsá; an alligator killed the harmonious Pingala (the first writer on Prosody), on the sea-shore. Of what estimation is genius with irrational and ferocious brutes!"

Although the arguments, on either side, are continued for several pages, they are not intermixed with any narrative illustration in the Pancha Tantra, or Kalíla wa Damna. On the contrary, the Hitopadeśa inserts here the stories of the Antelope and the Jackal; and the Crow, the Cat, and the Vulture. Afterwards the several works proceed in a similar manner to the visit of the Rat and the Crow to Manthara, the Tortoise; to whom, and the Crow, Hiraṅyaka, the Rat related his adventures.

The commencement of this story is the same in all, but the Arabic version here is singularly close. The

---

luded to in the Ṛig-Veda. As. Res. vol. viii, p. 378. [Wilson, Ṛig-Veda, Vol. I, p. 85.]

* [Rámáy. I, 46 Schl., 47 Gorr. Vishṅu Pur. p. 151 f., quoted by Benfey in "Mélanges Asiatiques," Vol. IV, p. 214.]

Hitopadeśa alone inserts the story of the young wife, who took her husband by the hair, and embraced him, to favour the retreat of her lover; a story well known in Europe, from its version by Marguerite of Navarre, in her "Stratagème d'une femme qui fit évader son galant, lorsque son mari, qui étoit borgne, croyoit le surprendre avec elle" [Nov. 6], and she borrowed it from the first story of the Mauvaise Femme*. It was made a similar use of by the Sieur D'Ouville**, Malespini [I, Nov. 44], Bandello [I, Nov. 23], and other raconteurs***. In place of this, the original, and the Kalîla wa Damna have the story of the woman, who exchanged picked for unpicked sesamum seeds, including that of the "Forester, Wild Boar and Jackal," which occurs a little farther on in the Hitopadeśa. A long train of adventures, told of a merchant's son, follows this, in the Pancha Tantra, only to shew that a man must obtain the wealth that is designed for him by fate. The close of this story is followed by one, narrated by Manthara, of Somillaka, a weaver, who is taught by some Spirits, that wealth is to be enjoyed, not hoarded; and this includes a story of the "Bull and the Jackals," to inculcate the folly of absurd expectations. These two last stories have, however, but little merit, and do not occur in the Arabic, any

---

* [Legrand d'Aussy, Fabliaux. Vol. IV, p. 188.]
** [Élite des contes. Rouen: 1680, p. 224.]
*** [Hitopadeśa traduit par E. Lancereau. Paris: 1855, p. 217-22. Hagen, Gesammtabenteuer, Vol. II, p. XXVII ff. Benfey, l. l., I, p. 367 f.]

more than in the Hitopadeśa. The latter story, with some variations, has given rise to an idiomatic compound in the Bengali language; and Bakáńḍapratyáśa, indulgence in unreasonable expectation, comprises the pith of this story; the Baka, or Vaka, a crane, being substituted for the Jackal of the original. A verse of interesting resemblance follows the stories. Manthara says to the Rat, "Dismiss all anxiety regarding your lost wealth, as it is said, 'He, to whom the Swan owes her white feathers, the Parrot his green hue, and the Peacock his variegated plumage, He will provide me sustenance.'"

The addition of the Antelope to the friendly society occurs here, in the same manner, in all. The story of "the Elephant, liberated from his bonds by the Rat," of which we have a familiar version in the apologue of the Rat and the Lion, next occurs in the Pancha Tantra*. In its place, in the Hitopadeśa, we have the double story of the Prince, the Banker's Son, and his Wife, and of the Elephant and Jackal. There is none in the Kalila wa Damna. The three works conclude with the same incident, the liberation of the Antelope from the hunter's snare, by the united efforts and devices of the Tortoise, the Crow, and the Rat.

This Tantra contains, in the original, eight stories. It is more amply illustrated in the Hitopadeśa, than in either of the other two works.

---

* [Benfey, l. l., I, p. 324 ff. H. Kurz ad B. Waldis I, fab. 14.]

SECTION THIRD.

INVETERATE ENMITY, OR WAR BETWEEN CROWS AND OWLS.

The third section of the Pancha Tantra corresponds with the eighth chapter of the Kalila wa Damna, and the third chapter of the Hitopadeśa. In the last work, however, the belligerent powers are the peacocks and the geese. The choice of the Pancha Tantra is the genuine one, no doubt; not only from the character of the work itself, but its connection with a particular grammatical rule. The Sútras of Pániní afford a precept for the use of a particular affix, to form derivatives from compound terms, when enmity is implied[1]; and this rule is exemplified by the form Kákolúkiká, in which káka, a crow, and ulúka, an owl, are compounded, to signify the natural antipathy that subsists between these birds. Now as language precedes grammar, this rule was invented to explain the purport of a word already in use; and as in all probability this word expressed a popular notion of great antiquity, its established currency influenced the author of the fables to select the owl and the crow for the purpose of his narrative. We can scarcely suppose, that it was an accidental choise, which afterwards gave rise to

---

[1] Pán. 4. 3. 125. [Benfey, l. l., I, p. 37. 835—39.]

the popular expression, and the introduction of the compound term; and which, consequently, would make the Pancha Tantra take precedence in date of the Sútras of Pániní. I may also add, that the substantive term Kákolúkika, which Pániní's affix (Bun) could form, appears very rarely, if ever, in the Pancha Tantra. The form used by the author of that work is more usually the attributive, Kákolúkíya, which is formed by a different affix (Chha).

The introductory matter of this section, descriptive of the quarrel between the Crows and Owls, and the consultations of the monarch of the former, with his five ministers, correspond very closely in the Pancha Tantra and Kalíla wa Damna; although they extend to a greater length in the former, and contain some matters curious in themselves, and reflecting light on several Hindu peculiarities: amongst these, the following enumeration of the officers of state, who are, or are not, to be relied upon with confidence, is quoted from the Mahábhárata, the Sabhá Parva[*], in which Nárada, it is said, communicated their names to Yudhishthira. The full detail is, however, not given in that work, but the passage does occur, and the reference indicates, at any rate, the existence of the Mahábhárata prior to the date of the Pancha Tantra[1].

[*] [The enumeration does not occur in the printed edition, but is alluded to in v. 171 f.]

[1] A similar list occurs in the Bhairavi Tantra. [Kosegarten's edition has some various readings, on which see Benfey, l. l., II, p. 483 f. and Mélanges As., IV, p. 253.]

The Officers to be distrusted are eighteen.

1	Mantri	The minister.
2	Purohita	The royal chaplain, or priest.
3	Senápati	The general.
4	Yuraraja	The young prince, associated in the empire, and designated as successor.
5	Danvárika	Warden, or chamberlain.
6	Antarvansika	The superintendant of the inner apartments.
7	Sannidhátryupadesblá	A sort of master of the ceremonies.
8	Jnápaka	A master of requests.
9	Aśwádhyaksha	Master of the horse.
10	Gajádhyaksha	Master of the elephants.
11	Koshádhyaksha	Superintendant of the treasury.
12	Baládhyaksha	Ditto of the forces, or perhaps the stores.
13	Durgapála	The governor of the fort.
14	Karapála	The ruler of the prisons.
15	Simápála	The superintendant of the boundaries, or lord of the marches.
16	Párishada	A companion.
17	Protkaśa bhritya	A courtier.
18	Átavikádhya	The forest chiefs, and others.

The fifteen, naturally attached to the monarch's cause, are

1	Janani	The queen mother.
2	Deví	The queen.
3	Kanchuki	The confidential attendant.
4	Málika	The chaplet weaver, or florist.
5	Śayyápála	The bed-maker.
6	Śayyádhyaksha	The superintendant of the beds.
7	Sámvatsarika	The astrologer, or time-keeper.
8	Bhishak	Physician.
9	Jalaváhaka	The cup, or water-bearer.
10	Támbúlaváhaka	The betel-bearer.

11	Áchárya	The preceptor.
12	Anga-rakshaka	The captain of the body guard.
13	Sthána-chintaka	Quartermaster.
14	Chhatradhára	The umbrella-bearer.
15	Vilásini	Female attendant and singer, &c.[1]

Besides these, spies were a very efficient part of the ancient Hindu regime. We have no particular enumeration of these, except its being observed, that for what is going on amongst his own party, the king's best spies are the physician, the astrologer, and the preceptor; and that men, who exhibit snakes and the like, are the best to observe the designs of the enemy.

We have then the cause of the enmity between these feathered tribes referred to the successful interference of a crow, in preventing the owl being chosen king of the birds, narrated in a similar manner in the Pancha Tantra, and the Arabic copy; it is omitted in the Hitopadeśa. That work, however, inserts two stories, those of the Birds and the Monkeys, and the Ass in a Tiger's skin, (the latter an apologue of very wide circulation); before the story, common to all three, of the Elephant and Hares, and the Reflection of the Moon.

The story of the Hare, the Sparrow, and the Cat, does not occur in the Hitopadeśa, although much of the discription of the hypocritical piety of the Cat is copied in the story of the Vulture and the Cat, in the first section of that work [p. 18]. Some of the com-

---

[1] It is by no means certain, that all these names are rightly interpreted, or even rightly extracted from the text; but the greater part do not admit of doubt.

ments, however, are spared. It may be observed, indeed, that a much more decisive vein of satire, levelled particulary at Princes and Devotees, runs through the Pancha Tantra, than either the Kalila wa Damna, or Hitopadeśa: thus the Hare observes, when he sees the Cat away, as it is said, "Trust not in low persons, who exercise austerities for their own nefarious designs. Penitents are to be found at holy shrines, whose only virtue is in their vaunts."

The story of the Three Rogues, who persuade the Brāhman that his goat is something else, and so induce him to leave it to them, is the next in the Pancha Tantra, and Kalila wa Damna: it occurs in the last section of the Hitopadeśa [p. 116]*.

An incident, rather than a story, next occurs in the Pancha Tantra, singly, that of a Snake killed by Ants. The device adopted by the king of the Crows, as narrated in the Pancha Tantra, and Kalila wa Damna, reminds the reader of the story of Zopyrus; the councillor Chiranjíva being, at his own suggestion, stripped of his feathers, and smeared with blood, and left at the foot of the tree, in which state he is found by the Owls, and brought to their king. The discussions regarding his treatment, between the king and his ministers, are to the same purport in both works; but they are more detailed in the Pancha Tantra, and illustrated by very different stories.

The first minister, Raktáksha, who recommends the

---

* [For the literature, imitations &c. see Benfey, l. l., I, p. 855 ff.]

crow's being put to death, narrates, in order to shew that no confidence is to be placed in a reconciled foe, the story of the Snake and the Bráhman's Son*, comprising a brief apologue of the Swans and the strange bird. Neither of these is in the Arabic, or Hitopadeśa: and they may be therefore translated:

"In a certain country dwelt a Bráhman, who reaped no benefit from the cultivation of his grounds. As he was reposing one day in the hot season under the shade of a tree, he dreamt that he beheld a large hooded snake, coiled upon an ant-hill, at a little distance; and waking from his dream, he concluded that the snake must be the tutelary deity of the spot, who was little pleased with him, as one from whom he had never received any veneration. The Bráhman determined, therefore, to worship him; and boiling some milk, he placed it in a vessel, and carried it to the ant-hill, exclaiming as he laid the cup upon the ground, 'Lord of the soil, I have hitherto been ignorant of thy place of residence, and, therefore, only have foreborne thy worship; forgive my negligence, and accept my oblation. So saying, he left the milk and went home.'

"When he visited the ant-hill on the morning following, he found in place of the milk a Dínár[1], and this

---

* [Benfey, l. l., I, p. 359—61. Weber, Ind. Stud., III, p. 341 ff.]

[1] A gold coin. That there existed some connexion between this and the gold Denarius of the Romans, is not improbable, as has been shewn in another place. As. Res. XV. The indication of treasure by the presence of a snake is a common superstition among the Hindus.

was repeated daily. At last, the Bráhman having
occasion to go to the village, appointed his son to
present the oblation of milk in his absence. When the
lad, upon the ensuing morning, found the Dinár as
usual, it occurred to him, that the mound must be
filled with coin; and that it would be the most eligible
plan to kill its serpent-owner, and seize at once upon
the whole treasure. Arming himself, therefore, with
a stick, he lay wait for the snake, as he was lapping
the milk, and struck him on the head. The blow failed
to kill the snake, and the animal, inflamed with
wrath, bit the lad with his poisonous fangs, so that he
immediately died. The body was burnt by his people,
who were at hand, and saw what had chanced. The
father returned on the day following, and when he
had heard the cause of his son's death, was satisfied
that the event was not unmerited; declaring, that
the vital elements will be ever snatched from those,
who shew no tenderness to those living creatures, that
repair to them for preservation, as happened to the
Swans and their Lake. The persons present asked
him to explain this allusion, and he thus replied:

"'In a certain country reigned Chitraratha, in one of
whose gardens was an extensive lake, guarded by his
troops. In this lake were golden swans, who moulted
a feather once in every six months. A large bird,
having joined them, was refused admission to their
troop; they claiming the exclusive occupation of the
pool by the fee of the moulted feather. After much
discussion, the stranger bird applied to the king, and

said, Sire, these swans have had the audacity to say, what have we to do with the king? we will not allow any one to reside here: and it was to no purpose that I expostulated with them on the impropriety of such language, and threatened to bring it to your knowledge. The king, having heard this, commanded his servants to go and kill the birds, and bring them to him; and they set off with this intent. When they approached the pool, an old swan, suspecting their purpose, persuaded the rest to fly away; and thus, although they preserved their lives, they lost the residence, which they refused to share with a guest.'

"Having related this tale, the Bráhman proceeded to worship the snake. The serpent, however, could not be tempted forth, but shewing himself at the entrance of his hole, he thus spoke: 'Avarice brings thee hither, and banishes all sorrow for thy son's fate, but there cannot be any cordiality between thee and me:' again, 'in the insane presumption of youth, your son struck me; I have bitten him, and killed him: how is it possible for me ever to forget his violence? how is it possible that you should ever forget his death? Take this jewel, therefore; depart, and never more approach this place.' Having thus spoken, and cast a gem of inestimable value to the Bráhman, he withdrew into his hole. The Bráhman took the jewel, but, considering its value much inferior to what he might have acquired by long assiduous homage, never ceased to lament the folly of his son."

The next story is also peculiar to the Panchu Tantra,

and indeed so decidedly of a Hindu character, that we need not be surprised at its omission, from the Arabic translation at least. It may be called the Fowler and the Pigeons. The fowler, having caught the female dove, is overtaken by a violent storm, and repairs for shelter to the tree inhabited by the male. Moved by the councils of his captive mate, and his own estimate of the rites of hospitality, he not only gives the fowler shelter in the hollow trunk, but collects dry leaves, and makes him a fire, and casts himself into the flames, to furnish his guest a meal. The bird-catcher liberates the dove, and she also throws herself into the fire; on which she and her lord assume celestial forms, and are conveyed to heaven in divine cars, agreeably to the text, that says, 'A widow, who burns herself, secures for herself and her husband enjoyment in Paradise, for as many years as there are hairs on the human body, or thirty-five millions[1].' The fowler becomes an ascetic, and voluntarily perishes in a burning forest.

The next story of the Husband, and his Wife, and the Thief, is translated in the Arabic, but does not occur in the Hitopadeśa. It has been imitated by the writers of Europe. The Bráhman, the Thief, and the Rákshasa, the next story, is the same with

---

[1] This text is attributed to Angiras, and forms part of the declaration or Sankalpa, pronounced by the widow at the time of her ascending the pile. — As. Res. vol. iv, p. 210. [Colebrooke, Essays, p. 71 f. Skandapurâṅa, Kâśikhaṅḍa IV, 59, quoted by Benfey, l. l., II, 495 & 542. I, 365.]

"the Ascetic, the Thief, and the Evil Genius of the Kalila wa Damna.

The next story, of the Prince who had a snake in his bowels, is peculiar to the Pancha Tantra. He is cured by his wife. The eleventh fable is the same with the Husband under the Bed, of the Arabic, which occurs also in the third section of the Hitopadeśa. The next story, again, is the same in the Pancha Tantra, and Kalila wa Damna, that of the Mouse turned to a young girl by a sage, and finally to a mouse again[*]. The Arabic translator, by his alterations, has lost the point of the story. He makes the sun &c. decline the marriage; but in the Sanskrit, the lady makes objections to all the proposed bridegrooms, till she sees the rat, when her natural propensities induce her to solicit her adoptive father to give her to him in marriage[**].

The next story of "the Bird that voided gold with its dung" is peculiar to the Pancha Tantra; so is that of "the Fox, who detects the presence of a Lion in a cavern[***]:" neither tale has much point. The story of "the Snake and Frogs[†]" is told in all three works; but in the Pancha Tantra it is interrupted by the following: viz.

"The Bráhman and his Wife.

---

[*] [See the literature for No. 8–11 in Benfey, l. l., I, p. 365–73.]
[**] [Benfey, l. l., I, 373 ff. A. Weber, Indische Studien, III, 345. Die Fabeln des Sophos. Posen: 1859, p. LIII ff.]
[***] [Benfey, l. l., I, 382. Die Fabeln des Sophos No. 45.]
[†] [B. Waldis, I, 17. Weber, Ind. Stud., III, 346.]

"There was a Bráhman, named Mandavisha, whose wife was a woman of loose character. She had a lover, to whom she was accustomed to carry delicacies and cates, which she prepared herself. Her husband, at last taking notice of this, inquired of her whither she took them, and to whom: she replied, I carry them as oblations to my tutelary goddess Deví, whose temple, you know, is close at hand. Pretending to be satisfied with this reply, the husband allowed her to proceed, but continued to watch her. As she found that he observed her, she went to the temple, and performed the customary oblations, and entered the building. Her husband immediately set off by another path; and getting into the edifice by a different entrance concealed himself behind the statue of the goddess. The wife, being afraid that her husband was still on the watch, determined to go through with the ceremony in earnest, and having presented the oblations, she thus prayed, "O! goddess, deign to inform me by what means my husband can be deprived of his eyesight." The husband, hearing this, disguised his voice, and answered, " Feed him daily with such cates as you have brought hither, and he will soon become blind." The wife returned home delighted, and put in practice the supposed instructions of the goddess. In a few days the Bráhman began to complain of dimness of vision, and shortly afterwards pretended to lose his sight. The wife, attributing this to the favour of the goddess, entertained no doubt of the fact; and in the confidence of not being detected, invited her gallant to come fearlessly to the house. The husband, however, now thoroughly apprised of the truth, lost no time in punishing her misconduct. Surprising the guilty pair, he beat the adulterer with his staff, till he expired; and, cutting off his wife's nose, he turned her away*."

The remainder of this section, and the destruction of the Owls by their more crafty enemies, corresponds in the Pancha Tantra, and Kalīla wa Damna.

The third section comprises seventeen stories.

SECTION FOURTH.
LOSS OF THAT WHICH HAS BEEN GAINED.

The fourth section of the Pancha Tantra, illustrative of the folly of losing what has once been acquired (*Labdha-praśamana*[1]) corresponds with the ninth chapter of the Kalīla wa Damna, which relates the story of "The Monkey and the Tortoise." The Arabic, or Pehlevi translator has, however, made rather short work with his original, and has turned the twelve tales of the latter into two.

The chief performers in this selection, and the cir-

---

* (Benfey, l. l., I, 385. In Kosegarten's text, and Benfey's translation, the name of the Brahman is Yajnadatta, and, more appropriately, Mandavisha the name of the serpent who relates the story.)

[1] It is also read Labdha Pranasana, and Labdha Pranāśa, but the sense is the same.

cumstances, out of which the tales arise, are the same; only, instead of a Tortoise, the treacherous friend of the Monkey is the Makara, a fabulous aquatic animal, which corresponds, in representation at least, with the Capricornus of the Greek Zodiac. The first story, narrated by the Monkey after his escape, is that of "the Snake and the Frogs." The former is introduced into his well by the King of the latter, to revenge him on his rebellious subjects. This being done, however, he devours the king's subjects, and finally the king himself. The moral is, "that hunger will be appeased, even in spite of crime*."

The next story is the only one of the section, found in the Arabic, that of "the sick Lion, the Jackal, and the Ass**."

The next story is that of "a Potter, who, having cut his forehead against some broken pots, is encountered, bleeding, by a Prince, and taken for a valiant warrior by him, in consequence of which he is enrolled amongst his guards. When the mistake is discovered, the prince orders him to withdraw: and when the potter requests that he may be allowed to stay, repeats to him the next story, that of "the two young Lions, and the young Jackal, brought up with them, but who betrays his origin by his cowardice, and is advised by the old Lioness, his adoptive mother, to withdraw

---

* [Benfey, l. l., I, 429.]
** [Benfey, l. l., I, 430 ff. Weber, Ind. Stud., III, 338. Die Fabeln des Sophos, p. LXXX.]

quietly, lest his foster brothers find him out and destroy him." The potter takes the hint, and walks quietly off.

The ensuing stories tend to the disparagement of the fair sex. The first is that of a Bráhman, who quits his home and family, and relinquishes half his life for the sake of a spouse, who, notwithstanding, deserts him for a lame beggar, and attempts his life: a story that is told also in the Daśa Kumára*. The next is to shew that there is no pleasing women, without complying with all their caprices; as the minister Vararuchi, to conciliate his wife, submitted to have his head shaved; and his royal master, Nanda, to gratify his queen, allowed her to put a bridle in his mouth, and mounting on his back, compel him to carry her about, neighing at the same time like a horse**.

The next story in this section is an apologue of very familiar character. "A washerman, the owner of an ass, dresses him up with the skin of a tiger, to frighten away intruders from his field: after a time the ass betrays himself by his braying, and gains a beating from the villagers." This is given in the Hitopadeśa, in the third section. [Fable 2.]***

The ninth tale is of a villager's wife, who is tempted

---

* [p. 150. Benfey, l. l., I, 436 ff. F. Liebrecht in Benfey's "Orient und Occident", I, 127. „Das Ausland", 1858, p. 845 ff.]
** [Benfey, l. l., I, 461 f. von der Hagen, Gesammtabenteuer, I, p. LXXV ff.]
*** [Benfey, l. l., I, 462 ff. II, 517. Weber, Ind. Stud., III, 338.]

to run away from her husband, and carry off his wealth. When she arrives, with her gallant, at a river, he persuades her to entrust him with the property, and her clothes, to convey them across; after which he is to return for her. This, however, he omits to do, and she is deserted. In this state she sees a Jackal approach with a piece of meat in its mouth. The Jackal, seeing a fish on the edge of the water, lays down the meat, to make the fish his prey: the fish escapes; and, in the mean time, a vulture carries off the meat. The deserted wife laughs at the incident, when the Jackal thus applies it to herself: "Your wisdom is double that of mine; for here you are, naked in the water, and have neither a husband nor a gallant*."

The story of "the Sparrows and Monkey," is the same as that of "the Birds and Monkeys," in the beginning of the third section of the Hitopadeśa.

The two next stories, which complete this section, are those of "the Jackal, who by his craft preserved the carcase of a dead Elephant from a Lion and a Tiger, and by his courage from another Jackal**;" and "the Dog who, in a famine, left his own town for another, but was driven back by the dogs of the strange place, and was glad to seek his own home again."

The Makara now retires, having previously been

---

* [H. Kurz ad B. Waldis I, 4. Weber, Ind. Stud., III, 359. Die Fabeln des Sophos. No. 31.]

** [taken, according to Benfey (I. 473) froh Mahábhár. I, 5567—92.]

told of his wife's death, and the invasion of his abode by an enemy: circumstances, omitted in the Arabic translation, as well as the stories to which they give rise.

There are twelve stories in this section.

SECTION FIFTH.
INCONSIDERATENESS.[1]

The fifth Tantra corresponds in purport with the tenth chapter of the Kalíla wa Damna, the Ascetic and the Weasel being intended to illustrate the folly of precipitancy. The Pehlevi or Arabic translator has, however, taken a similar liberty with his original as in the preceding section, and has reduced again twelve stories to two. The tales in the original, therefore, are mostly novel, and not very prolix. It may be observed, by the way, that in the last two Tantras of the work either the original compiler had exhausted his store, or less frequent additions have been made by subsequent hands; as the reflections and citations, which are most disproportionably interspersed in the three first sections, become now much less copious: an obvious improvement in the interest, if not in the utility, of the collection.

Vishńu Śarmá now remarked, "a man should never

---

[1] Aparikshita-káritwa, inconsiderate conduct; acting without previous investigation.

attempt a business which he has imperfectly seen or understood, transacted or investigated, or he will meet with such mischance as befel the imprudent Barber." The Princes asking him, to what he alluded, he thus proceeded:

"In the south there is a city named Pátalipura, in which Maṇibhadra, a banker, resided. Although attentive to his moral and religious duties, it was the will of fate, that he should lose his wealth, and be reduced to poverty. The insignificance, into which he consequently fell, preyed upon his spirits, and he indulged in such reflections as these:

"It is justly said, that amiable feelings, purity of manners, moderation, ability, suavity, and respectability, are qualities that shine with little lustre in the person of a poor man. Dignity, pride, discernment, conceit, or intellect are all lost, when a man is poor; as the freshness of the dewy season is dissipated by the breeze of spring. The most brilliant talents will be of little benefit to their possessor, whose thoughts are all occupied in devising means for the support of his family, and when, for the exercise of lofty fancies, are substituted clothes, rice, oil, salt and ghee. Men without wealth are of no note amongst their fellows. They perish, as they are born, unheeded, like bubbles on the stream."

"Impelled by these considerations, he determined to abstain from food, and so terminate his life. For what, he exclaimed, is the use of a miserable existence? With this resolve he fell asleep. In his sleep the

Padma-nidhi[1] appeared to him under the form of an old Jaina mendicant, and forbade him to despair. You have been, he said, a faithful worshipper of me, and I will not desert you. In the morning early, you shall see me again, as I now appear: do you then take a staff, and strike me on the head; on which I shall be changed immediately to a pile of gold. He then disappeared.

"When the merchant rose, in the morning, he recollected his vision, but could scarcely persuade himself, that it would so come to pass. He referred it to the subject of his previous thoughts; as it is said: To those who are in sickness, or in sorrow, whose

---

[1] The Nidhi is properly a treasure; and is especially a kind of wealth appertaining to Kuvera, the God of Riches. The nidhis, or their superintendants at least, are personifications; and are, as such, worshipped (See Megha Duta, in note ad v. 79). The worship is of the Tāntrika description. The Sáradá Tilaka, a celebrated authority of that school, contains the following directions for adoring the Sánkha and Padma-nidhis, in conjunction with Lakshmi, the Goddess of Prosperity. "1. Let the votary worship the Sánkha-nidhi, and his spouse upon the right hand of the Goddess: him corpulent, and her full breasted: both adorned with pearls and rubies, both exhibiting gentle smiles upon their lotus-like countenances, locked in each other's arms, and each holding a lotus and a shell, both scattering showers of pearls, and each bearing a conch upon the forehead. 2. Let him adore the Padma-nidhi, placed with his wife upon the left hand of the Goddess: both of the colour of minium, each in the other's embrace, and either holding a red lotus and a blue one: both employed in raining jewels, and either wearing a lotus as a crest: the male Padma nidhi corpulent, the female slender."

minds are occupied with anxiety or desire, the object of their waking wishes is presented in their dreams.

"At this time, the barber, who had been sent for by the merchant's wife, to pare her nails, arrived, and whilst he was busy at his work, the seeming mendicant appeared. Maṇibhadra immediately recognized the figure of his dream, and snatching up a stick, struck him on the head; on which the figure changed to gold, and fell upon the floor. The banker took the gold to an inner apartment, desiring the barber not to mention to any one what he had witnessed. The barber promised secrecy, and went home, but could not help thinking of the occurrence. These naked mendicants, he muttered to himself, are all of one fraternity, and if one is changed into gold by a rap on the pate, why should not any other be changed in a similar manner? I will therefore invite their principals to my house, and then with a few strokes of a cudgel I shall surely get a quantity of the finest metal. These ideas he revolved in his mind the rest of that day, and all the night. When morning came, he went to the Vihára[1], and facing to the north, perambulated the Jina[2] three times. He then went on his knees, and holding up his hands with reverence, lifted up the edge of the curtain, repeating in a high tone this stanza, "Glory to those Jainas who possess the only true knowledge: and are thus enabled to traverse the wild

---

[1] The name of a Bauddha or Jaina convent.
[2] The deified sage who is the object of Jaina worship.

ocean of human passions." And again, "The tongue
which glorifies, and the mind that is dedicated to Jina,
are alone to be praised, with the hands that are busied
in his adoration." Having uttered these, and similar
invocations, he repaired to the chief of the convent,
and kneeling at his feet, received his blessing. The
barber then, in an insinuating tone, requested the
favour of his coming, with his principal sages, to a
slight recreation at his house. The principal replied,
"How now, son; what is it you say? Are we Bráhmans, think you, to be at any one's beck and call?
No, no; at the hour when we go forth to gather alms,
we enter the mansions of those votaries only, who, we
know, are of approved faith. Depart, therefore, nor
reiterate thine offence." The Barber replied, "most
venerable Lord, I shall obey, and do as you command,
but I beg to mention, that I have a store of excellent
cloths, for covers to our holy books; and of the materials for writing, which will be fitly disposed of,
when time may serve." So saying he went home, and
provided some stout bludgeons, which he hid in a
corner; he then went back to the convent, and took
his station at the gate; and, as the different ascetics
came forth, he addressed them as he had spoken to
their principal. Tempted by the wrappers for their
books, they all listened to him favourably, and deserting their old acquaintances, followed the barber to
his house; as it is said: The naked ascetic, who has
abandoned his home, and all his possessions, is still
no stranger to the desire of worldly goods. When the

Barber had introduced them into his house, he took up his staff, and struck them on the head, so that several were killed in an instant. The rest then, with broken skulls, set up so loud a clamour, that the neighbourhood was alarmed, and the town guards[1] flocked towards the spot, to see what was the matter. As they approached, they met the Jaina mendicants, fleeing with broken heads, and covered with blood, from the barber's house. Having learnt the cause of their dismay, they proceeded to lay hold of the barber, whom they bound and carried to the police. When questioned as to his conduct, he justified himself by the example of Mańibhadra: but when Mańibhadra, being sent for, and examined, revealed the extact nature of the occurrence, he was of course dismissed, whilst the barber was hanged, as a punishment for his violent and inconsiderate aggression.

"When the barber was disposed of, the judges remarked, that he had deserved his fate, as it is well said, that which has not been tried, should not be attempted, and that which is done, ought first to be well considered, otherwise repentance will follow, as in the case of the Bráhman and Ichneumon. Mańibhadra asked how that was, and they replied.

"There was a Bráhman, named Deva Śarmá, whose

---

[1] The Purakoshiapálapurusháh: The men who guarded the avenues of the city. Possibly there may be some etymological connexion between Koshiapála (Sanskrit), and Kotwál (Persian), an officer of Police.

wife had one son; she had also a favourite ichneumon[1], that she brought up with the infant, and cherished like another child. At the same time she was afraid that the animal would, some time or other, do the child a mischief, knowing its treacherous nature, as it is said, "A son, though ill-tempered, ugly, stupid and wicked, is still the source of delight to a father's heart." One day the mother, going forth to fetch water, placed the child in the bed, and desired her husband to guard the infant, especially from the ichneumon. She then departed, and after a while the Bráhman himself was obliged to go forth to collect alms. When the house was thus deserted, a black snake came out of a hole, and crawled towards the bed where the infant lay; the ichneumon, who saw him, impelled by his natural animosity, and by regard for his foster brother, instantly attacked him, and, after a furious encounter, tore him to pieces. Pleased with his prowess, and the service he had rendered, he ran to meet his mistress on her return home, his jaws and face besmeared with blood. As soon as the Bráhman's wife beheld him, she was convinced that he had killed her child, and in her rage and agitation, she threw the water jar at the ichneumon with all her force, and killed him on the spot. She then rushed into the house, where she found the child still asleep, and the body of a venomous snake torn in pieces at the foot of the bed. She then perceived the error she had committed, and beat her

---

[1] Nakula: Viverra mungo, C. [Benfey, l. l., I, 479. ff.]

breast and face with grief, for the unmerited fate of
her faithful little favourite. In this state her husband
found her on his return. When he had told her the
cause of his absenting himself, she reproached him
bitterly for that greedy desire of profit, which had
caused all the mischief, forgetting, she said, the saying,
"Excessive cupidity is to be avoided, although all
desire of profit be not relinquished. The wheel whirls
round his head, who evinced inordinate avarice."
The husband asked her how that happened, and she
replied:

"There dwelt in a certain town four Bráhmans, all
intimate friends, and equally poor. They consulted
together what was to be done; for poverty, they
agreed, was intolerable. Patrons, however well attended, are dissatisfied; friends and sons desert the
poor; merit is of no avail, and misfortunes multiply.
Wives of the best family abandon their husbands;
friends transfer their attachment to more powerful
individuals. Again, let a man be brave, handsome,
eloquent, and learned, without wealth, he obtains not
any enjoyment, and is as a dead man amongst the
living. Better death, than poverty. Again, it is said,
"Arise, my friend, for a moment, and remove the
burden of indigence from my fate, that I may share
with you the felicity which death affords. It is better,
therefore, to go to the cemetery at once, and become
a corpse, than live in poverty." The friends assented
to this, and agreed, that every effort should be adopted
to acquire wealth, as it is said, nothing is obtained by

him who has not money. Let, therefore, the wise
man attach himself to its acquirement. Wealth is
acquirable by six means: begging, service, agriculture,
science, usury, and trade: of which, trade is the best,
as its profits are most independently realized; as it is
observed: "The food obtained as alms may be carried
off by crows; the favour of a prince or patron may
be withdrawn; agriculture is laborious; and the respect
to be paid to a preceptor in acquiring knowledge
is troublesome; usury brings poverty on other
people; so that the only method eligible is trade.
Money is made in trade in seven ways: by defective
weights and measures; by false statements of price;
by the lapse of deposits; by receiving the securities of
friends; by managing estates for others; by dealing
in perfumes; and by exporting goods for sale. In the
first case, it is pretended that the measure is full,
when it is not. In the second, selling a thing for
more than its worth is the natural practice, even of
barbarians. While a deposit is in his house, the merchant prays to the gods that the owner may die, when
he will make them suitable offerings. When a trader
sees an acquaintance coming to borrow, he pretends
to lament his misfortune, but is inwardly delighted.
In the management of estates is the reflection, I have
got hold of lands full of treasure. Of all goods[1], perfumes are the best: gold is not to be compared to the
article which is procured for one, and is parted with

---

[1] See remarks at the close of this Essay.

for a thousand. Exporting commodities is the proper
business of persons already wealthy; as it is said, 'Those
who are wealthy are heard of from afar.' Riches are
attracted by riches, as wild elephants are caught by
tame ones. Capital is multiplied twice and thrice over,
in repeatedly buying and selling, by those who have
knowledge, and travel to other lands. The idle and
weak alone are afraid of foreign countries. 'Crows,
deer, and dastards, die in their native place.'

Having thus reflected, the four friends determined
to quit their home, and set off together on travel.
The man, whose mind is intent on wealth, leaves his
friend and family, his mother and his natal soil, and
roams to foreign and ungenial lands, without a moment's
hesitation. After some days, the Bráhmans arrived
at Avanti (Ujjayiní), where they bathed in the Siprá,
and worshipped Mahákála[1]; after which they proceeded, and met with a Yogí named Bhairavánada,
with whom they formed an acquaintance, and who
invited them to his abode. He inquired of them the
purpose of their journey. They said, they were
pilgrims in search of magic power, repairing to the
shrine where wealth or death awaited them; as it is
said, 'The water that falls from Heaven may sometimes
flow in the realms below the earth. The force of fate
is inconceivable, and man is weak against it. The

---

[1] One of the twelve great Lingas, and well known to have
been especially worshipped at Ujjayiní. This Linga was destroyed by Altumsh, in 1231.

objects of man may be apparently attained by mortal efficacy: but that is fate; for when you speak of human qualities, you give that name to destiny; at the same time, ease is not here the source of ease, nor can it be enjoyed without exertion. The destroyer of Madhu (Vishńu) seized Lakshmí forcibly, and held her clasped in a firm embrace. Tell us, therefore, they continued, if you are acquainted with any drug of virtue, to carry us into secret chasms, and tame the imps of evil; or efficacious in the rites of charnel grounds. You, they said, are an adept; we are but novices, but we are resolute. None but the illustrious can satisfy the wishes of the worthy. The ocean alone supports the subterrestrial flame.'

The Yogí, finding them apt scholars, admitted their request, and gave them four magical balls, one a-piece, directing them to go to the northern side of the Himáchala mountains, where each, on the spot where the balls should spontaneously fall, would find a treasure. They accordingly went thither; and one of the balls soon fell on the ground. The Bráhman, to whom it belonged, with the assistance of the rest, dug up the soil, and there discovered a copper mine. He desired the rest to take as much as they liked, but they refused, determining to seek their fortunes farther. He replied, Go on, then, I shall return; taking therefore as much of the metal as he could, he went back, and the rest proceeded.

The ball belonging to another soon fell, and he dug up the spot, which proved to contain a silver mine.

Overjoyed, he exclaimed, "Let us go no farther, but take as much as we can, and then return." The other two, however, ridiculed his folly, and resolved to advance, hoping as they had at first met with copper, then silver, they should successively meet with metal still more valuable. So it proved, for the next ball that fell indicated a vein of gold, with which the man to whom the ball belonged entreated his companion to rest satisfied. The argument previously used, however, being justified by the discovery of gold, determined him to persevere, in the full confidence, that he should next come to a bed of diamonds. The discoverer of the gold mine declined accompanying him, and he went on alone —, the other promising to await his return.

The last Bráhman proceeded through solitary paths, scorched by the rays of the sun, and faint with thirst, till at last he came to a place which was whirling round, and on it stood a man, whose body was covered with blood, and on whose head a wheel revolved. He approached, and asked him who he was, and why the wheel was placed upon his head, and requested him also to shew him where any water was procurable; but he had scarcely spoken, when the wheel transferred itself from the crown of its late possessor to the head of the Bráhman. He exclaimed, How! what is this? and the stranger replied, You have taken the wheel from my head, and you must keep it, till some one like yourself shall come hither, with that magic ball in his hand, and shall address to you similar questions to those you have asked of me. The Bráhman inquired, how long a time he had passed in that plight. The stranger asked who was the present sovereign, to which the Bráhman answered, Víná-vatsa[1]. The man then said, When Ráma reigned, I came hither, impelled by my poverty, and guided by the magic ball, as thou hast been: I found a man here with the wheel on his head, and asking him such questions as thou hast put, the wheel was fixed upon my head. I have been here ever since. And how did you get any thing to eat? inquired the Bráhman. The other replied, This law was fixed by the God of wealth, who fears his treasure should be plundered. His fears are known to the Siddhi Nágas[2], who send

---

[1] Udayana or Vatsa, the King of Kauśámbí, is probably intended here; he was celebrated for his skill on the Víná, or Lute. This prince is the hero of the first chapters of the Vrihat-Kathá, which gives this account of his descent. He is the son of Sahasráníka, the son of Śatáníka, the son of Janamejaya, the son of Paríksbit, the son of Arjuna. The genealogy of Arjuna's descendants, which Dr. Buchanan Hamilton derives from the Bhágavata P., has no prince of this name. The son of Sahasráníka is termed Aśwamedhaja. The two works are also at variance, regarding the founder of Kauśámbí, the Vrihat Kathá ascribing it to Sahasráníka, which is so far apparently most correct, that various works concur in styling Vatsa king of Kauśámbí, whilst the Bhágavata, however, calls the founder of that city Chakra, the fourth prince from Sahasráníka. Hindu genealogies, Introduction 13, and table 9. [Lassen, Ind. Alt., I, XXVI.]

[2] The Nágas are the serpents which inhabit the region under the earth. Siddhi means superhuman power which may be ob-

men hither: but when a mortal arrives, he loses the
sensations of hunger and thirst, and is exempt from
decay and death. He retains alone the consciousness
of solitude and pain. But now excuse me, I am re-
leased, and shall return home. So saying, he departed.

The Bráhman, who had found the gold mine,
wondered why his companion tarried so long, and
becoming at last impatient, he set off in quest of him.
Tracing his course by the impressions of his feet, he
followed him to the spot where he stood, and beheld
him covered with blood, running down from his head,
which was cut by the sharp edges of the wheel. To
the inquiries of his friend he replied by telling him
the property of the wheel—, and what he had witnessed. On which the other reproached him, saying,
Did I not tell you to stop? but your lack of sense
could not allow you to take my advice. It is very
justly observed, 'Better sense than science; unless it
improve by knowledge.' Those who want common
understanding will as surely perish as did those who
revived the Lion. The man with the wheel asked how
that was, to which the other replied:

"There were four Bráhmans residing in the same
village, all intimate friends. Three were men of great
acquirements, but destitute of common sense. The

---

tained by their worship. Their being opposed to Kuvera, and
desirous of encroaching on his wealth, although here stated in a
popular form, is like many things in this work, no longer a
familiar notion amongst the Hindus.

fourth was an intelligent fellow, but equally destitute of learning. As they were poor, they determined at one of their meetings to go to some country where learning was patronized, and where, they were satisfied, they should speedily be enriched with presents from the king. They accordingly set off, but when they had gone some way, the eldest cried out, 'It never occurred to me before, that our fourth friend here is illiterate. He is a man of sense to be sure, but that will not entitle him to any rewards from the king; we shall have, therefore, to relinquish to him a part of our earnings, and it would be fairer, I think, for him to remain at home.' The second agreed in this opinion, but the third opposed it, saying, 'we have always been friends and companions from infancy, and let him, therefore, participate in the wealth we shall acquire.' This sentiment prevailed, and they all went on in harmony.

"As they passed through a forest, they saw the scattered bones of a dead Lion. 'I have met,' said one, 'with an account of a method by which beings can be re-animated: what say you? shall we try the experiment, and employ the energies of science to restore life and shape to these bones?' They agreed. One undertook to put the bones together; the second to supply the skin, flesh, blood, &c., and the other to communicate life to the figure. When the two first had accomplished their tasks, the third was about to begin his; but the fourth stopped him; 'Consider what you are going to do,' he exclaimed, 'if you give life to the lion, the consequence will be that he will devour us.' 'Away, blockhead,' replied the sage, 'I am not to project things in vain.' 'Wait an instant, then,' replied the man of sense, 'till I get up into this tree.' So saying, he climbed up into a tree at hand, and his learned associates accomplished their undertaking. A substantial living lion was formed, who fell upon the three philosophers, and destroyed them. When he was gone, the man of common sense descended from his hiding place, and reached home again in safety."

When he had finished, the man with the wheel exclaimed: "This is very unreasonable, that destiny should destroy men of great talents, and allow simpletons to escape; as it is said, 'See where Śatabuddhi (hundred-wit) is carried on the head, and there too is Sahasrabuddhi (thousand-wit), whilst I, who am Eka-buddhi (single-wit), still may gambol in the crystal stream.' 'How,' asked he of the gold mine, 'happened that?' The Chakradhara[1] replied, 'In a certain reservoir were two fishes, one named Śatabuddhi, the other Sahasrabuddhi. They had a friend, a frog, named Ekabuddhi, with whom they were in the habit of meeting and conversing at the edge of the water. When the usual party assembled, they saw several fishermen with their nets approach, and heard them say to one another, 'this pool is full of fish, the water

---

[1] From Chakra, a wheel, and Dhara, who bears; the use of this denominative may spare some repetition.

is but shallow, we will come to-morrow morning and
drag it.' They then went away. When they had
departed, the frog said to his friends, 'What is to be
done? had we not better make our escape?' at which
Sahasrabuddhi laughed, and said, 'never fear, they
have only talked of coming. Yet, if they should come,
I will be answerable for your safety, as well as my
own. I shall be a match for them, as I know all the
courses of the water.' Śatabuddhi said, 'My friend
here is very right; wherever there is a way for the
breeze, for water or its tenants, or for the rays of the
sun, the intellect of a sagacious person will penetrate.
By following his counsel your life would be in no
peril, even had you approached the abodes of the
manes. Stay where you are, even I will undertake
your safety.' The frog said, 'I have, perhaps, but
limited talent, a mere singleness of sense, but that tells
me to flee; and therefore, whilst I can, I shall withdraw with my mate to another piece of water.' The
frog left the pool that night. In the morning the
fishermen arrived, and the lake was so beset with
nets, that all the fish, turtles, crabs, and other tenants
of the water were made prisoners, and amongst them
Śatabuddhi and Sahasrabuddhi, in spite of their boasted cunning, were caught and killed. The frog saw
the fishermen on their return, and recognising Śatabuddhi on the head of one man, and Sahasrabuddhi
dragged along with cords by another, pointed them
out to his mate in the words which I cited."

The Bráhman of the gold mine answered, This may

be very true, but a friend's words are not to be despised, and you had better have listened to me, than followed the dictates of your own avarice and presumption. Well was it said, 'Bravo, uncle, you would sing your song, though I dissuaded you, and see what a splendid gem you have received as the recompense of your performance.' The Chakradhara asked, how was that? The other replied.

"In a certain village there was an Ass named Uddhata. During the day he carried the bundles of a washerman. At night he followed his own inclinations. During his nocturnal rambles he formed an acquaintance with a Jackal, in whose company he broke into enclosures, and feasted on their contents. On one occasion, when in the middle of a cucumber field, the Ass, exulting with delight, said to the Jackal, 'Nephew, is not this a heavenly night: I feel so happy that I must sing a song. In what key will you prefer it?' The Jackal replied, 'What nonsense, when we are engaged in plundering, to think of such a thing. Silence becomes thieves and libertines, as it is said, 'Let the sick man and the lazy refrain from stealing and chattering, if they would escape with life.' If your song be ever so sweet, should the owner of the field hear, he will rise, and in his rage bind and kill you: eat, therefore, and be silent.' The Ass replied, 'You can be no judge of the charms of music, as you have spent all your life in the woods. Observe, in the nights of autumn, in privacy with your love, the distant song of the singer drops like nectar into the ears.' The Jackal answered, 'may be so, but your voice is abominable, why should you let it lead you into trouble?' The Ass was highly affronted at this, and said; 'away, blockhead, do you question my musical proficiency? I know every branch of the science; for instance, there are seven notes, three scales, and twenty-one intervals, &c.'¹ The scientific combination of the parts of music is particularly grateful in the autumnal season. There is no gift of the gods more precious than music. Rávańa received the boon from the three eyed god (Siva), delighted with the rattling of dry tendons. How then do you presume to question my powers, or to oppose their exercise?' 'Very well,' replied the Jackal, 'let me get to the door of the garden, where I may see the gardener as he approaches, and then sing away as long as you please.' So it was settled; and the Jackal having provided for his own safety, the Ass opened his chaunt. The gardener was awakened by the noise, and rising immediately, repaired to the spot, armed with a stout stick, with which he fell upon the ass, knocked him down, and belaboured him till he was tired. He then brought a large clog, with a hole in it, which he fastened to his leg, and tied him to a post, after which

---

¹ The entire enumeration in the text is 7 swara, 3 grama, 21 múrchhana, 19 tála, 3 mátrá, 3 laya, 3 sthána, 6 yatis, 9 rasa, 36 varńa, 40 bháshá, 150 gítá. See the author's remarks, at the close of this essay. Mr. Wilson reads nara for rasa, and three divisions of yatis in place of 6 yatis.—H.T.C.

he returned home, and went to sleep. The Ass came to himself, and forgot his tortures in the recollection of his home and companions. As it is said, 'On a dog, a mule, and an ass, a good beating leaves but a momentary impression.' Accordingly, springing up, he forced his way out of the inclosure, carrying the clog along with him. As he ran off, the Jackal met him, and said, 'Bravo, uncle,' &c."

The Chakradhara having heard this story, answered, What you observe is very just; but you should recollect, that a man who neither exercises his own judgment, nor follows a friend's advice, brings on his own ruin, as was the case with Manthara, the weaver.

"There was a weaver named Manthara, all the wood work of whose loom was, on one occasion, broken. Taking his axe, he set off to cut fresh timber, and finding a large Sísu-tree, by the sea side, began to fell it. In the tree resided a spirit, who exclaimed on the first stroke of the axe, 'Hola, this tree is my dwelling, and I cannot quit it, as here I inhale the fresh breeze that is cooled by the ocean's spray.' The weaver replied, 'What am I to do? unless I get wood, my family must starve. Do you, therefore, look out for another house; quick, this I must have.' The spirit replied, 'You shall have any thing else you ask for; but not this tree.' The weaver then agreed to go home, and consult a friend and his wife, and return with his final determination.

"When the weaver returned home, he found there a very particular friend of his, the barber of the village, to whom he told what had occurred, and whom he consulted what he should request. The barber said: 'Ask to be made a king; then I will be your prime minister, and we shall enjoy ourselves gloriously.' The weaver approved his notion; but first, he added, he must consult his wife. To this the barber strenuously objected. A wise man, he argued, would confer on women food, clothing, and appropriate ornaments, but would never let them share his councils, as Bhárgava has stated, that where a woman, a rogue, or a child, had the management, the house was sure of going to ruin. A man would maintain his rank and respectability, as long as he associated with grave people, and entrusted no woman with his secrets. Women are engrossed with their own designs, and purpose only their own pleasure. They love their own children even no longer than they derive from them self-gratification.' The weaver admitted the justice of his friend's observations; but his wife, he said, had no other thoughts than for her husband's welfare, and he must take her advice. Accordingly he went to her, and related what had happened, what the barber had recommended, and asked her what she thought it would be most advantageous for him to solicit: she replied:

"'You should never listen, husband, to the advice of a barber; as it is said, 'Husbands should never take counsel with courtezans, parasites, mean persons, barbers, gardeners, and beggars. Royalty is a very troublesome thing, and the cares of peace and war, aggression and negotiation, defence and administration, never allow its possessor a moment's enjoyment. He, who is wise, will ever shun the station of a king, for which his own relations, brothers and offspring, would be armed against his life. I should recommend you, therefore, to be contented with your station, and only to seek the means of more effectually earning your livelihood. Ask for an additional pair of hands, and another head, with which you may keep a loom going both before and behind you. The profit of such a second loom will be quite sufficient to give you consequence and credit with your tribe, as we have already from those of the first quite enough for our own expenditure."

"This advice pleased the husband mightily: he repaired forthwith to the tree, and requested the spirit, as the price of his forbearance, to give him another pair of arms, and an additional head. No sooner said than done; and he immediately was possessed of two heads and four arms, with which he returned homewards, highly delighted. His new acquisitions, however, proved fatal: for as soon as the villagers saw him, they exclaimed, 'a goblin! a goblin!' and falling on him with clubs, or pelting him with stones, speedily put a period to his existence. Therefore, I say, &c."

The Chakradhara continued: Every one who is tormented by the devil of improper expectations naturally incurs ridicule, as it is said, 'He who forms extravagant hopes for the future will be as much disappointed as the father of Soma Śarmá.' How was that? asked the other Bráhman; and he with the wheel proceeded.

"There was an avaricious Bráhman named Soma Śarmá, who had collected during the day as much meal, in alms, as filled an earthen jar. This jar he suspended to a peg immediately at the foot of his bed, that he might not lose sight of it. During the night he lay awake some time, and reflected thus: That jar is full of meal. If a scarcity should take place, I shall sell it for a hundred pieces at least; with that sum I will buy a pair of goats; they will bear young, and I shall get enough by their sale to purchase a pair of cows. I shall sell their calves, and will purchase buffaloes; and with the produce of my herd I shall be able to buy horses and mares. By the sale of their colts I shall realize an immense sum; and with my money I will build a stately mansion. As I shall then be a man of consequence, some wealthy person will solicit my acceptance of his daughter with a suitable dower. I shall have a son by her, whom I will call by my own name Soma Śarmá. When he is able to crawl, I shall take him with me on my horse, seating him before me. Accordingly, when Soma Śarmá sees me, he will leave his mother's lap, and come creeping along, and some day or other he will approach the horses too near; when I shall be very angry, and shall desire his mother to take him away. She will be busy with her household duties, and will not hear my orders; on which I shall give her a kick with my foot. Thus saying, he put forth one of his feet with such violence, as to break the jar. The meal accordingly fell on the ground; where, mingling with the dust and

dirt, it was completely spoiled: and so ended Soma
Śarmá's hopes.'"

"There is a city in the north, named Madhupura,
of which Madhusena was king. A daughter was born
to him, who had three breasts. When the king heard
this, he ordered the chief attendant to take away the
infant, and expose her in the woods, so that the matter
should remain unknown. The attendant, however,
recommended that, as the birth of such an infant was
a very extraordinary event, it would be better to
consult the Bráhmans what was to be done, so that
the consequence might not be the loss of both worlds;
as it is said, a wise man should always inquire the
meaning of what he observes, like the Bráhman, who
thus escaped the grasp of the goblin. The king asked
how that was, to which the attendant replied:

"Chańḍavarmá, a Rákshasa, haunted a certain wood,
and one day laid hold of a Bráhman, who passed,
leaping upon his shoulders, and ordering him at the
same time to proceed. The Bráhman, overcome with
terror, obeyed; but as he went along, he observed
that the goblin's feet were particularly soft and tender,
and inquired of him how this happened. The Rákshasa

---

[1] A story of a monkey revenging himself on a king, who
had caused a number of tame monkeys to be killed, and the
marrow of their bones applied to relieve burns in his horses,
scorched by the stables being burnt, here follows; and is succeeded
by a tale of a monkey, a thief, and a goblin. Both are omitted,
as deficient in interest; the entire fifth section being too long for
insertion.

replied, I am under a vow never to walk, or touch the ground with my feet. After this, they came to a pool, where the Rákshasa said, Let me down, whilst I bathe, and perform my devotions; but beware how you leave the place till I come out of the water. The Bráhman obeyed; but when he had got rid of his load, he reflected, that now was his time to escape; for as the Rákshasa was incapacitated for walking, he would not be able to overtake the fugitive; accordingly he took to his heels, and effected his retreat in safety: therefore I said, &c."

The advice thus given by the attendant was followed by the Rájá: and having summoned the Bráhmans, he consulted them how he should act; to which they replied, "It is said, Sire, that a daughter whose limbs are defective or excessive will be the cause of death to her husband, and destruction of her own character: and a damsel with three breasts will inevitably be the source of evil to the parent, whose sight she may attract. Your Majesty should therefore take care to avoid seeing your daughter. Let any one, that will, marry her, stipulating that he leaves the country. In this way no offence will be offered to this world, or the next." The Rájá approved of this plan, and ordered the drum to be beat, and proclamation to be made, that whoever would marry the princess, and remove with her to a distant country, should receive a hundred thousand rupees. Notwithstanding this offer, no person came forward; and the princess arrived at adolescence, without any one proposing to espouse her. At last she found a husband.

In the city resided two paupers who were friends; the one was blind, and the other hunch-backed; the latter, who was named Manthara, persuaded the former to marry the princess, with whom, and the money, they should remove to a distant place, and lead a life of ease: or if by the evil nature of the princess he should die, there would at least be an end of his misery. The blind man accordingly accepted the terms of the proclamation; and having married the princess, and received the dower, set off with her, and his friend, to a distant residence.

After passing some time contentedly, the blind man giving himself up to indolence, and hunch-back conducting their domestic arrangements, the evil influence of the princess's deformity began to operate, and she intrigued with hunch-back. This couple then soon began to plot the blind man's destruction. With this intent hunch-back brought home one day a dead snake of a venomous nature, which he gave to the princess, and desired her to mince it, and dress it with proper sauces, after which she should give it to her husband, telling him it was a dish of fish. Manthara then went away, and the princess, delighted, cut up the snake, and set it to boil: then, having other matters to look after, she called to her husband, and desired him to attend to the stirring of the nice mess of fish she was cooking for his dinner. He obeyed her, licking his lips at the intimation, and stirring the vessel as it boiled. In this manner, hanging over the caldron, the fumes of the venom drew the tears so copiously from his eyes, that they gradually dissolved the film which obscured his vision, and he was restored to sight. As he looked into the boiler, he saw immediately that he was cooking the fragments of a black snake. He at once concluded what his wife's design was, but remained in doubt, who her accomplice could be. To ascertain this, he resolved to dissemble, and still affect his former blindness. Presently hunch-back returned, and the husband, watching his conduct unobserved, was soon satisfied of the good understanding that subsisted between his treacherous friend, and faithless spouse. He approached them unperceived, and suddenly seizing hunch-back by the feet, being a man of great strength, he whirled him over his head, and dashed him against the breast of the wife with such violence, that his head drove her third breast through her body to her back, and both she, and her paramour, instantly perished: therefore I said, &c.

The Bráhman who had found the gold mine then concluded, "It is well said, all prosperity proceeds from Fate; but, in compliance with Destiny, prudence is not to be disregarded in the manner in which you neglected it by not listening to my advice." He then left his friend to his fate, and returned to his own abode.

Vishńu Sarmá having thus terminated these narratives, asked the princes, what more it was necessary for him to say? The princes replied, Most worthy preceptor, we have learnt from you all that is essential to the duties of a king. Then we have only to wish, answered Vishńu Śarmá, that this Sástra may be considered as a mirror, reflecting light friendly to other sciences, and facilitating to those, who are acquainted with its contents, the acquirement of worldly wisdom.

When the king found his sons were instructed in this manner, in the course of six months, in the substance of all the Śástras, he was highly delighted with their improvement, and acknowledging that the sage had fulfilled his promise, loaded him with unprecedented wealth and favours.

The course of the narrative has interrupted our comments: it is therefore necessary to revert to them, to indicate a very few analogies which this section offers, and to notice one or two circumstances which are interesting as throwing light on a state of manners no longer known to the Hindus.

The first story, of the beggar turned to a lump of gold by a blow, occurs, with some variation, in the third section of the Hitopadeśa. It may be also considered as connected with the tale of the dervise Abounader, in the Oriental Tales[*]. The chief peculiarity, however, of this story is its correct de-

---

[*] [Cabinet des Fées, Vol. XXV, p. 130. Benfey, l. l., I, 477 ff.]

lineation of Jain customs; a thing very unusual in Bráhmanical books. The address of the barber, and the benediction of the Superior of the Vihára, are conformable to Jain usages. The whole is indeed a faithful picture: it is also unaccompanied by any sneer, or abuse; and the satire is rather levelled at the Bráhmans. The accuracy of the description is an argument for some antiquity; as the more modern any work is, the more incorrect the description of the Jainas and Bauddhas, and the confounding of one with the other.

The second story is in both the Hitopadeśa, and Kalíla wa Damna. It was an early favourite in Europe, and is found as a Fabliau, the dog being substituted for the weasel or ichneumon; an exchange in very good taste, when the scene is laid in Europe, but wholly foreign to the notions of the Hindus, amongst whom the dog has never been a domestic animal: whilst the neol or nakula, the viverra mungo, on the contrary, has always been a pet. The most pleasing form of this celebrated tale is the ballad of Buth Gellert*.

The passage of the third story, relative to the profits of trade, it is not very easy to render in a satisfactory

---

* [bedd Gelhart, i. e. the grave of Kilhart. E. Jones (Musical relics of the Welsh bards. London: 1808, Vol. I, p. 75.) mentions the common Welsh proverb: yr wy'n edivaru cymmaint a'r Gwr a laddodd ei vilgi, i. e. I repent as much as the man who slew his greyhound. See also A. Keller ad "Dyocletianus Leben." 1841, p. 53.]

manner, as the technical terms employed are no longer in use.

The Goshṭika karma appears to imply the management of lands for others, by the expression illustrative of it; but the Parichita-gráhakágama is by no means clear. One copy alone attempts to explain it. Parichitam ágachchhantan gráhakam utkanṭhayá vilokya śreshṭhí hṛidaye hṛishyate: The merchant is delighted at heart, when with affected sorrow he sees an acquaintance coming (as a borrower)*.

The musical pretensions of the ass, and the beating they procure for him, form a fable with which all children are familiar**. The recapitulation of musical terms that occurs, is, however, rather curious, and exceeds the limits, to which Sir William Jones and Mr. Paterson *** have carried their explanation of the musical language of the Hindus. The seven notes are common to the Hindu scale, and that of Europe. The Grámas are scales. Of these, the Madhyama Gráma is identified by Mr. Paterson with the major, and the Gándhára with the minor, mode. The Múrchhanas

---

* [The verses quoted above are found in Kosegarten's text inserted at p. 6 & 7 (Book I, vv. 6—20.) Benfey, I. 1., II, 5. translates *goshṭikakarmaoniyukta* by "an agent" or "broker", and *parichitagṛdhaka* by "a rich buyer". The former is rendered by Böhtlingk (Mélanges Asiatiques, IV, 209.) "the partner in a joint business", the latter "a customer".]

** [Weber, Ind. Stud., III, 352. Grimm, Reineke Fuchs. Berlin: 1834, p. CCIX.]

*** [Asiat. Res., IX, 456 ff.]

he considers as the intervals of the scale. There are seven to each grámn, or twenty-one in all. Tála is the division of time; and the Mátrás and Layas refer to the same, no doubt: the first possibly implying the duration of the bars, the second that of the notes, and the third that of the rests, or pauses. Of the remaining members of the list, in their purely musical sense, I cannot here attempt an explanation[1].

The story of the weaver may remind us of the three wishes, to which, however, in point and humour, it is vastly inferior[*]. That of Soma-Śarmá is given in the Kalíla wa Damna, and Hitopadeśa [IV, 8]. It is in substance the same also as that of Alnaschar, in the Arabian Nights. As related in the Ayár Dánish of Abúlfazl, it is translated in the first volume of the Asiatic Miscellany[**].

The story comprised within the last, of the Rákshasa who got upon the Bráhman's shoulders, contains the hint of the old man who proved so troublesome to Sindbad, in his fifth voyage; and who makes so prominent a figure also in the Hindi story of Kámarúpa and Kámalatá, translated by Colonel Franklin[***]. The

---

[1] As relating to vocal music, several of the terms may here be understood in their ordinary sense: mátrá refers to syllabic length, or vowel sounds; varnas are consonants; bháshá signifies language; and gítá tune or song.—H.T.C.

[*] [Benfey, l. l., I. 495 ff.]

[**] [Benfey, l. l., I. 499 ff. H. Kurz ad B. Waldis IV, 81. Grimm's Kindermärchen, Vol. III, 214.]

[***] [For the literature comp. Benfey, l. l., I. 534 ff., who refers also to Mahábh. XIII, 5885—5918.]

last story of the section is absurd enough; but it has a curious bearing, although perhaps unintentionally. The malformation of the heroine might be thought a satire on a very popular legend of the south of India, traces of which may be seen in their sculptures, particularly at Madura. According to that story, the daughter of one the early Pāṅdyan Kings was born with three breast. She was an incornation of Devî; and the third breast disappeared, when she espoused Śiva himself, in the form of Sundareśwara, the divinity that was ever afterwards the tutelary god of the Pāṅdyan kingdom, and its capital, Madura. A modification of this legend is also met with in Ceylon; the fair demon Kuráńí, having been born with three breasts, one of which disappeared on her espousal of Vijaya, the prince who first led a colony to that Island.— Davy's Ceylon, 294*.

NOTE.

The Hitopadeśa is not the only Sanskrit epitome of the Panchopákhyána, or Pancha Tantra. Another abridgment of it, following the original much more closely, both in the matter, and in the arrangement of it, is the Kathâmríta-nidhi (treasure of the nectar of tales), by Ananta-Bhaṭṭa, who describes himself in the introductory and concluding lines of the work as

---

* [Benfey, l. l., 1, 513—34.]

son of Nagadeva-bhatta, a Bráhman of the Kánwa branch. He professes to preserve in his epitome of the text the whole of the narrative, or story, but to abbreviate the poetical illustrations. The performance appears, so far as I have compared it with the original, to conform with the author's professed design in that respect.—H.T.C.

VII.
HINDU FICTION.

From the British and Foreign Review, No. XXI (July 1840), p. 224—274.

1. Essai sur les Fables Indiennes. Par M. A. Loiseleur Deslongchamps. Paris: 1838.
2. Somadeva's Mährchen-Sammlung, Sanskrit und Deutsch. Von Dr. Hermann Brockhaus. Leipzig: 1839.

THE controversy that was carried on towards the end of the last century between the advocates of the eastern or of the northern origin of European fiction, had reference especially to a particular class of creations, — to those of chivalric romance, — to the marvellous exploits that were magnified out of the traditional achievements which might possibly have been wrought by the companions in arms of Arthur and Charlemagne, elevated to the rank of knights of the round table, or Paladins of France. These narrations, although they no doubt derived much of their martial fierceness from the songs of the bards and scalds, and much of their machinery from the more graceful and inventive fancy of the Arabs, yet took their peculiar character from the people for whom they were composed, and were

moulded into the forms in which they were popular,
in unison with the temper and tone of the times in
which they were written, until they presented but few
and uncertain vestiges of their foreign original.

This was not the case with the different class of
fictions which, at a somewhat later date, formed an
important accession to the literature of Europe, and
which can most confidently be traced to the East.
Belief in the Asiatic origin of many of the fables and
tales of domestic life, which afforded instruction and
entertainment to the Middle Ages, has for some time
prevailed, and of late years the proofs have been
multiplied by the industry of Oriental scholars. The
evidence adduced has been of the most positive description. It is not built on probabilities, upon general
and indefinite analogies, or on partial and accidental
resemblances, but upon actual identities. Although
modifications have been practised, names altered,
scenes changed, circumstances added or omitted, we
can still discover the sameness of the fundamental
outline, and, amidst all the mystifications of the mas-
querade, lay our hands, without hesitation, upon the
authentic individual. We can also, in many instances,
follow the steps of the migration which the narratives
have undergone, and determine when and by what
means these Asiatic adventurers were naturalized in
the different countries of Europe in which they are
found. The inquiry, however, is yet in its commencement, and it seems highly probable that its further
prosecution will very extensively add to the testimonies

of the Eastern origin of many of the inventions, which, as Contes, Fabliaux and Novelle, constituted the light reading of the more civilized nations of the West in the fourteenth and fifteenth centuries.

Sir William Jones, in his Discourse on the Hindus[*], observes that they are said to have boasted of three inventions,—the game of chess, the decimal scale, and the mode of instructing by apologues. He does not cite his authority, and it may be doubted if the Hindus ever boasted of any such discoveries. As far as relates to teaching by apologues, although there can be no doubt that it was a national contrivance, devised by them for their own use, and not borrowed from their neighbours, yet there is no sufficient reason to suppose that it was originally confined to them, or first communicated by them to other nations. It has been urged with some plausibility, that the universal prevalence amongst the Hindus of the doctrine of the metempsychosis was calculated to recommend to their belief the notion that beasts and birds might reason and converse, and that consequently the plan of such dialogues probably originated with them; but the notion is one that readily suggests itself to the imagination, and an inventive fancy was quite as likely as a psychological dogma to have gifted mute creatures with intelligence, and supplied them with a tongue. At any rate, we know that, as an article of poetical and almost of religious faith, it was known to the Greeks at an early

---

[*] [Works, III, p. 44.]

date, for Homer is authority for the speech of horses. Without affirming the apocryphal existence of Aesop, we cannot doubt that fables, such as are ascribed to him, were current even prior to his supposed date; and we have an instance of the fact in the story of the Hawk and Nightingale of Hesiod[*]. Other specimens of the same class of compositions are afforded by the fable of the Fox and Ape of Archilochus, of which a fragment is preserved by Eustathius; and by that of the Eagle and the Fox, which is attributed to the same writer[**], and is an established member of all collections of fables, both in Asia and in Europe. Roman tradition, — it would once have been called history, — furnishes at least one well-known instance of popular instruction by fable, which Menenius was not likely to have learnt from the Hindus; and various examples of this style of composition are familiarly known as occurring in Scripture. Although the invention was very probably of Eastern origin, we cannot admit that it was in any exclusive degree a contrivance of the Hindus, or that it was imparted originally by them to other Asiatic nations. If such a communication ever did take place, it must have occurred at a period anterior even to Hindu tradition.

Although, however, instruction by apologues cannot, strictly speaking, be regarded as originally or exclu-

---

[*] [Erga 202—11.]
[**] [Comp. G. Bernhardy, Griech. Literatur. Halle: 1856, II, 1, p. 427 f.]

sively a Hindu device, yet the purposes to which the
Hindus directed it, and the mode in which they
employed it, seem to be peculiarly their own. Fable
constitutes with them practical ethics—the science of
'Níti' or Polity—the system of rules necessary for the
good government of society in all matters not of a
religious nature—the reciprocal duties of the members
of an organized body either in their private or public
relations: hence it is especially intended for the education of princes, and proposes to instruct them both
in those obligations which are common to them and their
subjects, and those which are appropriate to their
princely office; not only in regard to those over whom
they rule, but in respect to other princes, under the
contingencies of peace or war. Each fable is designed
to illustrate and exemplify some reflection on worldly
vicissitudes, or some precept for human conduct; and
the illustration is as frequently drawn from the intercourse of human beings, as from any imaginary
adventure of animal existence; and this mixture is in
some degree a peculiarity of the Hindu plan of fabling
or story-telling. Again, these stories are not aggregated
promiscuously, and without method, but they are
strung together upon some one connected thread, and
arranged in the frame-work of some continuous narrative, out of which they successively spring; a sort
of machinery to which there is no parallel in the
fabling literature of Greece or Rome. As far, therefore,
as regards the objects for which the apologues or
stories are designed, and the mode in which they are

brought together, this branch of literary composition may be considered as original with the Hindus; and it was the form of their fabling that served as a model, whilst at the same time the subjects of their tales afforded materials, to the storytellers of Europe in the Middle Ages.

That the *fables of Pilpay* were of Indian extraction was known to the orientalists of Europe in the latter part of the last century. They are so described by Assemannus, Fabricius, Schultens, and other scholars. Acquaintance with Sanskrit literature had not then been attempted, and the orientalists alluded to were therefore unaware that the Indian original, in one of its forms at least, was still in existence, and was still as popular in its native country as it had been for some fifteen centuries at least. The translation of the Sanskrit work, entitled Hitopadesa, or Friendly Instruction, by Mr. Wilkins and Sir William Jones, first added this fact to the history of Pilpay's fables, and it was confirmed by the publication of the text at Serampore, in 1804, with an interesting preface by Mr. Colebrooke, in which its relations to its Asiatic and European imitations are circumstantially particularized. The text has been twice reprinted; in London in 1810, and at Bonn in 1829. The history has been further investigated, and a very ample and interesting detail of the different translations and imitations of the Indian original is prefixed to the late Sylvestre de Sacy's excellent edition of its Arabic version, the "Calila et Dimna, ou Fables de Bidpai," published at

Paris in 1816*. The subject has been resumed in the Essais sur les Fables Indiennes of the late M. Loiseleur Deslongchamps; and all that is known respecting it has been collected by him with most commendable industry, extent of erudition and accuracy of research. His premature death has deprived not only this department, but other branches of Sanskrit literature, of a zealous and talented scholar.

The *Hitopadeśa*, although in much of its contents the same as the prototype of Pilpay's fables, is not in all respects the original. It is avowedly a compilation, and the compiler in the introductory lines specifies his having collected his materials from the *Pancha Tantra* and other books. He therefore apprises us of at least a nearer approximation to the original, if not of the title of the original. In all works of this nature, however,—in all miscellaneous collections of stories, interspersed with passages which are in most instances, and may be possibly in all, citations from other works, great liberties have always been taken, both in the East and West, by transcribers and translators, with regard to the contents of the original compilation. The outline has usually been preserved, the most striking stories have been repeated, and in general a similar succession has been followed; but new stories have been inserted, old ones omitted or

---

* [Comp. also Liebrecht's translation of Dunlop's "History of Fiction." Berlin: 1851, p. 194 ff. Die Fabeln Bidpai's. Uebersetzt von Ph. Wolff. Stuttg. 1837. Introduction.]

remodelled, and the intervening remarks and precepts
diversified at pleasure, so as to produce infinite variety
in the copies of a work nominally the same, and to
render it a matter of almost insuperable difficulty to
determine the priority of any particular version, in
composition or in date. It would be rash, therefore,
to affirm of the Pancha Tantra that it is the very
work[*] that was translated by order of Noushirván,
the king of Persia, into Pehlevi in the sixth century,
although there is reason to believe that it is of high
antiquity, even as now current. An analysis of its
contents has been published in the first volume of the
Transactions of the Royal Asiatic Society[**]; and from
various considerations there specified it may be rea-
sonably inferred that, in the condition in which it is
still met with, it is an ancient work. In the arrangement
of the chapters it conforms with the Arabic Kalíla wa
Damna more exactly than the Hitopadeśa; and this is
one argument in favour of its approaching more nearly
to the assigned date of the original, as the Arabic
translation is itself a work of the ninth century. The
correspondence, however, is not complete; and as far
as any inference may be drawn from its greater or
less exactness, there is reason to believe, as we shall
have occasion hereafter to show, that we have in the
Sanskrit language another form of part of Pilpay's

---

[*] [See however Benfey's Panchatantra, I, p. 5—8.]

[**] [See the preceding article.]

fables, which claims precedence even of the Pancha Tantra.

A version of the Pancha Tantra, as current in the South of India, has been published in French by the Abbé Dubois, but not entire. He has given only a selection of the stories, taken from three different copies, written one in Canarese, one in Telugu, and one in Tamil. It may be doubted if his principle of selection is the most judicious that could have been adopted. "Nous avons tiré de cet ouvrage tous les apologues qui peuvent intéresser un lecteur européen, et nous avons omis plusieurs autres, dont le sens et la morale ne pouvaient être entendus que par le très-petit nombre de personnes versées dans les usages et les coutumes indiennes auxquelles ces fables font allusion*." This is in fact to omit all that is most characteristic. Enough, however, is given to show that the vernacular representatives of the Pancha Tantra in the Peninsula correspond in plan, and in most of their many details, with the Sanskrit original. Some of the stories are additions: they are classed, like the original, in five books, whence the name of the work, Pancha Tantra, meaning 'The Five Chapters;' not, as M. Dubois explains it, 'Les Cinq Ruses.'

The earliest date at which we have evidence of the existence of this collection of fables is in the middle of the sixth century. Noushirvún, who reigned from a. d. 531 to a. d. 579, having heard of the work, sent

---

* [Préface p. VIII.]

his physician Barzûya to India on purpose to procure it. He brought it back, and by the king's command translated it into Pehlevi. He gave it the name of the Book of Kalila and Damna, from the names of the two Jackals, who are interlocutors in the first book of the collection. The fact of the translation of an Indian collection of fables into the language of Persia, at the period spoken of, rests upon the authority of a number of Mohammedan writers, some of whom were so near to the time at which the occurrence is said to have taken place, that they cannot be very far wrong in their chronology. The story is told by Firdausí in the Sháh Náma, and by Masúdí in his history called the 'Golden Meadows*,' who both wrote in the tenth century of our era; and a similar account is given in the preface of the Arabic translation, which was made in the eighth. M. De Sacy, therefore, is fully justified in asserting, "s'il est un fait que la critique la plus rigoureuse ne puisse contester, ce seroit assurement celui-là, quand même on n'auroit à faire valoir en sa faveur que cette imposante réunion de témoignages." (Calila et Dimna, Mémoire Historique, 2.)

A difficulty that has sometimes puzzled even those who feel little doubt of the Indian origin of the Kalila and Damna, or of Pilpay's fables, is the name of the author, which, according to the Mohammedan writers, was Bidpai, of which Pilpay is the European corruption. In the Sanskrit works, the Pancha Tantra and

---

* [Maçoudi. Paris: 1861. I, 159.]

Hitopadeśa, the author is not named. The stories are ascribed to a Brahman denominated Vishńu Śarman, who repeats them for the instruction of the sons of the king; but this is merely a part of the machinery, a dramatic impersonation. No satisfactory Indian original has been conjectured for the term Bidpai*. As Sir William Jones observes, Bid-pai in Persian means willow-footed, which is mere nonsense if applicable to a man; and Pil-pai elephant-footed, which is not much better. He is disposed, upon the authority of the author of the Anwári Soheilí, to resolve it into Baidya-priya, said by that writer, and by Abúlfazl, to denote 'friendly physician.' The character of 'physician' attributed to the first translator of the work, Barzúya, is in favour of some such etymology, and possibly the original term was merely the Sanskrit word Vaidya or Baidya, physician, or with the additional final vowel, which in Persian converts a definite into an indefinite noun, Baidya-i, a physician. It is easy to understand how this became Baidpai, for the only distinction between the two consonants is in the dots underneath them, a y having two dots, and a p three: the accidental addition of a third dot would therefore at once have changed Baidyai into Baidpai, and the mistake of a copyist will have been the source of the perplexity. According to M. De Sacy **, the original Arabic reads the name Baidaba, which he conjectures may be

---

* [Compare however Benfey, l. l., I, 32—35.]
** [Calila et Dimna. Mémoire historique, p. 17, Note.]

derived from the Sanskrit Vidván or Bidbán, a learned man. The common attribution of the character of physician to Bidpai is however in favour of Vaidya.

The Mohammedan conquest of Persia in the seventh century was the era of the destruction of the literature as well as of the religion and independence of the country. That the Persians had a literature is undeniable, as it is repeatedly alluded to by the earliest Mohammedan writers; and besides the reputed version of the Pancha Tantra into Pehlevi, both Tabari and Firdausi affirm that they derived their accounts, historical and poetical, of the kings of Persia from Pehlevi (that is, from Persian) records. The total disappearance of the national compositions and popular literature of Persia prior to the Mohammedan invasion is a remarkable circumstance, and one not easily to be explained; but it is sufficient to refer to it in this place as the occasion of a very inconvenient chasm in the history of fiction. It is now impossible to determine how far the literature of the Persians was the fountain of that fabling which the Arabs transmitted, or how far it was itself merely the channel by which a stream, originally springing up in India, was conveyed to the Mohammedans, and by them to the people of the farther west. The tradition that an envoy was sent to India to procure a collection of fables, intimates, however, that the Persians were rather the importers than the fabricators of such wares. The destruction, although rapid, was not immediate, and at any rate the Book of Kalila and Damna was spared for a season.

About a century after the subjugation of Persia it was translated from Pehlevi into Arabic by a native Persian, a convert to Mohammedanism, 'Abdallah Ibn Mokaffa', in the reign of Al Mansúr, the second khalif of the house of Abbás, who reigned from a. d. 754 to a. d. 775, the first khalif, according to Masúdí, who ordered tranlations of Persian and Greek works into Arabic to be made; amongst these was the 'Calila et Dimna.' The Pehlevi text then shared the fate of the other writings in the same language. The Arabic version still exists, and is the work which M. De Sacy published.

The Arabic prose translation of Ibn Mokaffa' was put into verse at the end of the same century, under the patronage of Yahya, son of Jaffir the Barmekide; and another metrical version was subsequently composed. In the tenth century it was translated into modern Persian verse by Rudeghí, a celebrated poet at the court of Nasr, one of the Sámání princes; and in the twelfth century, or a. d. 1121, a Persian prose translation was made by 'Abdul Má'li Nasr-ullah, who wrote under the patronage of one of the last kings of Ghizní, Behram Sháh. This work is still extant, and a detailed account of it is given by M. De Sacy in the tenth volume of the Notices et Extraits des Manuscrits. It has been eclipsed, however, in the estimation of the Mohammedans, by a more modern version of the Kalíla and Damna, composed about a. d. 1494 by Hosein Bin 'Alí, surnamed Al Wá'ez, who was patronized by Amír Sheikh Ahmed, surnamed Sohail, a chieftain commanding under Hosein Mirza, one of the last princes of the family of Timúr, who held his court at Herat. In honour of his patron, Al Wá'ez changed the name of his work to that of Anwári Soheili, under which it is well known, and is deservedly popular. It has been printed repeatedly in India, and portions of it have been occasionally translated. Much of the work very faithfully translates both the tales and the moral precepts and remarks of the Sanskrit original; and it is evident that the author must have had the original Sanskrit under his eye, for the moral and practical observations of the Hitopadesa reappear in the Anwári Soheili much more literally rendered than in the Arabic version of Ibn Mokaffa'. The translator has, however, reset the whole in a frame of his own devising, and has made many additions to the narratives from the general mass of Mohammedan and Hindu fiction, which, at the time and in the country in which he wrote, and under the political relations that had then long subsisted between Khorasan and India, had no doubt become intimately, and in many cases undistinguishably, intermixed.

At a period long antecedent to the composition of the Anwári Soheili in the East, the Kalíla and Damna had performed the first stage of its journey westward. It was translated from Arabic into Greek by Simeon Seth, towards the end of the eleventh century. Syriac and Hebrew versions were made probably about the same date, and from other copies of the original, as they offer discrepancies, which, although of little moment, show that different manuscripts must have been employed. From the Hebrew translation*, John of Capua, a converted Jew, executed, some time between 1262 and 1278, a version into Latin; it was printed in 1480, under the title of Directorium humane vite, alias Parabole antiquorum sapientum. This translation, as M. De Sacy remarks, is of the greatest importance in the history of the Kalīla and Damna, as it is the source from which, directly or indirectly, the translations and imitations in Spanish**, German***, Italian, French, and perhaps other languages, are derived, and is probably the channel by which the narratives and apologues originating with the Kalīla and Damna have passed into those collections of tales which became popular in the fourteenth and fifteenth centuries in Europe. An interesting specification of the different European versions, up to the latest date, is given by M. Deslongchamps.

In his résumé of the contents of the Pancha Tantra, which he has taken from the analysis of that work in the Royal Asiatic Society's Transactions, M. Deslongchamps has repeated, with several interesting additions, the identifications there intimated between the Hindu stories and their European reiterations. For these,

---

* [the tenth chapter of which was edited & translated in Benfey's "Orient und Occident", I, p. 481 ff. & 657 ff.]
** [ib., 1, 497 ff. published in Vol. LI. of the Biblioteca de Autores Españoles, p. 11—78.]
*** [ib., I, 138 ff. and 383 ff.]

however, we must be content to refer to his pages, and must pass to what constitutes a greater novelty in his dissertation, his account of 'Le Livre de Sendabad'.

The *Book of Sendebad*, according to M. Deslongchamps, is an oriental romance, of which translations or imitations exist in various European and Asiatic languages. Of these he specifies three as likely to be in an especial degree derived from the original. The Arabic story of a king, his son, his favourite, and seven vizirs; the Hebrew romance of the Parables of Sendebar, and the Greek romance of Syntipas; and from one of the two last, but more particularly from the Hebrew, M. Deslongchamps derives the History of the Seven Sages of Rome, Historia Septem Sapientum Romæ, which was composed by Dam Jehans, a monk of the abbey of Haute Selve, about the beginning of the thirteenth century, and enjoyed extensive popularity in Europe for three centuries afterwards. In confirmation of his view it may be remarked, that in a MS. of the Parables of Sendebar, which exists in the British Museum, it is repeatedly asserted in anonymous Latin notes, that the work was translated out of the Indian language into Persian and Arabic, and from one of them into Hebrew. Sendebar is also described as a chief of Indian Brahmans, and Biebar, the king, as a king of India.—Ellis, Metrical Romances, vol. iii.*

---

* [Benfey, l. l., I, 12 ff. 38 ff. and in Mélanges Asiatiques, III, p. 188. 192. 196 ff. A. Keller's Introduction before his edition

There is no doubt that the scheme of these different works is the same. In each a young prince is falsely accused by the wife of the king to his father, who determines thereupon to put him to death. The king, however, has seven ministers, and each of them in succession undertakes to defend the prince against the unfounded accusations of the queen. The charge and defence are both supported by a variety of stories, related alternately by the queen and one of the seven ministers or sages; and in the end the innocence of the prince is established. The stories vary to a greater or lesser extent in the several compilations, but many of them agree, and are traceable to Indian sources. Many of them differ; but the identity of the general plan cannot be an accidental occurrence, and it is quite sufficient to place beyond reasonable disbelief the existence of some common original. That the native country of that original was India, appears, from the circumstances above referred to, to have been matter of tradition; and that the tradition was not unfounded there is further evidence to substantiate.

The Arabic writer Masúdí has already been adverted to as evidence for the history of the Kalíla and Damna; he is likewise available for that of the work in question. In his Golden Meadows (Murúj-az-zeheb), in the chapter on the ancient kings of India, he speaks of an

---

of "Dyocletianus Leben." 1841. E. Carmoly, Paraboles de Sendabar. Paris: 1849. Introduction. H. Sengelmann, Das Buch von den sieben weisen Meistern. Halle: 1842.]

Indian philosopher named Sendebád, who was cotemporary with king Kúrush, and was the author of a work entitled, 'The story of the seven vizirs, the tutor, the young man, and the wife of the king.' "This is the work," he adds, "which is called the Book of Sendebád*." Masúdí died a. d. 956. It is clear from his description, brief as it is, that the main subject of the Book of Sendebád was the same as that of the Parables of Sendebúr, in which the name also is preserved, and with the Historia Septem Sapientum, where it is omitted. The Book of Sendebád, according to a more modern Persian writer, the author of the 'Mujmal at-Tawárίkh,' as quoted by M. Langles**, was written in Persia under the Arsacidan kings, and his account is confirmed by an Arabic historian, Hamza Isfahání; but they probably allude to a different work, the Adventures of Sindbád, which, although known to us as part of the Thousand and One Nights, does not properly constitute a member of that collection. However this may be, the testimony of Masúdí is quite sufficient for the determination of the Indian origin of this Book of Sendebád, in which we have no fabulous voyages or adventures, but a series of amusing illustrations of domestic manners, tending mostly to a calumnious depreciation of the female character.

---

* [Paris edition. I, p. 162.]

** [Voyages de Sind-bád le Marin. Paris: 1814, p. 139. See also H. L. Elliot, Index to the Historians of Muhammedan India. Calcutta: 1849. I. 265—7.]

The analysis which M. Deslongchamps offers of the Greek romance of Syntipas, compared with the Parables of Sendebár and the romance of the Seven Vizirs, affords several instances of narratives familiar to Indian fiction. One of the stories of the first sage, related in Syntipas and the Parables of Sendebár, the trick practised upon the parrot by the wife, that its information of her misdeeds may not be credited by her husband, and which is repeated in the Arabian Nights, the Seven Vizirs, the Directorium humanæ vitæ, Discorsi degli Animali, Giorni of Sansovino, is of Indian currency, and no doubt Indian origin[*]. The story of the woman, her two lovers, and her husband, occurs in the Hitopadeśa [II, 9]. One of the two stories of the third philosopher relates the adventures of a woman who goes to market to buy 'rice.' The two stories of the fourth philosopher are both Indian: one is that of the prince and merchant's wife of the Hitopadeśa [I, 8]; the other is found in a work to which we shall have occasion to recur, the Kathá Sarit Ságara. The fifth sage relates the remarkably popular story of the man who inconsiderately slew his dog, thinking that he had killed his infant, when in truth the animal had saved the child by destroying a serpent which had approached its cradle. This story is found in the Kathá Sarit Ságara, in the Pancha Tantra [V, 2] and in the Hitopadeśa, and there is in all of them a fitness in the incidents which is wanting in the version of the tale in

---

[*] [Benfey, l. l., 1, 271—275.]

Syntipas, the Parables of Sendebár, and the History of the Seven Sages, in all which also it occurs. The venomous snake is more suitable to India than to any European country; but there is a still more truly national circumstance in the description of the faithful animal by which the snake is killed, as a 'mungoose,' the fierce hostility of which creature to snakes, and its singular power of killing them, are in India so well known as to have become proverbial, and are verifiable by daily observation. It is doubtful if a dog has either any instinctive enmity to snakes, or any characteristic dexterity in destroying them. There is much more propriety in the beautiful Welsh tradition of Beth Gelert, where the slain intruder, who is killed by Lewellyn's gallant hound, is a wolf; but this is evidently an improvement upon the original narrative*. Several other tales are related in the story of Syntipas, which are indisputably of Indian origin, although modified in their details.

The analysis of the *Historia Septem Sapientum* shows that the monk of Haute Selve departed very widely from whatever form of the original may have served him for a model; and although he has adopted the plan, he has changed the persons, and either invented his fables, or borrowed them from other sources. The work is well known by the account given of it under its English form of the Seven Wise Masters, by Ellis, and it is not necessary, therefore, to allude to it

---

* [See above p. 76.]

more particularly. Those of its stories which are most unequivocally Indian, are that of the prince and merchant's wife; the dog, child, and snake; and the pie (or in the original, the parrot,) killed by its master for giving false witness, as he supposed, against his wife. The story of the monkey and wild boar is found, with some variations, in the Indian tales translated by Galland and Cardonne. An incident similar to that of the device adopted by Octavian to discover the friends of a dead body found in the royal treasury and suspended upon a gibbet, for the purpose of finding out who the person was, occurs in the Kathá Sarit Ságara. The story of the three corpses is evidently of the same origin as that of the hunchback in the Arabian Nights; and nothing can be more common in the fiction of the Hindus than the mutual love of two young persons utterly unknown to each other brought about by their mutual dreams, an instance of which occurs in the seventh and last story related by the queen. Although, therefore, the Seven Wise Masters, or the Historia Septem Sapientum, is undeniably indebted to other quarters for the bulk of its materials, yet some of them, as well as its general design, are as undeniably of Asiatic and Hindu invention.

Besides the migration westwards of these two works, the Fables of Pilpay and the Parables of Sendebár, in their general outline, as well as their component figments, no reasonable doubt can be entertained that various narratives of Indian origin found their way individually and unconnectedly to Europe. By what particular vehicles their transport was effected it is now unprofitable to inquire; but the intercourse with the East through commerce, literature, religion and war, was much more intimate and frequent from the early ages of Christianity down to the fifteenth century than it has ever been since the latter date, even than it is in the present day, notwithstanding the existence of the British empire in India. The greater proximity of Asia Minor to the countries of the South of Europe was one especial cause of the more intimate intercourse that subsisted between them; and the greater parity of civilization in which indeed the Asiatics had rather the advantage, was another. The political relations of the divisions of the Eastern and Western Empire necessarily preserved the provinces of either in a communication with each other, which could not speedily be forgotten; and although interrupted by the first violences of the Mohammedan conquest, it was readily renewed when the storm had passed, and the first khalifs of the house of Abbás encouraged the resort of merchants and scholars, both from the East and the West, to Bagdád. Upon their decline followed the Crusades, and the interest which they attracted to the scene of their achievements, and the numbers that, either as soldiers or pilgrims or traders, were constantly passing to and fro, continued to preserve that interest from decay, and were no doubt actively concerned in importing and disseminating the lighter oriental fictions of domestic life, as well as tales of chivalry and romance.

From the period subsequent to the establishment of the Khalifat, Europe received whatever literary articles were imported from the East through the medium of the Arabs. This did not imply that they were of Arab manufacture exclusively. The subjugation of Persia placed at the disposal of the Arabs whatever treasures they chose to spare from the destruction to which the mass was condemned; and it is upon record of the most indisputable authenticity, that the first Abbaside khalifs in the eighth and ninth centuries, from Al Mansúr to Al Mámún, patronised in an especial manner natives of India; and that Hindus of eminence in various branches of literature and science flourished at their courts. (Journal of the Royal Asiatic Society, vol. v.)

This, according to the same record, was the season at which the fictions of the Hindus were naturalized amongst the Mohammedans. It has even been asserted that *the Arabian Nights' Entertainments* had an Indian origin*; and there can be no doubt, that although in their actual form the collection has received contributions from other and comparatively modern sources, yet there existed at Bagdád a work upon a similar plan prior to the golden age of Arabic literature, and which served as the foundation of the Thousand and One Nights. For this Masúdí again is irrefragable authority. The passage was first brought to notice by the celebrated orientalist Von Hammer,

---

* [Lassen, Ind. Alt., IV, p. 902 ff.]

now Baron Purgstall, in the preface to his translation of some unedited portions of the Thousand and One Nights, or rather in the German translation of Von Hammer's French version by Professor Zinserling. The French translation, after passing through some adventures almost as wonderful as the original tales, was lost, on its transmission to England. As the passage did not occur in all the MSS. of Masúdí, Von Hammer subsequently published the original Arabic with a translation in the Journal Asiatique (vol. x. p. 253): the translation runs thus:—

"Many persons learned in the ancient history of the Arabs assert that these accounts (of the Garden of Irem) are romances and tales invented by persons who wished, by relating them, to conciliate the favour of their princes, and who became popular amongst their countrymen by learning and reciting such narrations. The traditions thus repeated are of the same class as the works which have come down to us translated from Persian, Indian and Greek, and they are composed in the style of the book denominated the Hazár Afsána, which is rendered in Arabic Alef Khiráfa, that is to say, The Thousand Tales; for the Arabic word Khiráfa corresponds with the Persian Afsána, and people call this book 'The Thousand Nights'. It is the story of a king and of his vizir, and of the vizir's daughter and her nurse; the two last are named Shirzad and Dinarzad. Such also is the story of Yalkand and Shimas, and the particulars which are found in it of the histories of the kings of India and their ministers, and in the story of Sindbad and other similar compositions."

There are some variations in the reading of this passage in different MSS. In the first version given by Von Hammer, he called the book 'Thousand and One Nights;' and a MS. in the British Museum confirms the translation denominating it the Alef leila wa leila, or Thousand Nights and One Night. M. De Sacy, however, in a memoir on the origin of the Arabian Nights published in the Mémoires de l'Académie, v. x. p. 30, translates it the Thousand Nights, which seems to be the correcter appellation. The difference is not very material, and the agreement is close enough to establish the Persian or Indian origin of the Arabic work. In its actual form however the latter is no doubt of much more modern aggregation. The prominent part assigned in the early stories to the Khalif Hárún Al-Rashíd could have been ascribed to him only some considerable period after his demise. In the story of the Barber of Bagdád, the barber observes that it is the 653rd year of the Hijra, a. d. 1255. The institution of Calendars, according to M. De Sacy, originated in the christian year 1150; and the title of Sultan of Egypt, which occurs in the story of Beder ud dín Hassan, was not assumed before the middle of the twelfth century. These and other considerations induced M. De Sacy to conclude that 'The Arabian Nights,' as now current, was compiled not earlier than the thirteenth or fourteenth century. The middle of the thirteenth century is the date conjectured by Galland, the original translator of these tales; but M. Caussin de Perceval, upon the authority of a MS. note, affirmed that the compiler was living in a. d. 1548. That some portions at least are as late as the end of the fifteenth century, is proved by one instance of internal evidence not yet noticed by any European critic.

In the tale of Prince Ahmed and the fairy Peri bhánu, the eldest of the three brothers, Prince Hosein, in search of some extraordinary rarity which may entitle him to the hand of the Princess Núr-an-nihár, repairs to the Indian city Bisnagar, the capital of a country of the same name, and a metropolis of extraordinary wealth and population. This is no doubt the Bijnagar of the Mohammedan historians of the South of India, and of the early European travellers in the Dekhin — the Vijayanagar of the Hindus; and we know from ancient inscriptions, as well as Indian history, that this city was not founded until the middle of the fourteenth century[*]. It could not have risen to a reputation which extended to Arabia earlier than the beginning or middle of the fifteenth, and any collection in which it is found must have been put together subsequently to that date.

It is not precisely determinable from the expressions of Masúdí whether the Hazár Afsána is considered by him as of Indian or Persian origin, and his translator leaves it equally undecided, although he leans to the latter,—"les mille et une nuits étaient originairement non des contes Arabes, mais des contes Indiens, ou plus probablement Persans." The appellation Hazár Afsána is Persian, and no doubt the Arabs received their first knowledge of the work through the Persian language. Another Arabic writer, since quoted by Baron Purgstall in the Journal Asiatique of August

---

[*] [Lassen, I. I., IV, 156—160.]

last, is evidence in favour of their Persian extraction. Abú Ya'kúb al Darak compiled a Fihrist, a catalogue raisonné of Arabic literature, in the Hijra year 377 (a. d. 987). Amongst a long list of romances and tales attributed to the Persians, Indians, Greeks, Babylonians and Arabs, mention is made of the Hazár Afsána as the oldest work of the kind; for it is said to have been the composition of Homai, queen of Persia, daughter of Ardeshir Dirázdast (Artaxerxes Longimanus), and a favourite book of Alexander the Great and his successors. The authenticity of these particulars may be thought questionable; but there is no disputing the proof given, that at the end of the tenth century there was translated into Arabic from Persian a collection of tales, which was the prototype of the Thousand and One Nights. The subject of the Hazár Afsána is said by Abú Ya'kúb to be the story of a king who married a damsel of royal blood, full of wit and intelligence, named Shehrazad, who was accustomed to amuse her husband by relating stories to him every night, until he interrupted her, and put off the conclusion to the following night. In this manner a thousand nights were passed. There was another female of the party named Dinarzad, who assisted the narratress. In the end the king became attached to Shehrazad, and spared her life. The author adds, that the Hazár Afsána contains a thousand nights and two hundred conversations by moonlight, and that he had several times seen a complete copy. He appears to have no great taste for the marvellous, as he concludes,

"It is in truth a book of frigid tradition." It is clear therefore that the opinion of Mr. Lane, in denying the Persian origin of the Arabian Nights, as far at least as their plan and principal performers are concerned, is wholly untenable.

That many of the stories current in Europe originated in Persian invention is not at all improbable, but unfortunately we have no means of verifying the fact. The contrary is the case with the fictions of the Hindus; for although this branch of their literature is yet imperfectly investigated, yet enough has been ascertained to determine the actual existence in Sanskrit, or in vernacular translations from it, of a very extensive literature of fiction, in which many of our European acquaintances are at once to be recognised. This is true not only of the Pancha Tantra and Hitopadeśa, but of other collections, such as the Vetála Panchavinśati, twenty-five stories of a demon; the Sinhásana Dwátrinśati, thirty-two tales of the animated images supporting the throne of Vikramáditya; the Śuka Saptati, the seventy tales of a parrot; and a variety of popular collections of a more miscellaneous description. One of the most interesting and extensive works of this class is now however for the first time made known to the European public by the industry and learning of Dr. Hermann Brockhaus, Sanskrit Professor in the University of Jena[*], the Kathá Sarit Ságara, or Mährchensammlung des Somadeva.

---

[*] [Since 1841 at Leipsic in the same capacity.]

The work of which a portion is now published in the original Sanskrit, with a German translation, the *Kathá Sarit Ságara*, or ocean of the streams of narrative, is more commonly known in India as the *Vrihat Kathá*, the great tale, or great collection of tales. The popular nomenclature is however erroneous, and the compiler of the Kathá Sarit Ságara declares expressly that his work is a compendium of a preceding and more comprehensive work, entitled the Vrihat Kathá, of which it contains the substance. It corresponds exactly with the original; there is not the least departure from it, only the style is more compressed in order to avoid the great prolixity of the primitive work. It has also been composed in verse, care having been taken to preserve the arrangement of the text and the interest of the stories. The author adds, that his object is "not a reputation for learning, but the hope of enabling the memory more readily to retain the complicated net of narrative invention."

"Mich ehrfurchtsvoll verbeugend vor Sarasvati, der Fackel um aller Worte Sinn zu erleuchten, beginne ich diese Sammlung, die das Mark der Vrihat Kathá enthält. Wie das ursprüngliche Werk, so ist auch dieses, man wird nirgends die geringste Auslassung bemerken; nur die Sprache ist gedrängter, um die zu grosse Ausdehnung des Buches zu vermeiden. Den Kräften gemäss habe ich mich bemüht, den passendsten Ausdruck zu wählen, und indem die verschiedensten Gemüthsstimmungen in den Erzählungen dargestellt worden, ist ein Werk entstanden, das zu den Gedichten gerechnet werden kann. Meine Arbeit entsprang nicht aus Begierde nach dem Ruhme der Gelehrsamkeit, sondern um leichter dem Gedächtniss das bunte Mährchennetz zu bewahren."

From this it is clear that the Vríhat Kathá was in all essential respects the same as the present work; but inasmuch as it was written in prose, and with that minuteness of detail which is the soul of all story-telling, it was without doubt a much more animated and interesting compilation.

The period at which the original Vríhat Kathá was compiled is uncertain, but it must have preceded the eleventh century, for that is the date at which its abridgment, the Kathá Sarit Ságara, was composed. This work derives a great part of its value from the circumstance that its date admits of positive verification; and although this is subsequent to the time at which Indian and old Persian stories first became accessible to Europe, in consequence of their translation into Arabic, yet it precedes the era of the actual migration of the stories to the West, and establishes their naturalization in India at a date anterior to the possible introduction of Mohammedan literature amongst the Hindus. Whether India was indebted for its stories to the Magian Persians is doubtful; to some extent it possibly was; at least it is very likely that under the Sassanian princes there was an active traffic in all sorts of fabrics—those of the imagination as well as of the hand—between India and Persia, making it difficult to attribute to either its own indigenous productions. However this may have been, it is very improbable, it is almost impossible, that before the inferrible date of the Vríhat Kathá, before the actual date of the Kathá Sarit Ságara, the Hindus should have been indebted to the Arabs for any of their storytelling. In truth, until the Arabs were saturated, as their own authors acknowledge, with translations from Persian, Indian and Greek, they were not a storytelling, not a literary, not a scientific people. They had some poetry, some romance; but the poems that were suspended at the Ka'aba, and the exploits of Antar, are of a very different description from the rich and diversified pictures of social life which at first evidenced the more advanced civilisation of Persia and India, and afterwards accompanied the progress of society in Bagdád, Cairo and Cordova.

The date of the Kathá Sarit Ságara admits of being determined with very tolerable precision. At the close of it, the author, Somadeva, states that he compiled it at the desire of Súryavatí, a dowager queen of Kashmir, for the amusement and instruction of her grandson, Harsha Deva, whilst under her guardianship. Harsha Deva reigned, as Professor Brockhaus mentions, about A. D. 1125; but the Chronicles of Kashmir, the Rája Taranginí, give us more exactly the time. Harsha Deva was, according to Somadeva's genealogy of him, the son of Kalasa, the son of Ananta, the son of Sangráma, kings of Kashmir in succession. The Rája Taranginí has the same series of descents, and both authorities designate Súryavatí as the wife of Ananta, mother of Kalasa and grandmother of Harsha. The period assigned for the joint reigns of Harsha's three predecessors in the Rája Taranginí is seventy-six years. Abúlfazl has the same names; but in Gladwin's translution of the Áyíni Akbarí the aggregate of the three reigns is but thirty-one years. The MSS. of the work are however, in the chronological tables which they contain, exceedingly incorrect. Diddá Rání, the predecessor of Sangráma, died a. d. 1025 (Asiatic Researches, vol. xv. p. 80), and seventy-six years added to this places Harsha's accession a. d. 1101[*]. According to the Kashmir Chronicle, however, Súryavatí burnt herself with her husband Ananta's dead body eight years before, or in a. d. 1093. The compilation of the Kathá Sarit Ságara must have preceded this event by some few years, so that we cannot be far wrong in assigning it to about a. d. 1088, to which therefore we fix the most modern limit of all the stories found in the compilation. The Kathá Sarit Ságara then, considered in itself, and still more especially as the representative of a still earlier composition, the Vŕihat Kathá, is the oldest extant assemblage of tales, except the Hindu original, and the first translation of the Kalila and Damna, and it is therefore indispensable to the history of fiction to determine what it contains.

The Kathá Sarit Ságara is a large work. It consists of eighteen books, subdivided into 124 sections. The portion published by Professor Brockhaus extends to

---

[*] [Troyer (Rájataranginí, Vol. III, p. 655) places the reign of Harsha from 1090—1102, Lassen (I. I. III. p. 1061. 1078,) end of 1091 to end of 1103. The latter places the termination of Diddá's reign towards the end of the year 1007 (I. I. p. 1046,) after 24 years' reign.]

but five books, comprising 26 sections*. The Sanskrit text occupies 469 pages, the German translation but 153, but it is very closely printed in a small type. Each book comprises a number of stories loosely strung together, by being narrated for the recreation or information of the same individuals, or arising out of their adventures. These are Vatsa, king of Kauśāmbí, and his son Naraváhana-datta. The marriage of the latter with various damsels of terrestrial or celestial origin, and his elevation to the rank of king of the Vidyádharas, a class of heavenly spirits, are the leading topics of most of the books; but they merely constitute the skeleton of the composition, the substance being made up of stories growing out of these circumstances, or springing from one another with an ingenuity of intricacy which, although the Abbé Dubois complains of it, is in reality one of the great charms of all such collections.

"Un autre défaut peut-être qu'on pourra reprocher encore à ces apologues, défaut dont au reste les compositions orientales présentent de fréquens exemples, c'est qu'ils s'entrelacent presque tous les uns dans les autres de sorte qu'une fable commencée donne lieu, avant qu'elle soit finie, à une seconde fable, interrompue bientôt elle-même par une troisième, et celle-ci par une quatrième**."

---

* [The text of Books VI, VII and VIII was published by the same (in Roman characters) at Leipsic in 1862, comprising sections 27—59, and an analysis of B. VI and VII in "Berichte der Kgl. Sächsischen Gesellschaft der Wissenschaften." Philologisch-historische Classe, Vols. 12 and 13.]

** [Le Pantcha Tantra. Paris: 1826. Préface p. XIII.]

This is no very grave imputation, for the Abbé admits that, "l'auteur ne manque pas de revenir à son sujet et de finir tous les récits commencés." In the Kathá Sarit Ságara the stories all wind up at the end of each book, or not unfrequently sooner. The action is never suspended for any very prolonged interval, and the complication is not of such a nature or extent as to convert variety into confusion. The stories are always characterized by the features of Hindu nationality, and are illustrative of Hindu opinions, usages and belief. They exhibit, in a striking and interesting manner, the peculiarities of the social condition of India; and in the exposure of its follies and vices furnish those delineations of the similar imperfections of all civilized society, of which the general applicability and truth have recommended their imitation to the satirists and storytellers of Europe. The greater number of them turn upon the wickedness of women, the luxury, profligacy, treachery and craft of the female sex. These attributes no doubt originate in the feelings which have always pervaded the East unfavourable to the dignity of the female character; but we are not to mistake the language of satire, or the licentiousness of wit, for truth, or to suppose that the pictures which are thus given of the depravity of women owe not much of their colouring to the malignity of men. The avidity with which this style of portraiture was adopted and improved upon in Europe, shows that either the women of Christian Europe were still more vicious than those of India, or the men were still less disposed to treat them with deference and esteem. It is in this respect that stories of domestic manners contrast so remarkably with the inventions of chivalric romance; and the homage paid in the latter to the virtues and graces of the female sex is a feature derived, in all probability, from that portion of their parentage which comes from the North, woman being ever held in higher honour amongst the Teutonic nations than amongst those of the South of Europe or of the East, and contributing, by the elevating influence she was permitted to enjoy, to their moral exaltation and martial superiority.

Although the text and translation of the Kathá Sarit Ságara are now published for the first time in a continuous form, yet a short extract from the text has been previously published by Dr. Brockhaus himself —the story of the foundation of Pátaliputra or Palibothra. A translation of a larger portion of the work was published in a Calcutta periodical, the Quarterly Oriental Magazine of 1824—25*, from which a notice of the original has been recently inserted in the account of India, which forms a number of the Edinburgh Cabinet Library. The Calcutta publication also had the merit of attracting the notice and exciting the interest of the present editor and translator, and thus leading to the publication which has given rise to our remarks.

Our readers would probably be little profited by any

---

* [Reprinted in the first volume of this division, p. 156—268.]

criticisms we might offer upon the result of the editorial labours of Dr. Brockhaus. It is sufficient to observe that the text is carefully printed, upon a careful collation of five entire copies and one imperfect copy. The last and three of the former are to be found in the invaluable collection of oriental manuscripts at the India House; a fourth is in the collection of the Sanskrit Professor of the University of Oxford, and a fifth was procured by Dr. Brockhaus from India. He has employed these materials with unremitting industry and judicious scholarship, and has given a very accurate typographic representation of his original. The mechanical execution of the work is creditable and the type distinct. Dr. Brockhaus has followed Professor Bopp's plan of separating conjunct words and marking the separation—a device which we think unnecessary, and one which is objectionable, as not unfrequently productive of greater uncertainty than that which it was intended to obviate. The translation appears to be in general executed with very commendable fidelity, without sacrificing to a servile adherence to the original all pretensions to elegance and spirit. For a vindication of these opinions we must refer to the book itself, whilst we proceed to offer a summary account of the whole of the original work, with reference especially to the light it may be expected to reflect on the history of fiction.

The first book is introductory, and refers the origin of the tales contained in the collection to no less a person than the deity Siva, who, it is said, related them in private conversation with his wife, Párvatí, for her entertainment. One of the attendants of the god, Pushpadanta, took the liberty of listening, and he repeated them, under the seal of secresy, to his wife, Jayá, a sort of lady's maid to the goddess. What woman, says the author, can restrain her tongue? Jayá takes an opportunity of intimating to her mistress that she is acquainted with the stories narrated by Siva, to the great mortification of Párvatí, who had flattered herself that they had been communicated to her alone. She accordingly complains to Siva of his having deceived her, and he vindicates himself by discovering the truth. Párvatí thereupon pronounces an imprecation upon Pushpadanta, condemning him to be born upon the earth as a man; and she sentences his friend Mályaván, who had ventured to intercede for him, to a like destination. The infliction of this punishment is a not uncommon fate of the subordinate divinities of the Hindus, when they incur the displeasure of the Dii majores, or even of holy sages. The degradation, however, endures only for a season, and terminates upon the occurrence of some preannounced catastrophe. On the present occasion, Párvatí tells the culprits that they shall resume their celestial condition when Pushpadanta, encountering a Yaksha, a follower of Kuvera, the god of wealth, "doom'd for a certain time to walk the earth," as a Pisácha or goblin, shall recollect his own former state, and shall repeat to the Pisácha the stories he overheard from Siva; and when Mályaván, falling in with the Pisácha, shall hear from him again the stories that his friend Pushpadanta had narrated. The recitation of the stories forms also the limit of the Yaksha's sojourn amongst mortals. This machinery is of course exclusively Hindu.

The two demigods, Pushpadanta and Mályaván, are born as two Brahmans, named Vararuchi and Guṅádhya, and their adventures as mortals constitute the subject of several tales. Some of these possess much local interest: we have in them literary anecdotes relating to celebrated works and authors, as to Páṅini the grammarian; notices of historical persons and events, as of the accession of Chandragupta or Sandrocoptus; and traditions of the origin of celebrated places, as of that of Palibothra already alluded to. The circumstances of these narratives are marvellous, it is true, and are not to be received as facts. In the absence of all authentic history and biography, however, they are not without interest, and perhaps not without value; and in the place in which they are found they are evidence of the early date at which popular belief assented to legends still current.

We find also in this portion of the work various incidents and tales which are of wide dissemination. One of the best-told stories in the whole work occurs here. Upakośá, the wife of Vararuchi, becomes, during the absence of her husband, the object of the addresses of the king's family priest, the commander of the guards, the prince's tutor, and her husband's banker. She makes assignations with them all: each as he arrives is quickly followed by his successor, and is secreted only to be finally exposed and punished. The story* is the same in all essential respects as that of the Lady of Cairo and her four gallants, in Scott's additional Arabian Nights; and that of the merchant's wife and her suitors in the tale of the king, his favourite, and the seven vizirs, translated by the same orientalist. It is also that of Aronya in the Persian tales; and it is also found as a Fabliau, that of Constant du Hamel, or 'la dame qui attrapa un Prêtre, un Prevot et un Forestier,' (Fabl. de Le Grand, iv. p. 246); and it is worthy of remark, that the Fabliau alone agrees with the Hindu original in the mode of putting the suitors out of the way, by hiding them in baskets and disrobing them under the plea of a bath.

There is in this part of the work some very curious matter, the purport of which it is not easy to conjecture, unless it conceal an intimation that the stories are of inferior, if not of foreign origin. Mâlyavân, or Gunâdhya, in consequence of a dispute with a rival Brahman, foregoes the use of the Sanskrit, Prâkrit and Desya, or vernacular languages. He afterwards learns the Paisâchi language, or that of the goblins, which enables him to receive the narrations as they are told him by the metamorphosed Yaksha or Pisâcha. Possibly the author thought some contrivance necessary to explain how the Pisâcha should be intelligible to the Brahman, and nothing more is meant than meets the

---

* [See above Vol. I, p. 169 ff.]

eye; but a hypothesis might be framed upon it, that the stories were translations, whence made, it would not be easy to explain, unless we call in Pehlevi, a language extinct or disused before the Kathá Sarit Ságara was compiled. However this may be, Guńádhya having heard the stories, extending to seven hundred thousand stanzas, wrote them with his blood, for there was no ink in the forest. He then offered the work to Sátaváhana, king of Pratishthána, who rejected it with abhorrence, on which the author kindled a fire in the forest, and reading it aloud, to the great edification of spirits and goblins, and birds and beasts, he burned it leaf by leaf as he finished the perusal. The news of this proceeding at last reached the king, and he repented of what he had done, and repaired to Guńádhya to solicit the gift of the work. The sage consented to present the king with the hundred thousand verses that had not yet been consigned to the flames. Sátaváhana took it to his capital, and having received an explanation of it from two of Guńádhya's disciples, he translated it from the language of the Piśáchas. Sátaváhana, as king of Pratishthána, it may be observed, is identifiable with the Sáliváhana, whose reign, a. d. 78, forms an epoch in the ordinary chronology of the Hindus[*]. It would seem as if tradition ascribed to him the patronage of this class of composition, and there is nothing very improbable in

---

[*] [See above Vol. I. p. 181.]

the supposition that the golden age of Indian fabling dates about the commencement of the Christian era.

The second book is supposed to commence that part of the original narrative which was not consumed, and records the adventures of Udayana, king of Kauśámbí, a prince of great celebrity in the plays and poems of the Hindus, and his marriage with Vásavadattá, princess of Ujjayiní. The third book describes his acquisition of a second bride, Padmávatí, princess of Magadha; and the fourth book the birth of the son of Vatsa, by Vásavadattá, Naraváhanadatta; at the same time sons are born to the chief ministers of Vatsa, and they become the companions and councillors of the young prince. The fifth book records the adventures of a mortal, who became king of the heavenly beings termed Vidyádharas, a class of spirits who reside upon the loftiest peaks of the Himálaya mountains, who possess superhuman longevity and faculties, and the knowledge of what is passing beyond their presence. They have in many cases been mortals, and are constantly connected with human beings in friendship and enmity, love and hate. The story of their king is told to illustrate the manner in which the destiny of Naraváhanadatta, who it is foretold will be king of the Vidyádharas, can be fulfilled. With this tale the publication of Dr. Brockhaus closes.

In the stories which this portion of the Kathá Sarit Ságara comprises, we have various details which are recognisable in the fiction of the West, some possibly accidental, but others of too peculiar a nature to have

occurred independently to different inventors. Thus
we need not identify Vatsa with Orpheus, because his
musical proficiency on the lute subdues the animals
of the forest to his will; nor is it necessary to refer
to the tale of Troy for the origin of a contrivance by
which he is taken prisoner, a hollow wooden elephant
instead of a horse, in which armed men are concealed;
although perhaps traces of some such stratagem were
scattered over the East long before it came to Virgil.
"Habebat poeta fabulam a multis tractatam et vul-
garem ante se positam." The case is different with
other analogies. Guhasena, a young merchant, is
compelled to leave his wife, Devasmitá, for a season,
on matters of business. The separation is painful to
both, and the pain is aggravated by fears on the wife's
part of her husband's inconstancy. To make assurance
doubly sure, a couple of divine lotus flowers of a red
colour are obtained in a dream, the hues of which,
the married pair are told, will fade, should either prove
untrue. Some such marvellous indication of unsullied
honour is exceedingly common in European romance.
It is not always the same. In Ariosto the test is a
cup, the wine of which is spilled by the unfaithful
lover who attempts to drink from it; this device also
occurs in the romances of Tristram, Perceval and La
Morte d'Arthur, and is well known by La Fontaine's
version, 'La coupe enchantée.' Spencer has derived
his Girdle of Florimel from these sources, or more immediately from the Fabliau, 'Le manteau mal taillé,'
an English version of which is published in Percy's

Reliques, 'The boy and the mantle.' In the Gesta Romanorum the test is the whimsical one of a shirt which will require neither washing nor mending as long as the wearer is true. There are not wanting, however, instances of such a test as that of Somadeva. In 'Amadis de Gaul' it is a garland; in 'Les Contes à rire' a flower, and in 'Perce Forest' it is a rose, which borne by a wife or maiden of immaculate virtue preserves its freshness, but withers if the wearer is unchaste[*].

Guhasena falls in with boon companions, who learning the purport of his lotus, and the virtue of his wife, set off, like Iachimo, to put it to the proof. They find an old Buddhist priestess willing to promote their designs. In order to shake the constancy of the merchant's wife, she visits her, and leads along with her a bitch held by a string, whom she takes an opportunity of feeding with a piece of meat strongly seasoned with pepper; the effect of the seasoning is to draw tears from the eyes of the animal; and when Devasmita inquires why the animal weeps, the old woman tells her that she and the bitch were in a former life the wives of a Brahman who was frequently from home in the service of the state; during his absence she amused herself as she pleased, but the other wife was of rigid virtue and turned a deaf ear to all her suitors. They have both been born again in their actual forms, and with a recollection of their former state of existence,

---

[*] [above, Vol. I, p. 220.]

and the once faithful wife now weeps for the penalty she pays for her coldness and cruelty. Now this contrivance is quite consistent with the Hindu notion of the metempsychosis, and is clearly of Indian origin. It was nevertheless naturalized with suitable modifications in Europe, although not directly from the Kashmirian compilation, for it was introduced into the West about the same time that the Kathá Sarit Ságara was compiled. It occurs in the 'Disciplina Clericalis'[*] of Petrus Alfonsus, a Spanish Jew who wrote about a. d. 1106. His materials were obtained chiefly through the Arabian writers, and it must have been by way of Bagdád that the story travelled from Hindustan to Spain. It was speedily taken hold of by the conteurs and trouveurs, and appears in Le Grand's Fabliaux as 'La vieille qui séduisit la jeune fille[**].' The French might almost pass for a translation of the Sanskrit. The woman gives "une chienne à manger des choses fortement saupoudrées de sénevé, qui lui picotait le palais et les narines, et l'animal larmoyait beaucoup." She then shows her to the young woman and tells her that the bitch was her daughter, "son malheur fut d'avoir le cœur dur...Dieu l'a bien vengé: voyez en quel état pour la punir il a réduit ma pauvre fille, et comment elle pleure sa faute." The story became extremely popular: it was inserted in the Gesta Romanorum as 'The old woman and her little

---

[*] [ed. F. W. V. Schmidt, No. XIV and p. 129 ff.]
[**] [ed. of 1829, Vol. IV, p. 50.]

dog*;" and it also has a place where we should little expect to find it,—in the Promptuarium of John Herolt of Basil, an ample repository of materials for sermons **! It is worthy of note that the European conteurs make the example effective,—female virtue yields to such a warning. The Indian narrative has a more moral dénouement. Devasmitá appears to relent, and invites her lovers to an entertainment, where they are plied with wine in which a narcotic drug has been infused, and when they fall asleep they are branded on the forehead with the mark of a dog's foot, and then turned out of the house. They return to their own country disappointed and disgraced. Devasmitá, fearing that her husband may be the victim of their revenge, follows them in the garb of a man and character of a merchant. She makes acquaintance with her husband, who does not know her in her disguise, and after a season applies to the king of the country to recover certain persons whom she denounces as her runaway slaves. These were her suitors, who are accordingly obliged to appear, and are claimed by Devasmitá as her slaves. She appeals to the brand on their brows in testimony of their servile condition; their turbans are removed, and the mark becoming manifest is

---

* [ch. 28. See Swan's translation, I, 347, and Grässe's transl. II, 259.]

** [Latin Stories, ed. by Th. Wright. London: 1842, No. XIII & p. 218. See also Loiseleur Deslongchamps, l. l., p. 107 f. and J. H. von der Hagen, Gesammtabenteuer. 1850. I, CXII ff.]

admitted as proof. Subsequently Devasmitá consents to accept a liberal ransom from them, with which she enriches her husband, to whom she makes herself known, and they return home together to be separated no more.

In the story of Śaktideva, which forms the main subject of the fifth book, we have, along with a genuine national charakter, many particulars found in other collections. The Princess of Varddhamána, when pressed by her father to marry, declares she will have no man for her husband but one who has visited the 'Golden City.' Public proclamation to this effect is made; and Śaktideva, a young and dissolute, but courageous and enterprising Brahman, undertakes to discover what no person is acquainted with, the situation of the city to which a visit is to win the hand of the princess. He first has recourse to an old hermit, who refers him to his still older brother, by whom he is sent on to a certain island— in which particulars Śaktideva resembles Mazin of Khorasan in his search after the island Wák-al-wák. In the voyages he consequently performs he is repeatedly shipwrecked, and on one occasion is caught in a whirlpool, like Ulysses, and escapes in a similar manner, by jumping up and clinging to the branches of a fig-tree,—the Indian fig-tree,—the pendulous branches of which are more within reach than those of the Sicilian fig can be, making it doubtful whether Homer did not borrow the incident from some old eastern fiction. From hence Śaktideva is conveyed

by a gigantic bird, one of the race of Garuda, the bird
of Vishńu, and prototype of the 'Roc,' to the place he
is in search of. The Golden City is the residence of
Vidyádharís, females of the Vidyádharas only, so
Wák-al-wák is inhabited by female genie alone. The
chief of the sisterhood welcomes him as her future
husband; but deeming it necessary to obtain her
father's consent, she and her companions depart to
ask his sanction. Śaktideva is left in possession of
the palace, with a recommendation not to ascend the
central terrace. He of course disregards the injunction.
He finds three pavilions on the terrace, enters them,
and discovers to his great horror the three apparently
lifeless corpses of beautiful damsels,—one of whom is
the princess of Varddhamána. Quitting the last
chamber he comes to a reservoir of water, by the side
of which stands a horse caparisoned. Śaktideva approaches to mount him, but the steed kicks him into
the reservoir. When he struggles to the surface he
finds himself in the midst of a well-known pond in his
native city, Varddhamána. Some similar incidents
occur in the story of Mazin; and the catastrophe, more
humourously but less poetically related, is that of the
third Calender in the Arabian Nights.

Again we find an analogy with the tale of Mazin, in
the consequence of Śaktideva's satisfying the princess
that he has been to the Golden City. She is in truth
a Vidyádharí, condemned for a time to wear a mortal
shape: the term has expired; she flies away to resume
her proper form, which was lying seemingly inanimate

in the palace of the Golden City, and thither Śaktideva sets off to recover her. On his way he meets with other two nymphs, whom he espouses: they prove to be the originals of two of the three lifeless bodies he had seen, and in fact are Vidyádharís. By his marriage with them he himself becomes a Vidyádhara, and then proceeds, without difficulty, to the island of the Golden City, where he finds the former princess of Varddhamána, as well as the queen of the female inhabitants of the island. He marries them also, and repairs with his wives to their common father, the king of the Vidyádharís, who resigns the sovereignty to him, to be exercised only until the son of Vatsa shall be born[*]. The occurrence of this event is the occasion of his appearance.

The main purpose of the sixth book is the marriage of the young prince with the daughter of Kalingasená, a princess sprung from a celestial nymph, and who at first had been enamoured of Vatsa, and desirous of becoming his wife. Vatsa is well enough disposed to marry her; but as he has two wives already, his chief minister suggests to him that he may be contented. A friend of the princess, a nymph of air, is also opposed to the match, and a variety of tales are recited on either side in support of the reasonings for and against the union. One of these is the story of the wife of a foolish Brahman, who liberates her husband from a bad bargain with a Piśácha or goblin, by a

---

[*] [See Vol. I, p. 268.]

device not of a very delicate description. The story was not the less acceptable to the conteurs of Europe, for the point is precisely the same as that of 'le petit diable' de Papefigue of Fontaine. In the end, a spirit of air, in love with the princess, assumes the semblance of Vatsa, and in his person weds her. She becomes reconciled to what is without remedy, and has a daughter, who is the bride of Vatsa's son.

In the next book Naravāhanadatta marries a Vidyādharī: the wedding is celebrated at the residence of the lady's father, on one of the snow-crowned summits of the Himálaya. When the married couple return to Kauśámbí the young bride persuades her husband to throw open the doors of the inner apartments, and allow free ingress to his friends and associates. "The honour of women," she affirms, "is protected by their own principles alone; and where these are corrupt, all precautions are vain." The object of this arrangement is not only, however, the emancipation of the women from jealous restraint, but provision for the carrying on of the series of tales, as the prince's companions are their ordinary narrators. The stories that then ensue bear hard in general upon the conduct of women; but some are told in their vindication. A king has many wives, and an elephant of celestial race. The elephant is struck dead by a bird of the Garuda breed, and the incident throws the prince into great affliction. A voice from the sky proclaims that the animal will be restored to life by the touch of a chaste woman. The king commands one of his wives to perform the operation. She puts her hand on the elephant, but there is no resuscitation; the rest equally fail. The king then turns them all off, and tries his luck elsewhere. He is invariably disappointed, and at last relinquishes his quest in despair. The moral of this story is the occasion and connecting link of the Arabian Nights, and is the burthen of that of Giocondo, as related by Ariosto*.

The eighth book is devoted to the further illustration of the mode in which the prince may attain the elevation that has been promised him, by the relation of the adventures of a prince named Súryaprabha, who became king of the Vidyádharas. The scene of action is mostly in the regions below or those above the earth, and the dramatis personæ are the Nágas or snake-gods of Pátála and the Vidyádharas of mid air. The stories have little of humanity to recommend them, and lose in interest what they gain in the wonderful. They serve to illustrate, however, the notions of the Hindus with regard to magic, and to those classes of creatures who hold a middle station between human and divine; and it seems not improbable that many of the incidents in the Thousand and One Nights, in which magicians, witches, Peris and Jins, are implicated, are traceable to these inventions of the Hindus. Beings of supernatural origin, or the possession of supernatural powers by mere mortals, have no doubt a place in every form of popular superstition, ancient

---

* [XXVIII, 7 ff.]

or modern; but there are some coincidences which cannot well have been derived from a mere community of imagination, and which are not very intelligible until they are traced to some one existing system. There are some peculiarities in Hindu belief which explain much of the magic in other collections. Thus the adept in the practices of the Yoga philosophy is supposed, amongst other marvellous faculties, to have that of quitting his own body and animating any other he pleases. Now this involves a doctrine of some of the Hindu psychological schools. Besides the gross external corporeal frame, the soul is invested with a subtile body, made up of the impalpable senses and rudiments of matter, and it is this vehicle of soul which migrates with it from one body to another after death, or may be made by the perfection of the Jogí in his exercises to travel at his commands. Frequent instances of this occur in Hindu tales: thus in the first book of the Kathá Sarit Ságara, Indradatta, the Brahman, takes possession of the dead body of king Nanda, recently deceased, leaving his own body in the thicket, intending to resume it. The minister, suspecting the nature of the king's recovery from apparent death, but wishing to keep him on the throne, the heir being yet an infant, commands search to be made for all dead bodies, that they may be burnt. Amongst them the deserted body of Indradatta is consumed, and he is obliged to remain in that which he had purposed to occupy only for a season. He is therefore known in tradition as Yogananda, or the magic Nanda. So in the case of the four Vidyádharís in the last book: their own bodies were left inanimate in the chambers of the Golden City, whilst they occupied persons of inferior excellence; and in this book Súryaprabha finds in Pátála a lifeless giant; he is told that it is his own proper form, and he consequently lays down the dwarfish human body he is incased in, and resumes that of his former gigantic self. There can be little doubt, that any such device occurring in the fictions of other countries is of Indian origin. There is one well-known exemplification of it in the story of Fadlallah, in the Persian tales, where the Dervish, who animates the body of the dead bird, avows he had learned the art from an ancient Brahman in the Indies. The substance of this story is given in an Italian work of the end of the sixteenth century, 'Peregrinaggio di tre giováni figliuoli del Re di Serendippo.' Translated from the Persian by M. Christoforo, Armeno. Venice: 1584. It has been thence transferred to the 'Soirées Bretonnes de Gueulette*.'

There seems no particular reason for an occasional metamorphosis, not uncommon in both Eastern and Western fiction, that of fairies into serpents, as in the story of Zobeide in the Arabian Nights. Hindu notions account for it at once. The Nágas of the subterrene regions are in their own persons serpents—demi-divine, but snakes nevertheless. They have, however,

---

* (Dunlop's History of Fiction. Transl. by F. Liebrecht. p. 411. Benfey, Pantchatantra, I, 125 ff. Cabinet des Fées, XIV, 326.]

the power of assuming human forms, and the snake maidens are of very slippery virtue as well as of exceeding beauty. They are very fond of paying visits to earth, where, upon an emergency, they drop the human shape and appear as snakes. Of the Vidyádharas notice has already been taken. They correspond with the benevolent Genii and Peris of Arabian and Persian fiction, whilst the malignant Genii are represented by the Rákshasas: of inferior spirits, goblins, ghouls, ogres, ogresses, and the like, there is no lack of counterparts in the Vetálas, Pisáchas, Yoginís and Dákinís, of the Hindus. Of the paraphernalia of magical machinery there is also abundance. Thus in the first book of the Kathá Sarit Ságara, Putraka, the reputed founder of Pátaliputra, or Palibothra, becomes possessed of a staff that creates what it delineates, a cup that is always full of meat and drink, and shoes of swiftness, or a pair of slippers that enables the wearer to travel speedily through the air. The latter virtue, for a given time at least, is also ascribed in the third book to certain mustard-seeds extracted from the navel of a corpse in which a goblin resided. Vidúshaka, the hero of the tale in which this occurs, possesses also a sword of sharpness, which nothing can resist. Nothing also is more frequent than for a sage, or magician, or an adventurer, to have a Vetála, a Rákshasa, or a Vidyádhara—a goblin, a giant, or a genie, for a servant or a slave. It is worthy of notice too, that the Rákshasa, who is a cannibal as well as a giant, like the 'Fee fa fum' heroes of this class, so well known in our nurseries, is as remarkable for stupidity as malevolence and cannibalism. The following story* exhibits both these characteristics:—

The Prince of Varddhamána.

"The sovereign of Varddhamána had several sons, of whom the youngest, Śringabhuja, was his father's favourite, being distinguished above his brothers for grace and beauty, skill in martial exercises, and gentleness of disposition. The partiality of the king, and the superiority of Śringabhuja, excited the envy and jealousy of his brothers, and they were not satisfied until they had devised a plan to effect his removal, and, as they hoped, accomplish his destruction, without their incurring peril or suspicion. There dwelt a Rákshas in the forests of Vaddhamána, who was the terror of the surrounding districts, appearing from time to time in the most hideous shapes, and carrying off cattle, and even human creatures, for his sustenance. Him the princes propitiated by prayers and oblations, in the hope of securing his assistance to get rid of their obnoxious brother. Their end was at last accidentally attained. In the course of his predatory excursions the Rákshas one day made his appearance on the field where the princes were engaged in the sport of archery, in the form of a large and uncouth crane. The youths proposed to try their skill upon the intruder, and directed their shafts against him, but in vain, the bird keeping at too great a distance, or, by changing his position, evading the arrows. Śringabhuja was not so easily baffled, and his weapon lodged in the wing of the crane, striking him as it seemed to the earth. The prince advanced to secure his prize, but the wounded bird contrived to retire as Śringabhuja advanced, first slowly, and as it seemed with pain, until he appeared gradually to acquire vigour, and at last flew off with the arrow adhering to his side. Śringabhuja, who had been drawn a considerable distance from the exercising ground, and unwilling to lose his arrow, followed the crane as long as he

---

* [VII, ch. 39; ap. Brockhaus, p. 110. Comp. R. Köhler in Benfey's "Orient und Occident," Vol. II, p. 113 ff.]

was in sight, and when the bird had disappeared, continued to trace him through the forest by the drops of blood which at intervals were visible on the leaves of the trees or on the turf beneath them.

"In this pursuit the day had elapsed, and the prince found himself at sunset in the vicinity of a spacious garden, adjoining to a place of vast dimensions and extent. Utterly unacquainted with the place he had come to, and being unable to follow the track through the gathering gloom, Śringabhuja determined to rest where he was for the night, and in the morning endeavour to retrace his steps. He accordingly entered the garden to learn from some of the menials of the palace the name of the person to whom it belonged, and to solicit the hospitality of its owner.

"In the mean time the princes returned home, and reported to the king that his favourite son had been carried off by the Rákshas, and had undoubtedly been made the monster's meal. The king and the mother of Śringabhuja were overwhelmed with affliction at this intelligence, the truth of which was confirmed by the failure of all the parties sent out in quest of the prince to discover any vestiges of him.

"After wandering some time through the garden without meeting with any individual, Śringabhuja came to a large and stately Baŕ tree, in the centre of a smooth grass plot, and beheld seated at its foot a nymph of uncommon loveliness, so that he was disposed to look upon her as the tutelary divinity of the grove. She was no less impressed by his appearance, and in an instant a mutual affection sprang up between them, before a syllable was interchanged. Recovering from his surprise, the prince advanced and saluted the damsel; and having informed her of his name and rank, and the circumstances which had brought him thither, inquired who she was and what she was doing there. She replied, I am named Rúpaśikhá, and am the daughter of the Rákshas, Agniśikha, who dwells in this palace, and who is the person you have wounded in the form of a gigantic crane. No archer but yourself in all the three worlds could have hit such a mark; but his wound is healed by the application of the divine remedies which he possesses, and he will no doubt welcome so heroic a prince to his castle, and hold him worthy of his alliance. The prince replied suitably to these gracious advances, and the damsel repaired to her father to announce their guest, declaring at the same time that she had set her heart upon having him for her husband, and that she would put an end to her existence unless her father consented to the match.

"Now Agniśikha, notwithstanding his canibalism and other fiendish propensities, was fond of his daughter, and was not overwise, so that he could be easily coaxed or terrified into a compliance with all Rúpaśikhá's wishes. He therefore told her to conduct the prince into the palace, and promised not only that he would not eat him, but that he would accept him as his son-in-law on certain conditions: he desired her at the same time to go and bring her sisters, and the espousals should take place forthwith.

"Rúpaśikhá, who was much shrewder than her sire, perceived his drift, and contrived to intimate to the prince how it might be counteracted. The party was collected; Sringabhuja having previously bathed, and been attired by order of Agniśikha in bridal vestments. To the prince's astonishment, he beheld a hundred maidens before him, all arrayed and decorated alike, and so perfectly similar in form and features that it was impossible to discriminate one from another. The father giving the prince a chaplet, desired him to place it on Rúpaśikhá's neck, and she should be his. Sringabhuja appeared to hesitate; but his mistress, as preconcerted, had suspended a small blossom from the hair that parted on her forehead, and guided by this signal the prince selected his bride.

"Agniśikha thus discomfited, then told the prince that the wedding could not take place before the next morning, as his brother Dhúmaśikha must be present at the ceremony. 'Do you,' he continued, 'go and invite him; he lives about twenty miles off in an old temple of Śiva in the forest; ask him to be here by day-break tomorrow, but do you return without fail to-day.' Sringabhuja readily assented; but before his departure, Rúpaśikhá, who guessed her father's purpose, provided him with a fleet horse, a handful of earth, a cup of water, a few dry sticks and a match, and told him what to do to escape from the snare that was laid for him; for she was a fairy, prescient of events and commanding the elements.

"Śṛingabhuja set off and soon arrived at his journey's end, where he found Dhúmaśikha, an old monster more hideous and savage than his brother. As soon as his message was delivered, the prince abruptly withdrew as he had been enjoined by his mistress, sprang upon his horse, and set off at full speed. When he had ridden a few yards he turned his head round and saw the cannibal close behind him, on which, in conformity to his instructions, he threw the handful of earth upon the ground, and an immense mountain separated him from his pursuer. He now relaxed his speed, but soon repented of having done so, as Dhúmaśikha was again close at his heels. He therefore, as directed in such an emergency, poured the water on the earth, and a broad and stately river flowed between him and the cannibal. The prince nevertheless urged on his horse, but to little avail, as Dhúmaśikha had traversed the stream, and was once more upon him. His last resource was his match and fuel. Setting the sticks on fire he cast them on the path of the Rákshas, who was immediately enveloped and destroyed by a mighty flame.

"Śṛingabhuja completed his journey, and alighting from his horse announced to Agniśikha the delivery of his message. The Rákshas, surprised at his safe return, began to think the prince something more than human, and to tremble for his own security. He therefore allowed the marriage to be consummated, stipulating only that Śṛingabhuja and his wife should continue to reside with him.

"For a time the young couple, delighted with each other, and therefore with everything and everybody about them, lived happily in Agniśikha's palace, till at length Śṛingabhuja began to pine for his parents and his home. His wife perceived what was passing in his mind, and readily agreed to accompany him. They departed clandestinely; but their flight was soon known to Agniśikha, who having the faculty of moving through the air, overtook them before they had completed their journey. On marking his approach, the prince, by his wife's desire, bid himself*, whilst she assumed the semblance of a wood-cutter, with axe and faggots in hand. As soon as the Rákshas saw the supposed woodman, he descended and asked him if he had seen a youth and damsel such as he described. Rúpaśikhá replied, 'Yes, they are further in the forest, in great grief, and are cutting faggots to burn the corpse of their father, one Agniśikha, who is just dead.' Agniśikha, alarmed to hear of his own demise, and not quite sure whether he was alive or not, immediately returned to his own palace to ascertain the fact. In the meanwhile Śringabhuja and his wife reached the capital of Varddhamána, where they were received with rapture by the prince's parents, and spent the rest of their days in uninterrupted felicity."

In the ninth book are narrated a number of stories for the consolation of Naraváhanadatta, on the disappearance of his favourite bride Madana Manchuká, their subjects being the temporary separation and final reunion of faithful couples. They wind up with a compendious recital of the adventures of Nala and Damayantí**, known to English readers as it occurs in its primitive form in the Mahábhárata, by the version of Mr. Millman. We have therefore one limit in its chronology determined. It must be older than the eleventh century. It is no doubt very much older, but so much is certain. The next book, the tenth, is of still greater importance than any of its predecessors in the history of fiction, as the fourth section of it constitutes one portion of the fables of Pilpay, the

---

* [or rather, he was made invisible by his wife, chádítaṉ vidyayá.]

** [ed. by H. Brockhaus: Die Sage von Nala und Damayanti. Leipzig: 1859. It forms the latter part of ch. 56.]

first book of the Pancha Tantra and Kalíla wa Damna, the story of the Lion Pingalaka, the Bull Sanjívaka and the two Jackals Damanaka and Karatáka. The stories and the order in which they succeed agree better with the tales and arrangement of the Kalíla wa Damna then even the Pancha Tantra, and it would appear therefore that we have in the Kathá Sarit Ságara an earlier representative of the original collection than even the Pancha Tantra, at least as it is now met with; a comparative catalogue of the contents of each may throw some light on the relationship of the different collections*.

Stories in the Pancha Tantra, Kalíla wa Damna, and Kathá Sarit Ságara.

Pancha Tantra.	Kalíla wa Damna.	Kathá Sarit Ságara.
Merchant and his Bull, Lion and two Jackals —forming the introduction and framework.	Same.	Same.
1. Monkey and Timber.	1. Same.	1. Same.
2. Fox and Drum.	2. Same.	2. Same.
3. King, Merchant and Slave.		
4. Adventures of an Ascetic.	3. Same.	
5. Magic Garuda.		
6. Two Crows.		
7. Crane killed by the Crab.	5. Swan killed by the Crab.	3. Crane killed by the Crab.

* [Benfey, l. l., I, 419 f.]

Pancha Tantra.	Kalila wa Damna.	Kathá Sarit Ságara.
8. Lion and Hare.	6. Same.	4. Same.
9. King, Flea and Bug.	8. Same.	5. Same.
10. Jackal dyed.		
11. Lion, Tiger, Crow, Jackal and Camel.	9. Same.	6. Same.
12. Titiibha and the Sea.	10. Same.	7. Same.
13. Tortoise and Geese.	4. Same.	8. Same.
14. Three Fishes.	7. Same.	9. Same.
15. Elephant and Sparrow, Woodpecker, Fly and Frog.		
16. Swan, Creeper, and Fowler.		
17. Ram and Lion. Battle between the Bull and Lion.	Same.	Same.
18. Lion, Jackal and Camel.		
19. King, General and Ascetic.		
20. Snake changed to a Man.		
21. Parrot and Death.		
22. Monkies and Fire Flies.	11. Same.	10. Same.
23. Honest Man and Knave.	12. Two Friends and Bag of Money.	11. Brothers and Bag of Money.
24. Crane, Mongoose and Snake.	4. Same.	12. Same.
25. Rats that eat Iron.	13. Same.	13. Same.
26. Two Parrots.		
27. King's Son and his Companions.	(14th Book.–King's Son and his Companions.)	
Death of the Bull.	Same.	Same.

There is only a difference of one story therefore between the contents of the Kathá Sarit Ságara in this section and of the fifth book of the Kalíla wa Damna, the four preceding books of which treat of new and introductory matters prefixed by the translator. The omitted story however is a remarkable one, and one of great popularity in Europe. It relates the adventures of a religious mendicant called Deva Sarman in the Pancha Tantra* and Hitopadesa**, but not named in the Kalíla wa Damna, who in his wanderings puts up at the house of a barber: the barber's wife goes to an assignation with a lover, and leaves her confidante in her place. The barber, imagining that his wife is present, and provoked at her misbehaviour, throws his razor at her in the dark, and deprives her of her nose. The wife returns, and finding what has happened, prays to the gods that if she is virtuous her nose may be restored to her; and as her face is found in the morning without any defective feature, her husband is convinced of her immaculate purity, and suspects her no more. That this story jumped with the humours of our forefathers is proved by its numerous repetitions and imitations, as, with some modifications, it occurs as the Fabliau of the 'Cheveux Coupés,' the 'Une verge pour l'autre' of the 'Cent Nouvelles Nouvelles,' a story in the Decameron, in the collection of Malespini, and in the Contes of La

---

* [I, 4. Denfey, l. l., I, 140 ff.]
** [II, 7. Brockhaus in "Berichte der Königl. Sächs. Ges. d. Wiss." 1853, p. 198 ff.]

Fontaine, and has been dramatized in the "Guardian" of Massinger. In the East it is found in the Tooti Náma, or Tales of a Parrot, the Bahár Dánish, and other popular collections *.

In the fifth section of the same book occurs the skeleton of the first book of the Hitopadeśa, the second of the Pancha Tantra, and seventh of the Kalíla wa Damna, the Mitralábha or acquirement of friends, as illustrated by the association of the Rat, the Crow, the Tortoise and the Deer. The identity is confined to the general outline however, and none of the episodical tales are inserted. The purport of the narration is to contrast the fidelity and attachment of which animals are capable with the treachery of women, in illustration of which follows a story of a jealous husband and his wife. A man had a very beautiful wife, of whom he was so devotedly fond that he scarcely ever suffered her to be out of his sight. Having occasion to go from home he took her with him, and during his necessary absence on business left her under the care of an old Brahman. Near the Brahman's house was a village of Bhils, foresters, and with one of them the wife eloped. The husband on his return having learnt what had happened, proceeded in quest of his wife to the Bhil village, and arriving there, whilst the men were out hunting, encountered his wife. She assured him that she had been carried away by force, and desired him to secrete himself in a cave till night, when she would

---

* (See above p. 14.)

escape along with him. He believed her, and hid himself; but when the lover returned in the evening the false wife betrayed her husband, and he was seized and bound to a tree in order to be offered as a human victim in the morning to the goddess Chaṅḍí. His prayers to the goddess however moved her to free him from his bonds, and he availed himself of his freedom to kill his rival and cut off his head. The wife had still art enough to persuade him of her innocence, and accompanied him in his flight, carrying with her the head of her Bhil lover. Upon their arrival at the first city they came to, she produced the head, declared it was her husband's and gave the real husband in charge to the police as the murderer. He was taken before the king, but the investigation established his innocence and his wife's guilt. She had her ears and nose cut off, and was deserted by her husband, who was now cured of his misplaced confidence in her affection. It may be remarked that frequent mention is made in the Kathá Sarit Ságara of the sacrifice of human victims by the barbarous tribes inhabiting the woods and mountains, who, although not Hindus, seem to have adopted as their favourite divinity some of the terrific forms of Durgá, and offered to her human sacrifices: the practice still prevails amongst them when it can be perpetrated with impunity, but it is contrary to the letter and to the spirit of the genuine Hindu ritual.

The sixth section of the tenth book contains the war between the Crows and the Owls, which forms the subject of the third books of the Pancha Tantra and Hitopadeśa, the eighth book of the Kalila wa Damna, and the fourth chapter of the Persian imitation of it, the Anwári Soheilí.

Pancha Tantra.	K. S. S.	K. D.	Anwári Soheilí.
Introduction — War of the Crows and Owls.	The Same.	The Same.	The Same.
	1. Ass in Lion's Skin.		1. The King and his Mistress.
1. Elephant and Hares.	2. Same.	1. Same.	2. Same.
2. Hare, Sparrow and Cat.	3. Same.	2. Same.	3. Same.
3. Brahman, Rogues, and Goat.	4. Same.	3. Same.	4. Same.
4. Snake killed by Ants.			
5. Snake and Brahman's Son.			
6. Swans and Strange Bird.			
7. Fowler and Pigeons.			
8. Husband, Wife and Robber.	5. The Same.	4. The Same.	5. The Same.
9. Brahman, Thief and Rákshas.	6. The Same.		6. The Same.
10. Prince with a Snake in his Belly.			
11. Husband under the Bed.	7. The Same.	5. The Same.	7. The Same.
12. Brahman and Mouse changed to a Girl.	8. The Same.	6. The Same.	8. Monkeys and Bears.
13. Bird that voided Gold.			9. The Same.
14. Lion and Fox.			
15. Old Snake and Frogs.	9. The Same.	7. The Same.	10. The Same.
16. Brahman and his Wife.			11. The two Sparrows.

Of these stories several are well known in the narrative fictions of Europe; some of the identifications are pointed out in the 'Analysis of the Pancha Tantra,' and others by M. L. Deslongchamps. Thus the first of the Kathá Sarit Ságara, which occurs in another book of the Pancha Tantra*, is a very common apologue in all collections; the third or second of the Pancha Tantra and Kalíla wa Damna has been imitated by La Fontaine in the fable of Le chat, la belette et le petit lapin**. The story of the Brahman who is persuaded to part with his goat is found in les Facécieuses nuits du Seigneur Straparole***. The fifth story, which is found in the Pancha Tantra alone, is considered by M. Deslongchamps to be the same as La Confiance perdue of Senecé†. It is also found in the collection of Marie de France, a fabulist of the thirteenth century. The husband, wife and robber, and the mouse changed into a girl, are both modernized by Fontaine; the latter he derived from the Livre des Lumières of Daniel Sahid; the former occurs in the Cent Nouvelles Nouvelles††. In this, as in the story of the bull and the lion, the Kathá Sarit Ságara agrees better than the Pancha Tantra with the Arabic work, and may, there-

---

* [IV, 7; above p. 46.]

** [ap. Robert, Fables inédites, II, 107. cf. Benfey, l. l., I, 350 ff.]

*** [Paris: 1857, I, XVI & p. 46. F. W. V. Schmidt, die Mährchen des Straparola. Berlin: 1817, p. 308. Above p. 37.]

† [Paris: 1855, p. 119. Le Grand d'Aussy, IV, 389. Kurz ad B. Waldis I, 26. Above p. 38.]

†† [La Fontaine IX, 7 & 15. Livre des L. p. 279. Cent N. N. 16. Above p. 41 f.]

fore, be of earlier date; at the same time the style of the stories is unequivocally that of an abridgement, and they no doubt existed in some more detailed arrangement, and very possibly associated with others not here inserted.

In the next section of this book occurs the excellent story of the monkey and Śiśumára or Porpoise. In the Pancha Tantra, the Makara, a nondescript marine animal, is substituted for the Śiśumára; and, in the Mohammedan versions of the story, a tortoise takes the place of the Hindu aquatic. There is a greater coincidence again between the Kalíla wa Damna and our text in this story than between the former and the Pancha Tantra, in which last the story includes nine others: in the Arabic work, and in the Kathá Sarit Ságara, it has but one, that of the sick lion, the jackal (or fox) and the ass. The monkeys and tortoises, so often introduced in these stories, are, as M. de Sacy remarks, evidence of an Indian origin. "Les singes et les tortues souvent mis en scène dans ces fables appartiennent plutôt à l'Inde qu'à la Perse."—Mémoire Historique, vii. But this is still more applicable to such entirely Indian animals as the Makara or Śiśumára.

We have in this section also what may be perhaps the original of another well-known Arabian story, one of the earliest in the Thousand and One Nights. Two young Brahmans travelling are benighted in a forest, and take up their lodging in a tree near a lake. Early in the night a number of people come from the water, and having made preparation for an entertainment retire; a Yaksha, a genie, then comes out of the lake with his two wives, and spends the night there; when he and one of his wives are asleep, the other, seeing the youths, invites them to approach her, and to encourage them, shows them a hundred rings received from former gallants, notwithstanding her husband's precautions, who keeps her locked up in a chest at the bottom of the lake. The Hindu story-teller is more moral than the Arab. The youths reject her advances; she wakes the genie who is going to put them to death, but the rings are produced in evidence against the unfaithful wife, and she is turned away with the loss of her nose. The story is repeated in the next section with some variation; the lady has ninety and nine rings, and is about to complete the hundredth, when her husband, who is here a Nága, a snake-god, wakes, and consumes the guilty pair with fire from his mouth.

In the commencement of the eighth section of this book we have the story of the mungoose, the snake and child (see p. 54), and in the same section is a long and not uninteresting story of two friends, Ghaṭa and Karpara. They become thieves, and break into the king's palace to plunder his treasure. While Ghaṭa keeps watch without, Karpara makes his way into the inner apartments, where the princess sees him, and falls in love with him. She gives him much valuable property, with which he despatches his companion to their home, and returns into the palace. He is surprised there, and by the commands of the king hung upon a tree. On his way to the place of execution, Ghata, who, alarmed at his friend's not returning, had come back to seek for him, sees Karpara led to the gibbet. Karpara, by signs unperceived by the guards, commends the princess to the care of Ghata; he by the same means expresses his promise to effect her rescue. Accordingly at night he enters the palace, liberates the princess from her bonds, and carries her off. When the king is apprised of this, he concludes the perpetrator of the deed must have been a friend of Karpara, and that it is likely, therefore, that he will attempt to obtain the body, in order to perform its funeral rites; he accordingly places guards around the tree on which the corpse is suspended, and commands them to arrest any one who shall display any particular grief on viewing the body, or shall seek to take it away. Ghata determines, as the king had anticipated, to procure the body of his friend, and commit it to the flames. He disguises himself as a countryman, with one of his servants as a woman, and another carrying a jar of sweetmeats, in which the narcotic juice of the Dhattura has been infused. Pretending to have lost his way, he approaches the guards, and, entering into familiar conversation with them, invites them to partake of his sweetmeats, his wife, he says, being very famous for her skill in making them. The guards eat and fall asleep, and Ghata cuts down and burns the body of Karpara. He afterwards contrives to carry off the ashes; and the king, finding precaution useless, causes it to be proclaimed that he will give his daughter and half his kingdom to the man who has done these deeds. We have in these incidents an obvious analogy to those of the story of the knight and his two sons in the History of the Seven Sages of Rome, as above intimated, and still more to some of the circumstances of the story of Rhampsinites, king of Egypt, as narrated by Herodotus, (Essai sur les Fables Indiennes,) if not to the leading incident in the tragedy of Antigone*. The Indian story continues in a strain intended to demonstrate the depravity of women. Ghatá is persuaded by the princess that the king's offer is merely a trap for him; and, instead of accepting it, he departs with her and a religious mendicant, his associate, to a distant country. On the journey his mistress and friend accomplish his murder. The princess afterwards abandons the mendicant, and leads a life of profligacy paralleled by similar instances, which grow out of the story of her adventures.

The eleventh book is occupied with one story only, that of Velá, a damsel married to a merchant's son; the leading incidents are their shipwreck, separation and re-union. It is only worth while to notice the frequency with which adventures by sea are narrated in this collection, and, indeed, in other works of the

---

* [Herod. II, 121. Keller, Dyocletianus Leben, p. 55. Keller, Li Romans des sept Sages, p. CXCIII. Liebrecht's transl. of Dunlop's History of Fiction, p. 197 & 264.]

same, or an earlier date, showing that at the period in question the Hindus were not accustomed to regard sea-voyages as either unlawful or unusual.

The twelfth book presents several examples of the transformation of human persons to animals, of which instances are so frequent in the Arabian Nights, although it may be doubted if the notion be an article of Mohammedan superstition. With the Hindus it is but the second step in the doctrine of the metempsychosis, as the belief that men and women become animals in a future life readily reconciles them to the admission of the possibility that they may assume brute forms even in this. They have also exemplifications of it in their mythology: and Vishńu himself, in three of his incarnations, is a fish, a tortoise and a boar. In the first section of this book of the Kathá Sarit Ságara, Vámadatta has a wife who becomes possessed of magical powers; he detects her in some of her vicious practices, and is about to put her to death, when she throws some dust into his face, and he is turned to a buffalo, in which state he is sold by his wife, and becomes a beast of burthen. Another female sorceress discovers his true nature, restores him to it, and gives him her daughter in marriage; she enables him also to transform his wife to a mare, in which form he inflicts upon her daily chastisement. There is no hesitation in recognising in the story the leading incidents in the stories of the old man and his two dogs, and of Zobeide and her two sisters, and particularly in the story of Syed Naoman in the Thousand and One Nights; in the latter of these the wicked wife is transformed also into a mare. In the fourth section again of this same book we have some transformations which call to mind the adventures of Apuleius in the Golden Ass, or the still more ancient metamorphoses of Circe. Bhímaparákrama, coming to Ujjayiní, puts up in the house of a woman, who receives him hospitably. He goes to rest; but, waking in the night, sees his hostess busy in preparing some dishes of fried barley-meal, and muttering charms over them. Suspecting her to be a sorceress, he watches his opportunity, and transfers the meal to some other plates, whilst he replaces it with meal he finds set apart. The sorceress invites him to breakfast with her, and, unwittingly eating the barley she had bewitched, is changed to a she-goat. Bhímaparákrama sells her to a butcher. The butcher's wife is a sorceress also; and, although unable to save her friend, determines to revenge her; she therefore finds the youth when asleep, and, by tying a thread round his neck, changes him to a peacock. He is found in this condition, and liberated by his friend Mrigánkadatta, prince of Ayodhyá. The connecting chain of the whole of the twelfth book is the marriage of Mrigánkadatta with the princess of Ujjayiní; but before this can be effected the prince incurs the displeasure of his father, and is banished with his ten companions, the sons of his father's ministers. They set off together for Ujjayiní. In passing through a forest they find an ascetic sitting under a tree; they inquire of him his purposes in such a solitude, to which he replies that underneath the tree is the dwelling of a Nága, a snake god, who is master of a miraculous sword, the holder of which enjoys superhuman powers; that this sword is to be forced from its possessor by incantations, in which he asks them to give him aid. They assent; his magic compels the nymph of the sword to issue from the tree, but her beauty so bewilders him that he pauses in his process, and forgets his art. The Nága avails himself of the opportunity, appears, and destroys the magician, and condemns the inconsiderate youths to a temporary separation from each other. They are ultimately re-united with the prince, and repeat to him their several adventures. The scheme of this series of narratives is similar to that of a very excellent and popular Hindu work, ascribed to Dańdí, a writer of the ninth or tenth century, the Dasa Kumára, the Ten Princes, in which a prince and his nine companions are separated for a season, and recount what has happened to each when they meet again. The stories, however, are different. There are in the eighth section of this book incidental passages of some interest in the history of Sanskrit literature: the adoption of names, persons and incidents, and even the plagiarism of expressions found in well-known compositions, as the dramas of Mádhava and Málati, and Vikrama and Urvasí, and the poem of the Megha Dúta, or cloud-messenger, a work of Kálidása, to the prior celebrity of which they therefore bear testimony.

The ninth section of the twelfth book also is of

importance in the same respect, in its subservience to
the history of Sanskrit writings, as it contains the plan
and details of a collection extremely popular in India,
existing both in Sanskrit and in all the vernacular
dialects that have any literature, Hindee, Bengali,
Mahratta, Telugu, Tamil, and the rest. This is the
Vetála Panchaviṁśati: twenty-five tales of a Vetála,
being related by a sprite, who haunts cemeteries and
animates dead bodies, to Vikramáditya, king of
Ujjayiní, according to the usual version, to Trivikrama
Sena, king of Pratishṭhána or Pythan, on the Godávarí,
according to the Kathá Sarit Ságara. The king receives for a long time from a religious mendicant daily
presents of a fruit, which he hands over to his treasurer; at last a pet monkey takes the fruit, and
breaking it open, a precious jewel falls from it. The
treasurer being questioned as to what he had done
with the fruits previously presented, reports that they
had been thrown behind a door, where they still are;
but being desired to produce them, discovers that
they have all decayed, leaving a pile of valuable jewels on the spot where they had been cast. The king
inquires of the mendicant how he became possessed
of these gems, on which it appears that he is a Yogí
or ascetic, engaged in rites for the acquirement of
superhuman faculties, for the accomplishment of which
a dead body is necessary; and he has been propitiat-
ing Trivikrama in order to induce him to aid his
operations, a man of undaunted resolution being alone

capable of conveying a corpse, or in fact a body in which a malignant spirit abides, from the tree where it is suspended. The king undertakes the exploit, braves with unshaken intrepidity the horrors of the charnelground, cuts down the body, and lifts it on his shoulders. He is surprised, however, to find it address him, and propose to beguile the way by a series of narratives. It is essential to the safe conveyance of the Vetála that it should be effected in silence, and he therefore cunningly contrives that the Rájá shall not observe the condition. At the end of each story he proposes to the Rájá some question, arising out of what he has narrated; Vikrama replies; the body flies back to the tree, and the Rájá has the trouble of returning, and again endeavouring to secure it. The Vetála at last, subdued by the prince's perseverance, becomes his servant, and apprises him that the ascetic has a plot against his life, which he instructs the Rájá how to frustrate. The spirit being placed before the ascetic is worshipped by him, and he then desires the Rájá to perform a reverential prostration to the Vetála. The Rájá answers he knows not how to do it properly, and begs the ascetic to show him. The ascetic accordingly casts himself prostrate on the ground, when the Rájá cuts off his head. He then returns to his palace, and ever afterwards commands the services of the Vetála. The Vetála Panchavinśati has appeared in an English dress, having been translated by Rújá Káli Krishna, a native gentleman of Calcutta, and printed there*. Some of the stories have been imitated in the literature of other countries. There is one remarkable tale, however, found in the Hindu version, which does not occur in this setting of the stories. This is the story alluded to by Gibbon, as accounting for the disgrace into which the empress Eudocia, the wife of Theodosius the younger, fell. A Brahman presents a beautiful fruit to the king Bhartŕi Hari; he gives it to his queen; she transfers it to a gallant; he hands it to a courtezan, by whom it is again brought as a present to the king, who thus detects his wife's infidelity. According to the story, and to popular tradition, Bhartŕi Hari, disgusted with the world, abandoned, in consequence of this occurrence, his throne, and retired to a religious life. The French translation of Moreri, relating the story as applicable to Eudocia, says: "L'empereur se chagrina au sujet d'un fruit qu'il lui avait donné, dont elle fit présent au Paulin et que ce dernier rapporta à ce prince, ce fruit fut une vraie pomme de discorde." The authority for the story is Theophrastus, whose history of the Roman empire closes in the beginning of the ninth century. From the literature of the lower empire the story became familiar to that of Europe, and is dramatized by Massinger in his Emperor of the East. The probability of its Asiatic origin is confirmed by its being incor-

---

* [Bytal-Puchisi. Calcutta: 1834.]

porated into the Thousand and One Nights, under the title of the Three Apples*.

The thirteenth book is short, and recounts the adventures of two young Brahmans, who effect secret marriages with a princess and her friend. The incidents are curious and diverting, but they are chiefly remarkable from being the same as the contrivances by which Mádhava and Makaraúda obtain their mistresses in the drama entitled Málatí and Mádhava, or the Stolen Marriage. (See Specimens of the Theatre of the Hindus.) The two next books, the fourteenth and fifteenth, are of less general interest than the preceding, the scene of action being laid chiefly amongst the fabulous regions of the Vidyádharas. In the first, the prince Naraváhanadatta makes an addition to his domestic arrangements of five Vidyádharí wives. In the second he is crowned emperor of the Vidyádhara race.

The connecting thread of the series of tales should here terminate; but in the next book, the sixteenth, we have an account of the death of Vatsa, who resigns his throne to Gopálaka, the brother of his wife Vúsavadattá, and, accompanied by his wives and ministers, goes to Mount Kálanjana, where a heavenly chariot descends, and conveys them all to heaven. Gopálaka, inconsolable for the loss of his brother-in-law, soon relinquishes his regal state, and making over Kauśámbí to his younger brother, Pálaka, repairs to the White

---
* [Nights 19—24.]

Mountain, and spends the rest of his days in the hermitage of Káśyapa. We have then an account of the son of Pálaka falling in love with a young girl of low caste, a Chándálí, and different stories illustrative of unequal matches, some of which have been told before. A very convenient doctrine is maintained by Pálaka's ministers, that the very circumstance of the prince's being enamoured of the Chándálí is a proof that she cannot be truly of so base an origin, but that she must be a princess or goddess in disguise; otherwise it were impossible that she should have attracted the affections of any noble individual. They therefore counsel the king to demand the nymph of her father. The father consents, on condition that the Brahmans of Ujjayiní eat in his house. Pálaka issues orders that the Brahmans, to the number of eighteen thousand, shall dine with the Chándála. They are of course in great alarm, as this is a virtual degradation, and loss of caste, and they apply to Mahákála, the form of Śiva especially worshipped in Ujjayiní, to know what to do. He commands them in a dream to comply, as Matanga, the supposed Chándála, is in truth a Vidyádbara. He had conspired against the life of Naraváhanadatta, in order to prevent his becoming emperor of the Vidyádharas, and had been therefore condemned by Śiva to live in Ujjayiní with his family as Chándálas. The curse was to terminate when eighteen thousand Brahmans should eat in his house; and this being accomplished, he is restored to his rank, and his daughter is a fit bride for the son of the king.

The principal feature in this tale deserving of notice is its intimation of an indignity offered to the Brahmans of Ujjayiní by a king named Pálaka, a circumstance which is either derived from an ancient play, the Mŕichchhakatí, or taken, as well as the drama from some historical tradition.

The two last books are composed of narratives told by Naravàhanadatta, when on a visit to his uncle Gopálaka at the hermitage of Káśyapa. He repeats those stories which were communicated to him when he was separated from Madanamanchuká, to console him under the anguish of separation. The first book treats entirely of the loves of Muktáphala Ketu, a prince of the Vidyádharas, and Padmávatí, daughter of the king of the Gandharbas. The former is condemned by a holy person to become a man, and he is thus for a season separated from the latter. He is, after a short time, restored to his station and his wife. The story is not without merit, but it is tedious, and relieved by no episodical tales. The last book is of a more diversified description, and has Vikramáditya or Vikramaśíla, son of Mahendráditya, king of Ujjayiní, for its hero, and describes his victories over hostile princes, and his acquirement of various princesses. These are interspersed with love adventures, some of which reiterate the calumnies against women, and with stories relating the tricks of professed cheats. Several of them have some curious matter, but nothing that reflects any particular light upon the migrations of storytelling.

The sketch thus given of the contents of the Kathá
Sarit Ságara will show that it has been judiciously
selected by Dr. Brockhaus for publication and translation. It is impossible that so voluminous a compilation should be without a due proportion of
tediousness and insipidity, and the spirit of the narrations is not improved by the substitution of verse
for prose. The verse is in general of very simple
construction, and the style is upon the whole sufficiently easy; the metrical arrangement, however,
involves a formality and sententiousness which are
inconsistent with the freedom that gives animation to
narrative. The work, however, is full of interest, as
abounding with pictures of national manners and
feelings, and as offering the oldest extant form of
many of the tales which were once popular in Europe.
It is not necessary to suppose that the West was, in
the middle ages, barren of invention; that the novelists
and fablers of Europe were destitute of imagination.
Many of these fictions are no doubt "native, and to
the manner born"; but it is equally indubitable that
they were indebted to the East for many of their
"findings", and that the Hindus occupy an early and
a prominent place in the History of Fiction.

VIII.

EXTRACTS FROM THE DAŚAKUMÁRA, OR THE TEN PRINCES.

From the Quarterly Oriental Magazine, Vol. V, (1826), p. 297–314;
Vol. VI, p. 106–124 & 211–227; Vol. VII (1827), p. 279–294;
and Vol. VIII (1828), p. 69–87.

FIRST SECTION.

In Pushpapurí, a city of Magadha, ruled Rájahansa, an excellent and accomplished monarch; his queen was named Vasumatí. He had three ministers, Dharmapála, Padmodbhava, and Sitavarmá, who were the royal councillors by hereditary succession; of these Sitavarmá had two sons, Sumati and Satyavarmá. Dharmapála had three, Sumantra, Sumitra, and Kámapála; and Padmodbhava two, Suśruta and Ratnodbhava.

Satyavarmá, the son of Sitavarmá, becoming disgusted with the world, went upon a pilgrimage to foreign lands. Kámapála, the son of Dharmapála, attaching himself to low company, parasites, actors, and women, led a vagabond life; and Ratnodbhava who was engaged in traffic spent much time in distant voyages;

the other brothers succeeded to the ministerial situations held by their sires.

It happened that a war broke out between Rájahansa and Mánasára, King of Málava, in the course of which the former led a powerful host against his enemy; he was encountered by the King of Málava, and a furious conflict ensued in which Mánasára was defeated, and taken prisoner. The king of Magadha was of too generous a character, to wreak his vengeance on a captive prince, and far from treating Mánasára with rigour, he immediately restored him to his liberty and his kingdom.

Rájahansa now ruled the whole world without a rival, or anxiety; still he was not happy: he grieved that his union had not been blessed with progeny, and to obtain children was the subject of his constant supplications to the Creator of the universe, Náráyańa. His prayers were not in vain: his principal Queen shortly afterwards conceived, on the anouncement of which happy event Rájahansa, inviting all his royal and princely friends, celebrated with great splendour the Símanta festival. On this occasion whilst seated on the Throne, the Chamberlain informed the King, a holy man had arrived at Court, who begged admittance to the presence; permission was granted. As soon as he appeared, Rájahausa recognised him through his disguise as one of his own confidential emissaries, and dismissing the Courtiers he withdrew with his ministers, and enquired smilingly what news the spy had brought. The spy replied: 'In obedience

to your Royal commands I entered the capital of the
Prince of Málava: his late overthrow rankling in his
heart he addressed himself to Maheśwara in the shrine
of Mahákála, and by the fervour of his devotion obtained a divine boon, a club endowed with the certain
power of slaying one individual: armed with this
weapon, confident of victory, and anticipating your
destruction Múnasára is levying forces to march against
your Majesty.' When the Ministers heard this intelligence, they advised the King to retire into the Fort,
and resign to them the conduct of the war; but he
disdained their council, and determined to meet the
enemy in person. Mánasára advanced into Magadha,
and the Ministers prevailed upon Rájahansa to send
the women to a place of security in the Vindhya
Mountains. The armies met on the confines of the
Province, and an obstinate engagement took place.
In the battle the Princes encountered, and Mánasára
directed the fatal mace against the head of the King
of Magadha; he missed his aim, but the blow killed
the Charioteer, and left the King senseless; the horses
being without a master ran off frightened towards
the Hills, and carried their unconscious Lord into the
thickets, which had given shelter to his household.

The troops of Magadha, seeing their Sovereign's fate,
fled in every direction; and the king of Málava, now
victorious, overran the Country, and established his
own residence at Pushpapurí. The Ministers of Rájahansa had all been left on the field, covered with
wounds, but not dead, and having recovered a little

with the fresh breeze of the morning, their first effort
was to seek for the body of the king: the search
proving fruitless, they repaired to the retreat in the
mountains, which concealed the Queen, and reported
to her the misadventures of the conflict, and the disappearance of her husband. Vasumati was resolved
not to survive her Lord, but was dissuaded by the
Ministers, especially as she would thus frustrate the
decrees of the stars, which had predicted her giving
birth to a lovely, valiant, and illustrious Prince.

The Queen was silenced by this opposition: she
held her peace, but kept her purpose, and at midnight
she stole forth to the neighbouring thicket, where,
fastening her veil round her neck, she attempted with
it to suspend herself from the branch of a Ber tree,
exclaiming "May that Lord whose beauty was as the
flowery bow of Káma be again my husband in a
future life." At that moment the king who had been
hurled out of his car on that very spot, and now recovered, heard and recognised the voice of his Queen:
he called to her, and she hearing his accents, hastened
to him agitated with doubt and alarm. Delighted to
find him still alive, she loudly called for assistance,
when the servants of the Rájá approached, and seeing
their master, joyfully prostrated themselves at his
feet: they then prepared a tent, had his wounds
healed without delay, and to console him cited the
example of Harischandra and other Princes who, after
experiencing adversity, had again obtained an imperial
dominion. After a time Rájahansa went with his

11*

attendants to visit Vámadeva, a holy sage, who resided
in the adjoining thickets, and having spent a short
time with him, requested his aid to recover his kingdom. The sage recommended him to remain tranquil,
assuring him that his Queen was about to give birth
to a son, who would revenge him on all his foes.
Vasumati shortly afterwards bore a Prince, who was
named Rájaváhana, and at the same time it happened
that there were born sons to the King's four Ministers,
the son of Sumati was named Pramati; of Sumantra,
Chitragupta; of Sumitra, Mantragupta; and of Suśruta,
Viśruta; these grew up together, the playfellows and
friends of the Prince.

One day a Brahman approached the King, and delivering a young boy to him thus said:

TALE.

Sire, being one day on my travels through a forest,
I saw a young woman in ragged and foul attire, weeping bitterly. Moved by compassion, I asked, why thus
alone in a dreary forest she was wandering, and in
grief. She replied, as well as her sobs would permit
her: "Praháravarmá, Prince of Mithilá, came to
Pushpapurí, when the Kings were assembled at the
Símantiní ceremony of the Queen of Magadha, and
afterwards accompanying the King against his enemy,
the Prince of Málava, shared the defeat of his Ally:
making his escape from the field, he marched towards
his own country with such of his followers as survived
the engagement, but proceeding through a wood was

unexpectedly attacked by the Śavaras, and most of his people were slain: with great difficulty he effected his escape, and secured the retreat of the females of his family, guarded by a select corps. I and my daughter who were the nurses of the Prince's two twin sons were unable to keep up with him in his flight; we were lost in the wood, and whilst thus deserted, a fierce tiger rushed open-mouthed upon me. I attempted to fly, but in my terror fell, and with me fell the boy I bore in my arms; he scrambled away, and hid himself beneath a cow, that lay dead near us. The tiger seized the carcase and was dragging it along, when an arrow from a Forester streched the monster lifeless on the ground. The forester pleased with the child's appearance took him up, and carried him away, whither I knew not, nor did I know where to seek my daughter and her charge: overcome with agitation and fatigue I became insensible, and was found in that state by a Cowherd, who conveyed me to his hut, and gave me food and shelter. Thus recovered I have issued forth to search for my nurseling, or to return at least to my Lord to inform him what has so sadly chanced." Thus having said she left me. Sympathising with the distress which the Rájá of Mithilá would suffer, I determined to seek his children. On my search I beheld a stately Temple of Chańdiká, and approaching it, beheld a number of mountaineers collected, amongst whom was a fair child, whom they had resolved to sacrifice to the Goddess, in gratitude for their late victory, and for the propitiation of the deity in future. They differed as to the manner of killing their victim; some proposing to suspend him to the branch of a tree, and strike off his neck with a sword; some to set him as a mark for their arrows, and some to let him loose, and chace him with dogs. I approached and addressed them, saying: valiant Foresters, I am an old Brahman, who some days ago missed my way as I passed through your woods with my young son. I left him in the shade, whilst I went to recover the track, and when I returned I had lost my boy; have any of you, worthy Sirs, encountered a stray child? They were pleased with my address, and producing the young Prince, asked if the boy was mine, I pretended that he was, and they resigned him to me. I received him and took my leave, and have brought him to you for protection.

The Rájá grieving for his friend Prahárovarmá's misfortunes gladly took charge of the Prince; he named him Upaháravarmá, and brought him up as if he had been his own.

On one occasion as Rájahansa was travelling to holy places, he came to a village of Foresters, when he observed one of the women accompanied by a child of extraordinary beauty, and enquired of her who he was; she replied that, when her people defeated the troops of the Mithilá Prince, her husband brought this boy to her from the field, which was very near the village. The King on hearing this was satisfied it was his friend's son, and prevailed on the woman to relinquish the child; carrying him to his residence, he called him Apaháravarmá and brought him up with his own son.

The pupil of the sage Vámadeva one day brought a boy to the King and said: Prince, on one occasion, when I had bathed at Rámatírtha and was returning, I encountered in a forest an elderly woman bearing a child new born. I asked who she was, why in that lonely place, and what she was doing with the babe; she said: "In Kálayavana Island dwelt Kálagupta, a wealthy merchant: he had a daughter named Suvŕittá, who was married to a man of great wealth and abilities, the son of the minister of the King of Magadha, Ratnodbhava; in due time the wife became pregnant, and her husband being anxious to return to his own country set off with her privately for that purpose: the ship they embarked in was caught in a storm, and dashed to pieces: fortunately Suvŕittá and myself, who attended her as her nurse, got upon a plank, and were borne to land; what became of the crew and Ratnodbhava we knew not: the fright brought on premature pains, and in this wood my mistress has just been delivered of this child: she lies by the side of a pool under a tree senseless with her sufferings, and I have left her, to seek for assistance, bearing with me the infant, as the mother is unable to take care of it. The old woman had scarcely finished when

a wild elephant sprang forth: she dropped the child,
and ran away: I hid myself in a neighbouring clump
whence I could see what chanced: the elephant picked
up the infant with its trunk, when a fierce lion rushed
upon the animal: the elephant in alarm cast the infant
from its uplifted trunk towards the boughs of a tree,
where an ape seeing the child, and taking it for
some sort of fruit, caught it in his arms; finding
his mistake the monkey laid the infant upon a net-
work of the crossing branches, and bounded away, and
the lion having killed the elephant likewise disappeared.
I then ventured from my hiding place, took the child
from the tree, and went in quest of its mother or
nurse. Having sought for them through the thicket
in vain, I brought the child with me to my superior,
by whose desire I transfer him to your royal care.

The King was much astonished at the strange
fortunes which had brought together the children of
his friends, and his own, and was deeply grieved for
the loss of his early associate Ratnodbhava: the brother
of that chief, Suśruta, was equally afflicted for the
loss of the father, and consoled by the preservation
of the child; and to him the King consigned the boy,
naming him Pushpodbhava, and directing him to be
brought up with the Prince and his young companions.

———

One day Rájahansa observed the Queen nursing a
strange infant, and approaching her he asked whose
the child was. The Queen replied: I was awakened

in the night by a celestial female, who delivered to me this infant, saying, I am the beloved of Kámapála the son of your Minister Dharmapála; my name is Tárávali, the daughter of Manibhadra, and by the command of the King of the Yakshas, I bring you this my son to be a servant to your son, whom future fame awaits, your Rájaváhana. So having said she disappeared, before I had recovered from my astonishment, and left the infant in my hands.

Rájahansa was not less astonished by the Queen's relation, and receiving the child he named him Arthapála, and gave him in charge to his uncle Sumitra to be brought up with the other Princes.

On another occasion one of Vámadeva's pupils brought a most lovely boy to the presence of the King, and said: I went, oh Monarch, in pilgrimage to the Káverí River, and there I saw an old woman on the bank with a child in her lap weeping violently. I asked the cause; she replied: formerly Satyavarmá, the son of Silavarmá, minister of Rájahansa King of Magadha, came to this holy spot, and taking up his abode in a neighbouring Agrahára[1], he married Kálí the daughter of a Brahman: she proving barren, he espoused her younger sister Gaurí, by whom he had a son: the elder sister conceived a violent hatred for the child, and one day

---

[1] A sort of secular convent; lands and houses granted to Brahmans and their families.

seized an opportunity of pushing me, who am its nurse, along with the infant, into the stream. I supported myself and the child as well as I could, till we reached a floating tree, clinging to which we were borne along with the current to this place: on the tree was a black snake, by which I was bitten, and the poison spreads through my frame, so that I cannot long survive, and then what is to become of my child? so I thought, and as I thought, I wept.

She had scarcely finished, when she fell on the ground lifeless. I endeavoured with charms and drugs to arrest the venom, but it was too late; then committing her body to the flames, I took the child, and not knowing where to find the abode of its parents, I have brought him to your Majesty.

The King accordingly received the boy, and gave him to be reared under his uncle Sumati, naming him Somadatta, and directing him to be educated with the Prince and his companions.

So these boys were associated and went through their education together: they were taught to write and speak various tongues; the Holy Sciences, Policy, Rhetoric, History, and sacred Record (Puránas), Metaphysics, Astrology, Law, and the morals of Princes, according to Káutilya, and the Kámandakíya; and to play on many Instruments, and the sciences of Music, Medicine, and Magic: to manage the Horse, Elephant, and Car, to use various weapons; to excel in thieving, gaming and other such practices; and the King seeing their youth, and skill, and valour, felt proud of his juvenile band, and confident of triumphing with their aid over every danger.

SECOND SECTION.

On one occasion Vámadeva approached the King, surrounded by these Princes, each as lovely as Káma, and valiant as Kárttikeya; he returned the King's salutation with his benediction, the prostration of the Princes with his embrace, and thus addressed the King: "The time is arrived for your son to set forth to conquest: let Rájaváhana attended by his companions depart." Accordingly Rájaváhana, attended by his associates appointed to the various offices of state, took leave of his father in a propitious hour, and directing his course by the auspices he noticed, entered the Vindhya forest: there he saw a man covered with scars, with a body as hard as iron, and of hideous aspect; by his cord he seemed a Brahman, but in all other respects a Barbarian. Rájaváhana, receiving his respects, said, "How is it you reside in this lonely spot, fit only for the deer? why wear you this sacred cord, and yet by these wounds appear a savage woodman?" To this the stranger replied:

In this wood, oh! Prince, resided many Brahmans who followed the usages of the barbarians, and ate with them; foregoing the study of holy writ, the observances of their tribes, and their moral and social duties; of one of these I am the son, my name is

Mátanga: on one occasion with a party of savages I
harried the neighbouring country. We bound the old
men and the women, and brought away wealth and
captives, and destroyed all else. On our return I observed a party of my associates menacing a Brahman
with death. I commanded them to forbear, but they
reviled, and fell upon me, and left me dead. I went
to the city of Souls, and beheld its mighty King seated
upon a lofty throne studded with splendid jewels. I
bowed before him; he looked at me, and calling to
Chitragupta said: 'This man's hour is not yet come.
He dies in defence of a Brahman. That one virtuous
act effaces all his former sins. Let him behold the
penalty paid by the wicked, and then restore him to
his former body.' Chitragupta then shewed me where
the wicked were beaten with red-hot clubs, hurled
into caldrons of scalding oil, pulverized with pestles,
or pealed with adzes, and then giving me friendly
counsel he dismissed me. Restored to my former
body, I found the Brahman I had rescued sprinkling
me, as I lay apparently fainting, with cool water; my
friends who had heard of my encounter then arrived,
and carried me home, and dressed my wounds, and
the grateful Brahman still staid with me, and gave me
instructions: he taught me to read, to understand the
sacred Books, and to look on Śiva with the eye of
wisdom. He then left me. After his departure, I
abandoned my former life, quitted my family and
home, and came to abide here, in undisturbed meditation upon the one God of all worlds. Something I

have to say to you, but alone; follow me. The Prince withdrawing with him, he thus continued: Last night Śiva imparted to me a dream, saying, 'On the bank of the River of the Daṅḍáraṅya forest, behind the Sphaíika linga, is a stone marked with the feet of the daughter of the Mountain Monarch: near that is a Chasm: in it is a Copper-plate, on which is written the means of making you sovereign of Pátála: your associate in this must be the Prince who to-day or to-morrow will come hither. You have come as he foretold, and now give me your aid. The Prince assented, and at midnight, leaving his friends asleep, accompanied Mátanga to a distant thicket: when his followers woke and missed him, they sought him in every direction, but their search proving vain, they agreed to separate, and after prosecuting their enquiries for some time, rendezvous finally at Ujjayiní.

Mátanga aided by the Prince, entered the Chasm, obtained the Talisman, and penetrated the path to Pátála. On arriving near a city they paused in a grove on the edge of a Pool where, agreeably to the directions of the plate, Mátanga made a fire, and offered Ghee, whilst the Prince stood watch against intrusion. Whilst thus employed, he was surprised to see his companion cast himself into the flames, and thence again rise in an angelic form. On this a damsel richly arrayed, and numerously attended, approached the grove: she presented to the Brahman a splendid jewel, and to his enquiry who she was replied in tones of exquisite sweetness.—

I am the daughter of the King of the Asuras: my name is Kálindí. Vishńu, impatient of my father's fame, destroyed him. A Saint, in compassion of my sorrow for his loss, announced that some heavenly-formed being would become my husband, and cherish these domains. I have awaited your coming, as the Chátaka expects the rain, and hearing of your arrival, I have come with the concurrence of my council, and the guidance of my desires, to offer the kingdom and myself, twin wives, to your espousal. Mátanga readily assented, married the Damsel, and became the King of Pátála. Rájaváhana took leave of him, receiving his thanks, and the jewel given him by Kálindí, which had the property of dispelling thirst and hunger: he returned by the Chasm to the place where he had left his followers, and finding no trace of them, set off to seek them. In his peregrinations he arrived in the city of Ujjayiní, and entering a Garden saw a man borne in a litter with his wife, and attended by his followers, approach. When they met the Prince, the man sprang from the litter exclaiming, my master! and fell at his feet. The Prince at last recognising him embraced him, and said, 'Somadatta, where have you been so long; what has befallen you; where do you go now; and who is this Damsel? declare.' Somadatta, after recovering from his agitation, thus replied:

THIRD SECTION.
SOMADATTA'S STORY.

"Whilst wandering in quest of your Highness, I arrived oppressed with thirst on the borders of a tank; as I stooped to drink the cool water, I saw a most brilliant diamond on the sand. I picked it up, and went on my way. After some time, I entered for shelter and rest into a Temple, where I saw an old man with several boys, whom I respectfully saluted. He said, 'you see me living here with these orphans in this dreary place, and subsisting by charity.' I enquired of him who was the sovereign encamped in those tents I beheld, his name, and what was the cause of his coming hither. The old man answered:

'The camp belongs to Mattakála, King of Láta; the King of this country is Víraketu; his daughter Vámalochaná was celebrated for her beauty, and this coming to Mattakála's ears, he demanded her in marriage. Her father refused to assent, but was compelled by Mattakála's superior force, and gave her up. Mattakála now takes her with him to his own country to espouse her there, and is on his way, but halts here to hunt. Mánapála, the minister of Víraketu appointed to guard the Princess with a strong escort, encamps separately, and mourns his master's disgrace.' Finding the old man so intelligent, and pitying his state, I gave him the jewel I had found; he accepted it with many blessings, and departed with his scholars. Overcome

with fatigue I fell asleep and was awakened by a loud
outcry of "this is the thief," when looking up, I found
the old man bound and guarded; the guard quitted
him and seized me, and without listening to my defence carried me off, tied hand and foot, and threw
me into prison, amongst a number of people they
called my confederates. I learned from my fellow
prisoners that they were the servants of the minister,
who at their master's instigation had broke by night
into the apartment of the King of Láta, hoping to kill
him, but he was not there, and missing him, they
plundered the apartment, and carried off the valuables
into the woods: the next day they were overtaken,
and brought back with their spoil, excepting one gem
of great price, which was not to be found, and which
was accidentally the one I had met with. The identity of our fate produced a friendship between us, and
taking an opportunity we broke out of our prison,
and fled to the camp of Mánapála. When he heard
my story from his people, he treated me with kindness. The King of Láta sent to reclaim us by an in-
solent message, which still more incensed the minister;
"who is this King, he cried; what have we to do with
him," and he sent back the messengers with disgrace;
their report inflamed Mattakála to rage, and although
slightly attended, he immediately attacked our camp,
where Mánapála, who expected and desired the contest,
was fully prepared to receive him; he provided me
with arms, a chariot and steed, and directed his troops
to follow me, confiding in my prowess. We rushed

to the encounter. I met the King of Láṭa, struck him from his chariot, and cut off his head; his troops fled, and we plundered their camp. The minister welcomed me with honour: the King who had beheld the conflict rewarded my exertions with his daughter's hand and adopted me into the empire as Yuvarája. Nothing was wanting to my happiness but your presence, and I was now on my way to the shrine of Mahákála, where a Seer predicted I should find my lost friend." Whilst thus engaged in converse, they saw a man advancing who proved to be Pushpodbhava; they hastened to embrace him, and after their first greetings had passed, he thus related his adventures.

SECTION FOURTH.
STORY OF PUSHPODBHAVA.

When we found that your Highness did not return, we set off severally in search of you. After I had passed some time in the pursuit I one day rested myself in the shade of a tree, at the foot of a mountain, when suddenly a speck appeared, and a man fell upon me; he lay senseless awhile, till I brought him to himself, when I enquired his story. He thus replied:

'My name is Ratnodbhava, I am the son of Padmodbhava, the minister of the King of Magadha. I went as a merchant to Kálayavana Island, where I married a merchant's daughter. I was returning with

her, when we were wrecked near shore, and all were
drowned except myself. The loss of my wife, however, overwhelmed me in the depths of despair; and
although the counsel of a holy Seer, whom I encountered, led me to hope her recovery, at the end of
sixteen years, I threw myself from off a precipice.'
At this moment his story was interrupted by the sound
of a female voice, exclaiming; "why throw yourself
into the flames, when sixteen years will restore your
husband and son!" On hearing this I said, 'Father,
you have much to say, but stay awhile, and let me
see what this means.' I accordingly ran off to where
I beheld a blazing fire, and a woman about to throw
herself into it; I seized her, and her attendants, and
brought her to my father. I then asked them, what
they were doing in this lonely wood; the oldest replied: this is Suvŕittá, the daughter of Kúlagupta,
merchant of Kálayavana. When she was coming back
with her husband, our vessel was wrecked near the
shore, and I her nurse, and she, escaped upon a raft.
Being near her time, she was delivered of a son in the
forest, but the boy was carried off from me unhappily
by an elephant. A Seer told us, sixteen years would
restore us to her child and husband; we have resided
that time in a holy house, but the patience of my
mistress being now exhausted, she has determined to
cast herself into the flames. Knowing that this was
my mother, I prostrated myself at her feet and pointed to my father. My parents recognized each other,
and mutually rushed into each other's arms, when

blessing and embracing me they sat down in the shade
of a tree, and I related to them all that had befallen
me. Leaving them in the cell of a sage, I prosecuted
my search for you. Wandering through the Vindhya
Forest, I came to some ruins, where I observed the
signs of buried treasures, I dug them out, and found a
heap of Dínárs; thence going into a camp, I bought
oxen and bags, and returning to the spot, loaded them
with the treasure. I thence rejoined the camp, and
forming a friendship with a merchant's son, travelled
in his company to Ujjayiní. I brought my parents
thither and, with the assent of the King of Málava
obtained by the aid of Bandhupála my friend's father,
lived there. I made frequent excursions in search of
you, but my friend Bandhupála at last advised me to
forbear, as they were fruitless, and that he would
impart to me signs of your near approach. In expectation of this I visited him daily, and here saw Bálachandriká, a lovely maid whose beauties struck me
to the heart; she herself was not unmoved, and by
her looks expressed the emotions of her bosom. I
was, therefore, encouraged to form a plan for our
union. On one occasion I accompanied Bandhupála
to a garden in the suburbs of Ujjayiní, to watch for
omens of your coming, where, whilst he listened to
the language of the birds, I wandered through the
groves, and coming to the bank of a pool beheld Bálachandriká. I approached her and avowed my love,
and sued for its return; and encouraged by the privacy
of the place, she banished her diffidence, and thus ad-

dressed me: 'Youth, Mánasára, when advanced in
years, crowned his son Darpasára sovereign of Ujjayiní: he in the hope of overcoming the world has
gone to Rájagiri to practise austerities, leaving the
Government to the sons of his paternal aunt Dáruvarmá and Chandravarmá. Dáruvarmá, disregarding
the restraint of his elder brother Chandravarmá,
commits all sorts of atrocious acts, and seizes the wives
and wealth of his people: he has seen me, and professes such love as you offer me: as, however, I have
discouraged his suit, and he is regardless of feminine
purity, he seeks to appropriate by violence the person
he will not gain by affection. In constant alarm of
his attempts, I live wretched. So saying she wept
bitterly. I dried her tears, and soothed her appre-
hensions, vowing to effect the death of Dáruvarmá.
I desired her therefore to circulate a report that a
Yaksha was a candidate for her charms and occupied
her chamber, and to promise that, if any would
encounter, and overcome the Goblin, he should be
rewarded with her hand. If Dáruvarmá hearing this
should desist, it would be well; and if he persevered,
her friends should say to him that it would not be
proper for the minister of Darpasára the King of the
world to suffer violence in their mansion, and that he
should take Bálachandriká to his own dwelling in the
presence of the people, and there dispose of her as he
pleased. If he consented to this as he probably would,
I undertook to accompany her as a female attendant,
dressed in a woman's garb, and thus having gained

admission, I would kill him with my hands and feet:
then, still in the capacity of an attendant, follow her
fearlessly forth; after which we would apprise the
family of our mutual love; and they no doubt
would consent to our marriage. She agreed to
what I proposed, and reluctantly departed. On
returning to Bandhupála he told me to expect
your return in thirty days, and we then repaired
home, and things occurring as I had expected,
I accompanied Bálachandriká to the chamber of
Dáruvarmá, where I fell unexpectedly upon him, and
pummelled him to death, then rushing forth called
loudly for assistance. The people thinking he had
been killed by the Goblin, and censuring Dáruvarmá's
rashness in incurring such peril, entered in crowds,
full of alarm and curiosity, and in the bustle we withdrew.
When some days had passed we went through
the ceremony of exorcism, and I espoused the damsel.
On this day, as announced by Bandhupála, I came
forth to seek you, and have found you."

The Prince now narrated to Pushpodbhava his own
adventures and those of Somadatta, and they all repaired
to Ujjayiní, where the Prince passed for the
son of Pushpodbhava's preceptor, and was soon distinguished
for his eminent acquirements.

SECTION FIFTH.

The season of spring had now arrived, and the youths and damsels of Ujjayiní celebrated the festival of the deity of amorous desires. On this occasion, Avantisundarí, the daughter of Múnasára, attended by her friend Bálachandriká and female train, went forth to the gardens of the suburbs, and worshipped Káma at the foot of a Mango tree. Desirous of beholding the Princess, Rájaváhana, accompanied by Pushpodbhava, entered the gardens, and after roaming through its pleasant paths, came to where the Princess stood. Beckoned by Bálachandriká they approached, and the figure of Rájaváhana made an immediate impression on the bosom of Avantisundarí. She thought him Káma approaching to grant a boon in person to his worshippers, and trembled with emotion, like a creeper waving in the breeze. He was no less struck by her charms. The Princess asked her friend to tell her who the youth was, but unwilling to declare the truth before so many witnesses, she answered generally, that he was a young Brahman of great learning, valour, skilled in magic, and entitled to her reverence. Hearing this the Princess was highly delighted, and bade him to be called, when giving him a seat she offered him the customary homage. Rájaváhana immediately recognised the Princess as his wife in a former birth, then named Yajnavatí, and took occasion to recall the circumstances to the recollection of the Princess: she remembered it, and all her ancient love revived.

Whilst thus engaged, the Queen of Mánasára, attended, came to view her daughter's pastimes. Báluchandriká gave the signal to her husband, and he and Rajaváhana hid themselves amongst the trees; after a short time the Queen returned, and her daughter attended her to the palace. The affection of Rájaváhana and the Princess continuing to become more intense, they sought anxiously for an interview, which at last was thus effected: walking in the garden, where Rájaváhana first saw the damsel, he encountered a Brahman of sumptuous apparel, and splendid appearance: they exchanged salutations, and the stranger called himself Vidyeśwara, a magician: they soon formed a friendship, and he engaged to assist Rájaváhana to obtain his mistress. On the ensuing morning Vidyeśwara, well attended, went to the palace, and was announced by the Chamberlain; he was invited by the Prince into the inner Court, where after song and music he beguiled all the spectators with the whirls of his wand, so that the Prince and all his Court were confounded, and imagined they perceived strange sights, as if innumerable snakes rolled along on all sides, and vultures darted down, and bore them away in their beaks: he then exhibited the story of Hiraṅyakaśipu as torn by Nŕisinha, and filled the Rájá with surprise: at the end he offered to exhibit him still more pleasant sights, and to perform a marriage by spirits, between the seeming Princess, and the Prince destined to be her lord.

The King assented, and the imagination of the courtiers being deceived, Rájaváhana and the Princess, who were ready to play their parts, were married in their presence, with all the customary rites: at the close of the ceremony, the magician ordered audibly all his attendants to disappear, and the Princess and Rájaváhana withdrew unnoticed into the inner apartments. There, whilst spending his time in enjoyment, the Prince related to his spouse the secrets of the fourteen worlds.

Having heard the description of the universe from the Prince, Avantisundari replied, 'What return can I make my Lord for the delightful entertainment and instruction I have received from him? I have nothing to requite such favour with, but my permission for him to share undisturbed by my jealousies, or doubts, the embraces of Saraswati[1].' In such conversation and mutual enjoyment they passed their time. On one occasion they beheld in their dreams a Swan, and wakened at the vision: on waking the Prince found his feet fast tied together by a silver chain, like the lotus bound with lunar beams. The Princess perceiving it screamed with apprehension; her screams were echoed by her attendants; their cries brought the guards to see what had chanced, and they discovered the Prince: not daring however to approach him, appalled by his royal radiance, they hastened to

---

[1] The Goddess of Literature and the Arts.

communicate the circumstance to Chandravarmá. He
came, foaming with fury, like the flame of fire, and
seeing the Prince, recognised him as the friend of
Pushpodbhava, the husband of Bálachandriká, for
whose sake his younger brother had perished: 'how,
he exclaimed, can Avantisundarí have thus forgotten
her rank to treat such as we are with disdain, and
decline to such a base and false adventurer as this!
But this must be remedied: she shall see her new Lord
this very day exalted to the dignity of the gibbet.'
Rájaváhana, finding resistance hopeless, submitted to
his fate, and recommended patience to his wife, reminding her, that the Swan had foretold a period of
two months as the limit of this ill fortune. He was
sent to prison. When the old King and Queen of
Málwa heard the story, and considered that Rájaváhana, by whatever means, was now their son-in-law,
they opposed the execution of the sentence, and
threatened to put an end to their own lives if it were
accomplished. Chandravarmá persisting in his purpose, but unwilling to cause the destruction of the
elder Princes, wrote to Darpasára for his commands,
and in the mean time seized Pushpodbhava also, with
all his family, threw him into prison, and confiscated
his effects. The Prince like a young Lion was secured in a wooden cage, and would have been starved
to death, had he not been preserved from the distress
of hunger, and thirst, by the magical jewel he had
formerly received; and which he had preserved in his
hair. Chandravarmá being engaged in an attempt to

compel the King of Anga to give him his daughter in marriage, proceeded against that Prince, carrying Rájaváhana incaged along with the army, with which Champá was invested. The King of Champá, Sinhavarmá, issued with his forces, impatient of aggression, and unable to await the arrival of his numerous allies. Notwithstanding their valiant exertions, the army of Sinhavarmá was defeated, and himself taken prisoner. Chandravarmá detained him, but ordered him to be taken care of; not purposing his death through the love he bore his daughter Ambálikà, also named Abaláratna, whom, she having likewise fallen into his hands, he resolved in conformity to the calculations of the Astrologers to espouse that evening. During the celebration, a Courier arrived from the Northern Mountains with the reply of Darpasára, which ran thus:—"Fool! what respite shall be granted to the violator of the secret chambers? Why listen to the imbecility of age? let me hear that the love-crazed Idiot is put to death with the tortures he deserves; as to the girl, throw her into chains, and let my younger brother Kírttisára share the same fate." On receipt of this, Chandravarmá ordered Rájaváhana to be brought before the palace gate next morning, and his own elephant also to attend; intending that the criminal should be crushed to pieces by the elephant; after which he would proceed to encounter the allies of the King of Anga. The dawn arrived: Rájaváhana was led forth, and the elephant was brought. At that instant, the silver chain fell spontaneously from the Prince's ancles, and assuming the semblance of one of the Nymphs of Heaven, stood before him, and thus addressed him: "Prince, condescend to hear me; I am a Nymph of Heaven, the daughter of Somaraśmi; and Suratamanjarí is my name: once I traversed the Mandodaka Lake, in the bosom of Himálaya: my course was impeded by a flight of Swans: to make my way amongst them I waved my hand, and in the act of waving my hand, my bracelet slipping off fell upon the head of Márkańdeya Muni, as he stooped to perform his ablutions in the wave. Incensed by the affront, he denounced a curse upon me, and sentenced me to take a metallic form; then relenting, he limited my transformation to a period of two months, during which I have been attached to your feet, as the chain from which you are just liberated. After my transformation I was found, and known for what I was, by the Vidyádhara Viraśekhara, the son of Mánasavega, the son of Vegaván, a Prince of the family of Ikshwáku. Víraśekhara had formed an alliance with Darpasára, in enmity of Naraváhana, the grace of the lineage of Vatsa, and Darpasára had agreed to give him his sister Avantisundarí in marriage. The Vidyádhara, anxious to see his intended bride, descended one night upon Ujjayiní, and entering the palace unperceived beheld the Princess sleeping in your arms: enraged at the sight, he determined to expose your person to the fury of the Prince of Ujjayiní, and with this view passed me as a fetter round your feet. To day my curse expires;

I have been your servant for two months. Is there any thing I can do to oblige you?" The Prince replied: Go, bear the news of my liberation to my other life, and cheer his sinking spirits! And then dismissed the nymph.

When the Apsará had disappeared, a sudden cry arose, that Chandravarmá was killed, stabbed by a single thief as he took the hand of Ambáliká, and that a hundred others had fallen by the same hand, as he was resolutely forcing his escape. On hearing this Rájaváhana leaped upon the elephant, knocked down his driver, and forcing the animal into the press, called to the valiant youth to join him, promising to aid his retreat: the youth advanced, and before he could be prevented sprang on the elephant. Rájaváhana, with no less joy than surprise, recognised in him his friend Apahárावarmá, who also knew him: after a momentary embrace they seized the weapons which the elephant carried, and fought their way through all opposition, levelling Chandravarmá's chieftains with the ground. At this time another army made its appearance, and fell upon the host of Chandravarmá. After some interval, a person on a swift elephant advancing to the friends, announced to Apahárावarmá, that the host now engaged was that of the allies of the King of Anga, whose advance he had been sent to accelerate, and whose efforts were attended with success, as the army of Chandravarmá was broken, and dispersing. Apahárávarmá then presented the person to Rájaváhana as his friend, and other self, Dhanamitra.

Dismissing Dhanamitra then to liberate the King of Anga, and dispose of the spoil, Apaháravarmá and the Prince withdrew from the city, and alighting from the elephant sat down on the border of the Ganges under the shade of a Rohin tree. While thus seated, a splendid Troop advanced, whom on their near approach Rájaváhana knew to be his friends, Upaháravarmá, Arthapála, Pramati, Mitragupta, and Visruta, attending the King of Mithilá, Praháravarmá; the King of Kásí, Kámapála; and the King of Champá, Sinhavarmá. The Prince rose to receive them, and after their first congratulations were exchanged, he narrated to them at their request his own adventures, and those of Somadatta and Pushpodbhava. His other friends in turn recounted to him the incidents which had severally befallen them, Apaháravarmá thus commencing:

STORY OF APAHÁRAVARMÁ.

When we dispersed in search of your Highness, I took the direction of Anga, and arrived at the Ganges, near Champá. At a short distance from the city resided a holy Saint named Maríchi, of whose wonderful powers I heard frequently from passengers on the road. I was therefore desirous to see and consult him respecting your fate, and repairing to his hermitage beheld under the shade of a young Mango tree a wild looking Devotee: sitting down by him, I asked him respectfully where the great Seer Maríchi was, of whom I wished to enquire the destinies of a dear

friend. The Seer, for it was he himself, thus spoke:
There was such a sage formerly, in this retirement;
a Damsel named Kámamanjarí once approached him;
large tear-drops fell like stars upon her breast,
and as she bowed in homage to the holy man,
her long dishevelled tresses swept the ground. She
had scarcely attempted to impart her grief, when a
vast crowd, led by the Damsel's mother filled with
apparent rage, arrived, and thronged around the hermitage. The sage moved with pity addressed the
Damsel, and demanded the cause of her distress.—
She thus replied: 'these people round me would best
accomplish this world's desires; mine seek the world
to come, and therefore I prostrate myself at your feet,
the asylum of the afflicted.' The mother here interrupted her, bowing to the ground: 'great Sage! permit
your slave to say without offence, that in this I follow
the duties of my profession. With women of my cast
if we have daughters, we cultivate their beauty from
their birth; we carefully nourish them with choice
viands, and from five years of age they never see a
man, not even a father. On their birth day, and
every festival, we celebrate auspicious rites: we train
them thoroughly in foreign literature; we instruct
them to read and write, and express themselves with
elegance and wit, we rear them to understand flowers,
perfumes, and confectionery, and accomplish them in
drawing, painting, dancing, singing, in playing musical
instruments, and in dramatic representation: we have
them instructed in grammar, in logic, and astrology,

and teach them to earn a livelihood, to excel in sportive graces, to be skilled in games of chance or strife, to appear in gay and elegant raiment at public festivals, to speak in praise of public characters, to recommend talent to patronage, and want to charity. When this is accomplished, we grant them to one whom they may love, to one who may passionately love them, or to such as are amiable, respectable, learned, skillful, and above all, who are independent: to such we deliver them for a price proportioned to their means, but if we have given them to be trained by others, the teacher shares the remuneration. In all circumstances, however, the mother or grandmother must never be disobeyed. Now this Damsel has abandoned the duties prescribed by her fate; she has fallen in love with a young Brahman whose form is his whole fortune, and has at her own expense indulged her passion; her admirers are repulsed and enraged, her family ruined; from my reproaches she has fled to take up her abode in the woods, and if so, then what is to become of us, who depend upon her for subsistence?' She ended with a flood of tears.

The Rishi then addressed the Damsel:—"a life of devotion is a life of suffering; its object is either absorption or paradise: the first is only attainable by the perfection of wisdom, a thing not easily effected; the second is within the reach of all who discharge the duties of their station. It were well therefore that you return to obedience, and your mother." To this she replied: 'if I find not protection from you, I shall have recourse to the Lord of flame.' The Muni finding her determined, recommended her friends to leave her alone for a few days, in which time she would grow weary of an ascetic life, and return to her home, and they obeyed, and left the Damsel. A very little time had elapsed before her charms, her devotion, her graceful accomplishments, and elegant and serious conversation, made an impression on the Sage's heart. On one occasion he addressed her: "say, child, in what degree does Dharma (virtue), excel Artha (wealth), and Káma (pleasure)?" She replied, 'you mock me to ask my opinion, yet as it may be only a proof of your kind wish to hear me prattle, I will speak.

Without Dharma the other two properties are unproductive, but without regard to them Dharma alone is the creative cause of final happiness: it is the object of the soul, attainable by meditation, whilst unlike Artha and Káma it is not affected by external agents: where there is a fund of moral merit, that is not injured by the occasional prevalence of the other properties, or if affected, it is recovered by a little exertion, and eradicating the fault secures not a slight reward.

Hence the passion of Pitámahá for Tillottamá; of Siva for the Muni's wife; of Krishńa for his sixteen hundred concubines; of Prajápati for his own daughter; of Súrya for a mare; of Anila for a lioness. These acts of the Gods were worthy of Demons alone, but by the virtue of divine wisdom they did not destroy the moral worth of the individuals: a mind that is purified by piety admits no soil, any more than the atmosphere can be defiled by dust. I therefore hold that Artha and Káma are not to be regarded as comparable in the hundredth degree with Dharma.'

Having heard this, the passion of the Sage was augmented, and he replied, "Damsel, you have spoken well; the piety of those who know what truth is is not incompatible with earthly enjoyment, but we from our birth are unable to judge of the real merits of Artha and Káma. It is necessary to note what are their natures, their circumstances and their results." She replied, 'of Artha the essentials are accumulation, increase, and conservation, the concomitants agriculture, pasturage, trade, and government, and its consequence devout duties and alms. Káma is the various intercourse of the sexes, yielding pleasure to the passions; its concomitants earthly splendor, and beauty; its fruit mutual gratification, delightful recollections, self-satisfaction, supreme and present pleasure. The duties of an ascetic are severe, and imply liberal gifts, perilous conflicts, and crossing deep waters.' Hearing this, the Muni, overcome by fate, her eloquence, and his own infirmity, forgot his devotions, and became her prize. She prevailing on him to accompany her ascended a car, and with him at her side returned to her own house by the high street. As they passed, the Criers announced the next day as the festival of Káma. In the morning she made the ascetic discard his usual attire, bathe, and perfume himself, and put on a flowery garland, to appear as a votary of the

God of love, and led him, who could not bear to be
separated an instant from her, by the public and most
frequented roads through the bands of Káma's votaries
to the gardens in the suburbs, where the King sat,
surrounded by hundreds of Damsels. On her approach the King said, "Damsel, sit down with the
Sage." She paid her obeisance smilingly, and sat
down, on which one of the train rose, and addressed
the King: 'Sire, I confess myself vanquished, and own
myself the Damsel's slave.' A general murmur of
applause followed: the Damsel was then rewarded by
the Prince with valuable jewels and dresses, and with
the applause of the citizens she returned home. On
the way she thus spoke to the Sage; "grave Sir, accept
my thanks, your servant has been favoured; now so
please you, return to your pious purposes." As if
struck by a thunderbolt, he heard her, and replied:
"fair Damsel, what means this? whence this indiffer-
ence? where is the affection you professed?" She
smiled and replied: "Sir, the Damsel who in the assembly confessed herself defeated formerly defied my
being able to conquer your affections; I accepted the
challenge, and it was agreed upon between us, that
the loser should become the servant of the other. By
your favor I have won the wager." The Seer, when
he heard this, was filled with surprise, and mortification, and falling as it were from the clouds, he
recovered his senses, and returned to his solitary
dwelling. That same Rishi, shamed by a girl, behold,
brave youth, in me; the passion I then felt once sub-

dued, my devotion has been rendered more intense. The question you would ask I shall in no long time be able to answer, and in the meanwhile do you abide in yonder city, Champú, the capital of Anga." At this time it was sunset, and with the Muni's assent I passed the night at his hermitage, listening to his conversation, till we fell asleep. In the morning when the first red rays glowed above the eastern mountain, I paid my homage to the Lord of day, and preceeded to the city. As I advanced, I passed a Vihára[1], where seated under an Asoka tree, in a grove by the road side, I beheld a miserable Bauddha mendicant: the tears fell down from his filthy breast.—I sat down by him, and asked him, 'what is this penance and why these tears? if not a secret let me know the cause.' He answered: "my name is Vasupálita, I am the eldest son of the Banker Nidhipálita, an inhabitant of Champá, where I was distinguished by the epithet of the Ugly; there was another youth, called the Handsome, he was as clever as beautiful, but possessed of little wealth, and as I was opulent, the ill-disposed made these properties the cause of enmity between us. After much dissension and mutual abuse we agreed at last that the merit of a man was not to be decided by beauty or fortune, but its surest test was woman's love, and he who could win the choicest of our Damsels should be owned the victor. Of all our girls Kámamanjarí was the most distinguished, and we therefore

---

[1] A convent of Bauddha ascetics.

both addressed ourselves to her: my advances were
most favourably received, and she became the mistress
of my house, my heart, my wealth, and my existence.
She availed herself of her influence to appropriate all
my means, and leaving me not even any clothes to
wear, turned me out of my own mansion. Unable to
face the ridicule and contempt of my fellow-citizens,
I came and took my abode in this Jaina convent where
under the tuition of a holy Sage I sought the path to
final felicity. I fear I have mistaken the road, and in
deviating from the faith and observances of my pro-
genitors I follow an impure track, as if it were that of
virtue; disregarding the Vedas and Smritis (Codes of
law), abandoning the distinction of my caste, and constantly listening to blasphemy against the Gods. On
this account I seek these shades, to bewail my hapless
lot in privacy." Moved to pity for his grief, I advised
him to be patient, and promised I would endeavour to
redeem his property for him. I then left him, and
entered the city, preparing to encounter the tricks and
frauds of the rogues with which Champá notoriously
abounded, and to reduce some of them who had enriched themselves at their neighbour's cost to their
primitive poverty.

I therefore early entered the gambling houses,
and associated with the gamesters, and was never
satisfied with observing them skilled in the twenty-
five sorts of games, knowing how to cog a die, and
shift a card without being perceived; to reply to any
reflection on their play with abundant abuse, to en-

gage in affrays as prodigal of life, to admit the faith of their President, to argue or contend in order to enforce payment, to wheedle the resolute, and bully the timid; able to make partisans, to profess or proffer secret advantages, to disclaim a bet, to divide peremptorily the spoil, to mutter abuse. I laughed at one who made a blunder in his play: his partner swelling with rage said, 'what do you, who seem so fond of laughing, pretend to teach us? let him alone, he is but a novice; but if you are disposed, you shall find your match in me.' The Chairman assenting to this, we played. I won 16,000 Dínárs of him, half of which I gave to the President and the Assembly, and with the other half I rose to go into the town: the party were loud in my praise, and the President requested me to put up at his house, where I was splendidly entertained. He, on whose account I had first played, put great faith in me, and looked upon me as his other self; his name was Vimardaka, and by his means I became most thoroughly acquainted with the city. On a night as dark as the throat of Śiva, putting on a black jacket, and a sword under my arm, with a scoop, a whistle, tongs, a sham-head[1], magic powder, a magic light, a measuring thread, a wrench[2], a rope, a lamp, a beetle in a box[3], I went to the house of a celebrated usurer. I found his strong box, and

---

[1] Or perhaps a mask.
[2] Called Karkaṭaka, a Crab.
[3] [or a box containing winged insects] to put out the light.

brought it away. As I passed along the main road,
I saw a sudden blaze like the fall of lightning, and on
nearing the object I met a lovely Damsel, richly attired, who I thought at first was the presiding Goddess
of the city. She stopped alarmed. I asked her who
she was, and whence, to which she hesitatingly replied:
"A merchant lives in this city, named Kuveradatta.
I am his daughter: my father betrothed me from my
very birth to Dhanamitra, the son of a wealthy man
in this city, but he upon his death purchased with
profuse liberality the condition of a pauper, and although he has thus gained the epithet of munificent,
yet being now destitute, my father refuses to give me
to him for a wife: he is now desirous of marrying me
to a merchant of great opulence, named Yathártha:
the marriage is fixed for to-morrow morning, and to
avoid this union, agreeably to a promise formerly
made to my beloved, I have deceived my father, and
am making my escape to my lover's house. I learnt
the way in my early youth, and have love to attend
my steps: let me pass, and take this casket." So
saying she put it into my hands, but pitying her state,
I said, 'come on, fair maiden, I will lead you to your
lover;' and proceeded a few steps, when we saw by
the light of their torches the city-watch all armed,
and numerous, approaching. The Damsel was alarmed. I told her not to fear; my sword was to be
trusted, but that for her sake I would have recourse
to stratagem. 'I will affect to sleep, as if overcome
by poison, do you say to these people thus: We

entered the city this night: my husband here was bitten by a snake in this place: if any one of you know a charm to remove the poison, have pity on my desolate condition, and restore my Lord to life.'

The Damsel, whose own terrors fitted her to enact this part, did as I desired; I assumed the appearance of profound fainting: one of the train professing himself an adept tried his skill upon me, but in vain, and he proclaimed me defunct: 'there is no hope, he said to the Damsel, be of good cheer, we will burn the body to-morrow; who can oppose fate!' So saying they passed on. When they were off, I rose and accompanying the maiden to her lover, thus addressed him: I am by profession a thief, and in my travels encountering this maiden coming to you with no companion but her affection, I have attended her through compassion hither. I resign to you also this casket of splendid gems. He replied: 'youth, you have brought me a present, for which I have not words to thank you; I cannot speak my wonder at what you have done, and yet it seems marvellous to yourself. You have made me your slave. What folly do I utter! how can I propose so worthless an object as this body for the gift of my love:—a body that is your present; for had I not obtained her, I should have soon parted with it in death.' So speaking he fell at my feet. I raised him, embraced him, and enquired his intentions; he replied he could not continue to reside in the city with safety, upon marrying his mistress without the concurrence of her parents, and therefore purposed leaving Champá that very night, unless I should disapprove of it. I replied that change of country was nothing to a man of talents and spirit, but that he should consider the tender age, and timid disposition of his future bride rendered foreign travel, and separation from her first home, painful tasks to her, and that it did not appear impossible for him to stay at home with impunity. Follow my advice, I said, let her conduct us to her own house, and do as I direct. He assented, and we repaired thither; she served as a spy and guide, and we stole every thing except the earthen pans. Leaving the Damsel, we went and hid our booty, and then proceeding, we encountered a party of citizens, but just before they reached us we found an elephant resting by the road side, whose rider we dismounted, and ascended ourselves. The elephant it happened was a savage beast, and tore and trod on all he approached. We arrived at the house of the lady's lover, and passing on into a grove, caught hold of the branches above, by which we held till the animal passed away, when going home we bathed and reposed till sun-rise, when after the performance of our customary rites we went abroad to hear of the stir we had made. The merchant had sent some cash to his intended father-in-law Kuveradatta on hearing of the robbery, but had put off the marriage for a month. I then advised Dhanamitra to take a handsome leather bag, and go to the King, and say: 'your Majesty knows that I am Dhanamitra, the sole heir of Vasumitra: being reduced to poverty, I was despised of men, and

Kuveradatta who had promised his daughter to me, whilst wealthy, now retracted his promise; in grief for which I repaired to a neighbouring wood, and was about to cut my throat, when an ascetic of the Śaiva faith prevented me, and rebuked me for my despair, saying, there were many ways of recovering lost wealth, but none to redeem lost life; that he was perfect in the art of multiplying treasure, and possessed a purse, which would yield any sum I might want, and which, as he no longer required it, he would give me; that, if I should be ever under the necessity of relinquishing it, I must recollect, it would be available only to merchants, and courtezans, and that, should any wish to benefit by it, they must first restore whatever they might have dishonestly gained to the right owner, and give what they possessed to the Brahmans: after which, performing worship to the bag, and depositing it at night in a secure place, they would find it in the morning full of treasure. So saying he gave it me, and vanished. I have not thought proper however to retain it without leave from your Majesty.' The King being pleased by the offer, will desire you to do with it as you please, and then do you ask the Prince to protect you against it being stolen, after which go home, and give away every thing you have. Afterwards fill the bag by night with some of the stolen booty, and in the morning take it out before all the people. When Kuveradatta hears this, he will esteem his present intended son-in-law as nothing, and will himself give you his daughter.

Yathártha will be affronted, and in his rage he will endeavour to ruin Kuveradatta, but you should anticipate him, and reduce himself to rags.

So it happened: in the mean time Vimardaka the gambler by my instructions excited the wealthy lover's enmity against Dhanamitra, whilst Kuveradatta wished to give the latter his daughter, and still more incensed the former.

At this time Rágamanjarí, the younger sister of Kámamanjarí, being to sing at the public rooms, the people in their best garbs were collected: when the dance began I was struck with admiration and love, and how it happened I know not, but I caught her attention, and she smiled significantly on me as she withdrew. I returned home and under pretence of a head-ache went to bed. Dhanamitra knew by his own experience the truth, and comforted me by expatiating on her good qualities, and the certainty of our coming together. He told me that she had declared her determination to be won only by merit, and to become no man's expect by marriage: that her sister and mother had applied to the King to complain of her, and prevailed upon him to declare, that any one who should carry her off without their assent, should be punished as a thief: hence without wealth she was not attainable from her kindred, nor without merit from herself. I therefore opened a negociation with Kámamanjarí by her principal agent, a servant who was a female mendicant of the Bauddha order, and promised to steal Dhanamitra's purse, and give it

to her, if she would give me Rágamanjarí: accordingly
I wedded the latter. By my directions a violent
quarrel took place in the exchange between Vimardaka
and Dhanamitra, in which the former, as the friend of
Yathártha, told the latter to look to his magical bag,
or he might lose it: accordingly, the bag having disappeared, Dhanamitra complained to the King, and
he summoned Yathártha, and desired him to produce
Vimardaka, but the latter was not to be found, for I
had sent him in search of you to Ougein, and the suspicions of the King being thus confirmed, the merchant was sent to prison.

After a time Kámamanjarí, being desirous of availing herself of her prize, restored the property of
Virúpaka to him, and he abondoning the society of
ascetics returned to his own profession again. Kámamanjarí then gave away all that remained of her own
effects. Dhanamitra, instructed of this by me, informed
the King of it, and stated what he suspected must be
the cause of such liberality in so covetous a person.
She was accordingly summoned, and being advised
by me of the probable motive, it was a question what
was to be done: at last her mother suggested that
they should assert that they received it from Yathártha,
with whom, it was known, they were on intimate
terms. The King hearing this accusation ordered him
to be put to death, but was prevented by Dhanamitra,
in consequence of whose intercession the King contented himself with confiscating all his wealth, and
banishing him from his dominions; some of his trea-

sures were made over to the luckless Kámamanjarí, and I took Rágamanjarí to a house full of gold and jewels.

Man, however ingenious, cannot avoid his fate. I was one day enjoying the pleasures of the table with my mistress, till I was completely intoxicated, and as drunken people follow the practices to which they are naturally or customarily addicted, I promised to fill the house that night with the collected spoil of the city. In spite of her entreaties I set off, armed only with my sword; at her desire her nurse Śrigáliká followed me: my manner attracting the notice of the guard, they arrested me, and after a very feeble resistance I fell. Śrigáliká came up as I was bound, and the tumult dissipating my drunkenness, I considered what was to be done. I therefore called out to Śrigáliká, 'away, you old devil, you are disappointed in your plans to bring that covetous Rágamanjarí and my false friend together, having borne off his bag, and your daughter's ornaments, I am now ready to die with pleasure.' She took the hint, and addressing the guard with tears and sobs, said: "very true, Sirs, all my property has been stolen of late, pray let me ask this fellow some questions." They desired her to approach, and she prayed me most pitifully to tell her what had become of her daughter's property, and threw herself at my feet. I pretended to relent, and stooping to raise her, whispered to her what was to be done. On which she blessed me aloud, and withdrew. I was carried to the guard.

The next day Kántaka, the chief magistrate, who had lately succeeded to his father's place, and who was young, silly, arrogant, and vain of his person, threatened me, if I did not restore Dhanamitra's purse, and the property of the people I had robbed, I should see the end of the eighteen punishments, and death. I laughed at him, and told him that, though I might give up all the other wealth I had stolen, I would never restore my false friend's magical purse, and I was accordingly punished with stripes, but in vain, as I defied my judge. In this manner, sometimes threatened, and sometimes soothed, several days passed, during which my wounds were neglected and spread. At last, one evening, Srigáliká with a smiling countenance, and handsomely dressed, approached me, as my guards were a little removed, and embracing me said: "you are fortunate, your plans have not been neglected; I spoke to Dhanamitra as you desired me, he accordingly complained to the King, that in a fit of jealousy you had stolen his purse, and your wife's casket, and run away, in which you had been seized by the watch; that you had restored the casket, and might be prevailed on to give up the purse, in which case he solicited the King's mercy for you. I also, procuring the necessary means from Rágamanjarí, secured the interest of Mangáliká, the nurse of the Princess Ambáliká, and became soon a very great favourite with the latter. One day the flowers in her ear being loose, I pretended to adjust them, but let them fall, and then picking them up,

and pretending to throw them at the pigeons, I threw
them upon Kántaka who was entering the prisons
which are below the female apartments. He thinking it a mark of kindness looked up to our window,
and was confirmed in his fancy by the smiles of the
Princess, and my signs; so he went away, deeply
wounded with the venomed shaft of love. In the
evening I took a basket sealed with the Princess's
signet, containing perfumes, pán, a dress, and ornaments, from her to Rágamanjarí, but conveyed it
instead to Kántaka's house, who, plunged in passion's
ocean, hailed me as his friendly bark. I augmented
his passion by describing in most piteous terms the
condition of the Princess, and pretending that she had
sent him these tokens of her affection. I said to him:
your signs of auspicious elevation are not likely to be
in vain. A neighbour of mine, a cunning man, has
told me, this kingdom shall fall into Kántaka's hand;
he bears the marks of it: and accordingly the Princess,
the only child of the Rájá, has fallen in love with you:
however much the King may be displeased, he must,
through fear of his daughter's death, consent, and you
will then be Cæsar at least, and what will not follow?
how are you to get into the apartments? I will tell
you: there is not above three spans between the
prison, and the palace wall. Do you procure some
skillful hand to aid you alone in making a hole through
the wall; once in, I will be answerable for our guards
and her attendants, who are all well affectioned.
'Well said,' he replied; 'there is a thief equal to the

sons of Sagara at a mine; if I can secure him, the job is done. Who should that be, and why not procurable? I enquired. 'It is the man,' he answered, 'who stole Dhanamitra's magic purse.' I tell you what, said I, go swear you will liberate him if he does the work properly, then fetter him again, and representing his obstinacy to the King, you will get him out of the way: so that your object will be gained, and there will be no fear of the secret being discovered. He was pleased with my council, and has sent me to communicate with you, whilst he remains without." I praised Srigáliká's address, and desired her to introduce the judge: he entered, and took a faltering oath for my liberation. I understood his sense, and swore never to divulge the secret. He set me at liberty, and had me well fed and taken care of for some days: we then set to work to break the palace wall; beginning in a dark corner, I made a hole with a crow (snake-headed). Whilst employed thus, I considered that the purport of his oath was to murder me, and that I was therefore fully justified in effecting his destruction. Having made the breach, as he extended his hand to help me through, I kicked him on the breast, and then knocking him down dispatched him with my knife. I then desired Srigáliká to shew me the way into the inner apartments, that my labour might not be wholly unprofitable, and I might carry off something of value. I entered the chamber, and found the Princess sleeping securely on a white couch, like lightening on the fleecy clouds of autumn. The sight arrested my attention, and instead of plundering the apartment I was robbed of my heart. I did not dare to wake her, lest her alarm should summon her attendants to her aid, and I should be apprehended, and put to death. I picked up a pencil, therefore, and with the smoke of the lamp sketched her sleeping, and myself kneeling at her feet, with this motto:

> Your slave, thus kneeling at your feet, implores you.
> Sleep not, but wake, for him who here adores you.

Then finding some superior betel, I extracted the juice, and cast it upon a pair of Chakwas painted on the wall. After which I took off her ring gently, and exchanged it for my own, and then effected my retreat: repairing to the prison I went to Sinhaghosha, one who had been a chief of Police, but afterwards was my fellow captive, by which we became friends, and I recommended to him to say as the means of being enlarged, that he had detected Kántaka breaking into the palace, and in edeavouring to arrest him had killed him. I then set off with Śrigáliká. On our way we encountered the watch: I could easily have escaped, but what was to become of the old woman. After a moment's thought I assumed an attitude of rushing upon them, and called out: If I am a thief do you seize me, but let this poor old woman go. Śrigáliká guessed my purpose and said: 'my good friends, this is my son, he has been long afflicted by a demon, and has been taking medicine: being something recovered yesterday, I gave him better food, his best clothes, and let him go to day where he pleased:

at midnight he was again seized by the fiend; he has killed Kántaka, and exclaiming, he would have the Princess for his bride, he ran off into the public road: I followed him as fast as I could. Pray, pity my trouble, bind him, and give him over to me.' As she thus exclaimed, I cried out: away old woman! who shall fetter the wind? shall the crows presume to pounce upon the hawk? absurd! And away I ran: she then abused them for letting me escape, and crying and scolding followed me. Thus we arrived at home, when I cheered Rágamanjarí who had pined in so long an absence. In the morning I saw my friend Dhanamitra, after which I went to the Sage Maríchi, whose cause I had avenged, and who having resumed his holy practices, and recovered his superhuman knowledge, announced to me your approach. Sinhaghosha was placed in the situation of Kántaka by the King, who was pleased with the service he was supposed to have rendered. The passage into the interior of the palace was still open to me, and by the agency of Śrigáliká I obtained possession of the Princess. In those days Chańdavarmá being refused the daughter of Sinhavarmá, and being highly enraged, besieged the city. The King Sinhavarmá, impatient of the outrage of the enemy, and mistrusting his friends, marched out of the city, and he was defeated by the superior numbers of the enemy, and taken prisoner. The Princess Ambáliká was likewise seized and carried to the palace of Chańdavarmá, where the marriage was to be solemnized at the close of the night. I had also prepared the nuptial bands to be bound at the house of Dhanamitra. I told him that the allies of the King of Anga were close at hand, and that he should collect the chief men of the city, and joining them unobserved bring them as fast as possible, when they should find the enemy without a head. He set off for this purpose: I remained, and taking advantage of the confusion, and crowd assembled at the wedding, I slipped in, armed, along with the Brahmans, when seizing the hand of Ambúliká, whilst Chańdavarmá invoking the fire to witness, according to the Atharvańa rite, put forth his arm to take her, I dragged her aside, and stabbed him in the belly with my dagger: then baffling those who sought to seize me, I made my retreat to this place, bringing with me the Damsel, whose fear I dissipated with my endearments, and bore her to a private apartment. At that moment I heard your voice, as welcome as the muttering clouds laden with the first dews of the season. What ensued you already know.

Rájaváhana, having heard of this narrative, addressed Apaháravarmá, and acknowledged that he had acquired such proficiency in so difficult a practice as to overcome Karńísuta: he then desired Upaháravarmá to relate his adventures, who bowed and thus obeyed.

STORY OF UPAHÁRAVARMÁ.

During my peregrinations I came to Videha, and just without the city of Mithilá rested myself at the threshold of a temple, when an ancient female devotee

gave me welcome, and water for my feet; she looked
at me attentively, and after a time burst into tears, of
which I enquired the occasion. She replied: Praháravarmá was the King of the city of Mithilá, and the
particular friend of Rájahansa, King of Magadha;
their Queens Vasumatí and Priyamvadá were equally
attached to each other. The latter with her Lord
went to visit her friend, upon the birth of her
first child. Whilst at Pushpapura, a war broke
out between Rájahansa, and the King of Málava,
in which the former was utterly overthrown. When
Prahàravarmá returned to his country, and found
that the throne had been seized by Vikatavarmá
and the other sons of his elder brother Śankara, he
resolved to repair for assistance to his sister's son,
the King of Suhma. With this intent he entered the
forests, and was there attacked by the Barbarians,
and plundered of every thing. I fled with the youngest
child in my arms, and to avoid the shower of arrows,
plunged into the thicket; the child was there knocked
from my grasp by a tiger; he hid himself in the carcase of a cow; the tiger was killed by the arrow of a
forester, and the child carried off by the Barbarians,
whilst I remained insensible. A cow-herd found me,
and conveyed me to his hovel, where he dressed my
wounds, and tended me, until I had nearly recovered.
As I regained my strength, I became impatient to re-
join my master, and was meditating how to effect this
purpose, when my daughter with a youth arrived at
my dwelling. She related to me her adventures, the

defeat of the troops, the loss of the young Prince, her captivity by a forester who sought to win her affections, and his attempt to put her to death when she refused to listen to his suit, her preservation by the youth in her company and who had subsequently espoused her. The youth was a servant of the King; and attended by him we overtook Prahúravarmá and Priyamvadá, and afflicted them with the loss of the Princes. Praháravarmá was baffled in his efforts to recover his dominions, and he and his Queen were both made prisoners. Their misfortunes affected me so strongly that I determined to adopt a mendicant life, whilst my daughter in despair took service with Kalpasundarí. Had the sons of Praháravarmá lived, they would have been of your years, and the oppression of their parents would not be attempted with impunity. So saying, she wept violently. When I heard her story I told her to be comforted, and reminding her of the Muni to whom she had applied in the forest, [I told her how he had applied in the forest,] I told her how he had found and brought up the child, and that in fact I was that infant. I then vowed to destroy Vikatavarmá but it was necessary to proceed with caution as he had many brothers, and the people were generally attached to him, whilst on the other hand even my parents did not know me, much less any other persons. I therefore resolved to wait for a favourable opportunity of executing my designs.

I now entered the temple where my old nurse provided me with every necessary, and kept me from observation. I passed the night in meditation on the means of procuring access to the inner apartments of the royal palace, as the fittest scene for my intended operations, and enquired of my nurse, as soon as the day had dawned, whether she were acquainted with the secrets of the Harem. I had scarcely spoken, when a female appeared. The old woman as soon as she saw her exclaimed. See, my dear daughter, our master's son. She welcomed my recovery with tears of joy, and when the feelings excited by our interview had subsided, began to tell us the state of affairs in the palace. The Queen, she said, was highly displeased with her Lord: her name was Kalpasundarí: she was the daughter of Kalindavarmá, King of Kámarúpa, and excelled the Apsarasas in beauty and accomplishments. Vikaśavarmá was excessively attached to her alone, although he had many other women in his palace.

On hearing this, I told her to carry to the Princess garlands prepared by me, and to inflame her resentment still more against her Lord, by citing to her the example of Vásavadattá, and other distinguished females, who obtained Lords of equal value with themselves, and bringing to her knowledge whatever private favours the King had bestowed on other females of his establishment. After which she should come, and report the results to me. My agents, both mother and daughter, diligently promoted my designs, and in a few days my nurse told me that the Queen considered herself as ill-matched as the lovely Mádhaví to the bitter Nimba, and was plunged in despair. What, said she, is now to be done? I gave her a picture of myself, and desired her to put it in the way of Kalpasundarí: she did so, and the Queen was immediately struck by the performance, conceiving it to be a work of fancy, and highly creditable to the painter's skill. My old nurse told her that the world was large, and handsome as was the picture, she did not doubt the reality might prove as charming; but she enquired, supposing that such a youth were found, with talents, graces, and rank to correspond, what might he expect. Kalpasundarí replied: 'Nothing, for what have I to offer worthy of such a prize? my body, heart, and being, were of infinitely less value; but if this be not a fiction, let me at least behold the original.' To this the old woman replied, "It is no fiction: there is such a youth, the son of a King, who having beheld you at the vernal festival was penetrated with the arrows of Káma. He applied to me to procure him access to your presence, and conceiving you to be made for each other I promised him my aid. The Chaplets I bring you are the work of his hands, and this his picture is painted by himself. If you are desirous of beholding him, his talents and valour will make way to you, and I have no doubt you will see him this very day." The Queen reflected a little, and then replied:

'Mother, I can have nothing to conceal from you. My father was the attached friend of Prahárovarmá, and my mother equally devoted to his Queen: these two agreed that, when they should have children of a different sex, their offspring should be married. As it chanced, however, that the sons of Priyamvadá were lost, my father gave me in marriage to my present husband, a wretch of cruel and unjust temper, misshapen body, and uncultivated mind, a boasting liar, a forfeiter of his word, and vain only of his ferocious valour. I hate him not the less that he passes his time with my rivals, especially a low and miserable creature, Ramayantiká, a woman who has the audacity to measure her state with mine, and whom he has dared to decorate with flowers plucked from the Champa that I had planted, and reared as if it had been my child. I hear these things from my faithful attendant Pushkariká. The man is detested, and I am scorned: what more is necessary? the fear of futurity is obscured by present sufferings, and the female heart can ill restrain the passion love inspires, when its gratification is impeded only by duty to one we hate. Let your friend therefore come this day to the Mádhaví bower in the garden.' My nurse promised that I should, and having communicated the conversation to me, I had only to accomplish her engagement.

When the night set in, and the vapours rose in the west round the setting sun, as from the fume of a vast and red hot coal dipped in the ocean, I retired to repose, and to reflect that, if I sinned in intriguing with another's wife, I might claim some extenuation in the important objects which induced me to it, the recovery

of my birthright, and liberation of my parents. In
such meditation, and in considering how my friends,
and Prince would judge of my conduct, I sank into
repose. In my sleep Ganeśa appeared, and encouraged
me to persist; and I rose, determined to proceed.
Káma, unoccupied that day elsewhere, plied me with
his shafts, so that by the evening I was impatient to
see the Queen. As soon as it was dark I repaired to
my assignation, clothed in dusky raiment, grasping
my trusty sword, and prepared with all implements
necessary for my purpose. When I arrived at the
palace I crossed the ditch by a bamboo ladder concealed previously near the spot by Pushkariká, and
which again served me to scale the wall. I let myself
down on the other side by the projecting steps of the
Masonry. I then slowly passed the Bakula bower,
and Champaka avenue. I heard at a little distance the
cries of the Chakwas. I then turned to the north by
the Bignonias, and having leaped over the canal that
ran to the palace, proceeded on a gravel walk bordered
by red Aśoka trees and Jasmines. I again turned to
the west by a Mango grove, and there distinguished
the Mádhaví bower, shining gently by the lustre of
the gems that gleamed from an open casket upon an
inlaid couch in the centre. I entered an inner appart-
ment, separated by a wall of flowers, and branches,
and a door of the same materials. There I found
a couch of flowers, caskets of Lotus leaves, an
ivory-handled fan, and vases filled with fragrant
waters. I sat awhile inhaling the odours about

me, when I heard the gentle tread of feet approach: leaving the Chamber I hid myself behind a tree. Kalpasundarí now arrived and not finding me there, broke out into the most passionate regrets at her disappointment, calling upon Kámadeva to know what crime she had committed, that he thus exposed her to the flames of despair, and yet refrained from reducing her to ashes. I then appeared and consoled her distresses: we soon felt implicit confidence in each other, and how impossible it was ever more to separate. I therefore instructed her what plan to pursue.

By my desire she was to shew my portrait to the King, and ask him whether he did not think it surpass mere mortal beauty: 'to this, I continued, he will say yes: then do you tell him that an old female devotee has instructed you, how by particular charms, and sacrifices, to become invested with this very form, but it must be done at night, and alone, presenting to Fire a hundred sticks of sandal, Agurn, and handfuls of camphire, and silk garments, preceding it in the day by a public offering to the same element, with all due ceremonies: then you are to sound a bell, on hearing which your husband is to come, when if he will acknowledge to you all his secret purposes and plans, have his eyes bound, and embrace you, this form shall be transferred from you to him, you becoming the same as you were before. Tell this to the King, and leave it to him to determine, advising him to call his counsellors, and people together, and be guided by their advice. There is no doubt he will comply. When the

royal sacrifice is performed in these garden walks, and
the smoke of the oblation fills the air, I will enter and
secrete myself in this bower.' I told her also to reproach him in seeming sport with his infidelity, and
threaten him not to fulfil the rite, and desired her to let
me know his reply. I then left her, Pushkariká effacing
the marks of my footsteps as I retired. In a short time
every thing turned out as I expected, and the rumor
run through the city that the Rájá was about to obtain,
by the magic skill of the Princess, a most celestial
figure, and that there was no trick in this; for it was
to take place in the garden of the palace, in the presence of the chief Queen, and had received the concurrence of the ministers. The efficacy of jewels,
charms, and drugs was pronounced wonderful. So it
took place, and when clouds of smoke spread from
the palace adding gloom to the shade, I entered the
garden. Kalpasundarí soon hastened to me, and told
me that she had addressed the King, as I had told
her to do, on which, falling at her feet, he vowed,
that he never more would seek the love of any other
woman. I have now come here, she continued, your
bride, the former evidence of our marriage was Káma,
but now let these sacred flames bear witness to our
union. I desired her to withdraw, whilst I completed
our plan. I then struck the bell, and she muttered in
low sounds, like the herald of fate. The King approached; she then retired, and I remained, engaged
apparently in the oblations when he arrived, and as
he stood in fear and doubt, I said, declare again, and

take the holy fire to witness, you will never when you
assume this form prove unfaithful to me. This dissipated his doubts; he was satisfied it was the Queen,
and no imposition; and therefore began to make such
a vow. I then smiled, and stopped him, saying: I will
not exact your oath. What woman need I fear? and
if the Apsarasas be attracted, follow your inclinations.
Now then reveal your secrets, and having uttered
them take this form. He replied: I have plotted with
my ministers to convey poisoned food to my father's
younger brother Prahāravarmá, who is in prison, intending to give out that he has died of an old disease.
My own younger brother Viśokavarmá I am about to
send with an insufficient army to Puṅdra, where he
must perish. An old merchant of Panchála, and Paritráta, my merchant, are employed by me to get from
Khanati, a Yavana, a jewel of inestimable value for a
little price, and my managing man Śatahali has been
authorised by me to destroy Anantasíra, a powerful
landholder, by exciting troubles on his estates, and
leading a force to support them.

Having heard his secrets thus related, I said to him:
receive the reward of your actions! On which I drew
my sword, and cut him in two, and making a copious
offering of ghee to the Lord of flame, threw his body
into the blaze, where the whole was speedily reduced
to ashes. Then cheering my mistress who with the
timidity of her sex was agitated with apprehension, I
took her by the hand, and returned with her to the
palace, where summoning all the attendants I received

their homage. I then retired to rest in the royal apartments along with my bride, from whom I learned the customary practices of my predecessor. In the morning, after bathing, and the usual auspicious observances, I repaired to council, and addressing my ministers, said: 'With my figure, Sirs, I have changed my temper. Let my uncle be liberated, and restored to his Sovereignty, and I will shew that obedience I owe him.' Sending for my younger cousin, I told him, 'The people of Puṅdra at present have been urged to despair by distress, whilst we are in plenty; it is only necessary to protect our harvests from their depredations, and it is needless for you to march against them.' To the jewel dealers I sent, and told them that I thought it but just, that a suitable price should be given for an article of value, and directed them to pay the owner of the diamond the price he demanded. I then called Śatahali, and said, as the chief fault of Anantasíra was his attachment to Prahâravarmá he was no longer an object of resentment, and as my uncle was restored to dignity we should desist from all aggression upon his friends. By these orders the Officers of my Government were satisfied of my identity, and delighted with the amendment of my character. My parents were set at liberty, and reseated on the Throne. After a short time my nurse, by my instructions, revealed the whole truth to my parents, and I had the happiness of prostrating myself at their feet. I was also installed in the Yuvarájya by my father's commands. It only now remained to complete my felicity, to be reunited to your Highness, and I was meditating the means of finding you, when letters from Sinhavarmá, my father's ancient friend, solicited my aid against the hostile advances of Chaṅḍavarmá. I was united with him in the command, and arrived at this place, now rendered illustrious by your auspicious presence.

Having thus concluded, Rájaváhana observed that the important objects his friend had accomplished excused his single deviation from moral rectitude, and that the schemes of the prudent were certain of success. Then turning to Arthapála, with an encouraging look, the Prince requested him to relate his adventures.

STORY OF ARTHAPÁLA.

I engaged with our other friends in search of your Highness, and after some time spent in traversing this sea-encircled earth I arrived at Káśipurí, Váráṅasí, where I bathed in the pure transparent waters of Maṅikarṅiká, and paid my adoration at the shrine of Avimukteśwara the foe of death. I then proceeded south of the city, where I met a man of stout, robust make, tightly girded, and his eyes red with incessant weeping. It appeared strange to me that a man of such singularly powerful make should give way to despair, and determined to ascertain the cause of his affliction. I therefore addressed him, saying, 'Brother, your appearance indicates some desperate purpose; if not a secret, I should be gratified to know what has caused your evident grief, and whether I can be of

use to you.' He looked at me awhile, and then said:
"I have no objection to relate my story to you." We
accordingly sat down under a Karavíra tree, and he
thus proceeded: "I am the son of a man of property,
and my name is Púrṅabhadra. I was accustomed
always to follow my own inclinations, and in spite of
my father's cares addicted myself as I grew up to the
profession of a thief. Being detected robbing the
house of a trader in this city, I was confined, and
sentenced to death. I was accordingly led forth in
front of the palace gate, and in the presence of
Kámapála, the chief minister, a wild elephant was let
loose upon me, and approached amidst the clamour of
the multitude, clattering his bells still louder, and curling his trunk to seize me. I was not accustomed to
fear, and encountering the animal I struck him with
the uplifted logs in which my arms were wedged: he
reeled and retreated. His driver enraged had recourse
to abuse, and the liberal application of his heel and
his goad, and at last again forced the elephant to the
encounter. I repeated my blow with greater violence,
and the animal, who was for a moment stunned, no
sooner recovered, than he turned tail, and fled: his
driver brought him up a third time, but he retreated
again as soon as he saw me preparing to attack him,
and all his guide's efforts were now in vain. When
the minister observed this, he sent for me and said:
'The elephant you have discomfited has been hitherto
as irresistible as death himself. So much valor merits
not so vile a fate. Desist therefore from the unworthy

practices you have followed, and adopt a more creditable life: what say you? Will you enter into my service?' With all my heart, I replied. I accordingly attached myself to him, and he treated me as a friend. When he felt confidence in me he one day communicated to me his story at my request.

Dharmapála was the minister of Ripunjaya, the King of Kusumapura, a man of profound understanding and great learning: his son, equal to him in all respects, was named Sumitra. I am his younger brother by a different mother. As I spent much of my youth amongst improper persons, my elder brother reprimanded me for it. I did not much relish his reproofs, although they were kindly urged, and therefore withdrew from my home. Wandering about the world, I came to this city, Kási, where I saw Kántimatí, the daughter of Chandasinha, the King, playing at ball with her damsels in a grove dedicated to Káma. I was the prize of her beauty, and in time effected a private union with her. The fruit of our secret love was a son, of whom she was privately delivered: her attendants, apprehensive that the infant might lead to a discovery, told the mother it was still born, and carrying it away, exposed it on a mound, whence a woman of low caste was employed to carry it to a cemetery. As she returned along the road by night, she was seized by the guard, and being threatened with severe punishment unless she gave a satisfactory account of herself, she betrayed our secret. The King was immediately informed of it, and by his commands

the woman led him to the place of my concealment,
the grotto below the artificial mound, where I lay
unsuspectingly asleep. I was immediately seized and
carried off to the place of execution. The executioner
aimed the fatal blow at me, but fate so willed it that
he missed the mark, and only cut asunder the cords
that bound me: before he could recover, I sprang
upon him, wrested the sword from his gripe, and dis-
patching him and several of his assistants made my
escape. As I wandered alone without shelter, I was
addressed as I passed through a forest by a damsel of
celestial beauty, attended by a train of females, but
seemingly immersed in grief. She approached me,
and decorating her lovely forehead with the tiara
radiance of her hands she invited me to sit down with
her at the foot of a stately Banian tree. I accepted the invitation, and asked her the motives
which induced her to detain me; who she was, and
where was her abode. In a honied stream of eloquence
she replied:

"I am named Tárávalí, and am the daughter of Mańibhadra, King of the Yakshas. Having paid a visit
to the venerable Lopamudrá, the wife of Agastya, I
was returning from the Malaya Mountains, when I saw
in a charnel ground at Benares an infant weeping. I
took him up and feeling compassion for his helpless
condition conveyed him to my father. My father carried him into the presence of the Lord of Alaká. The
friend of Śiva sent for me, and said, 'daughter, how
feel you for this infant?' As if I had given him life,

I replied. The God said, 'the poor child speaks the truth,' and then he related to us a long narrative from which I found that Śaunaka, Śúdraka, and Kámapála were one person in different lives, and that Bandhumatí, Vinayavatí and Kántimatí were also the same individual; other wives of these persons were in like manner reborn, amongst whom in the time of Śaunaka I was named Gopakanyá. When you were Śúdraka, I was again your wife in infancy; but when you grew up, your affection was chiefly given to Vinayavatí, who was thence born again as Kántimatí, whilst I was born again in my present form. After relating these events, Kuvera directed me to take the child to the wife of Rájahansa, where he might be brought up along with Rájaváhana, and by the advice of my elders I have come to lay myself at the feet of one, who by the will of fate has so often overcome the power of death." When I heard this narrative I embraced her, shedding tears of delight, and spent some time with her in a palace suddenly reared in the forest, and in the midst of more than mortal enjoyment. After a few days I expressed to Túrávalí my desire to be avenged on Chańdasinha for the jeopardy in which he had put my life. My new spouse smiled, and said, 'you shall see Kántimatí, I will bring her here.' Accordingly, at midnight, the palace of the King of Káśi was transported to us, and entering his chamber I took up the sword lying at his pillow, and woke him from his sleep, saying: 'behold your son-in-law; I gained possession of your daughter without your concurrence,

and am now come to wipe away my fault.' In terror
of his life, the King bowed down to me, and said:
"The fault was mine, who like an idiot, or one possessed, repaid with death the honor you had conferred
upon me; now deign to dispose of my daughter, my
kingdom, and my life, at your pleasure." His submission appeased me, and being restored to his Capital,
he celebrated publicly my espousal of his daughter,
Tárávalí, repeated to Kúntimatí the different trans-
migrations we had undergone, and we lived happily
together; the King conferring on me the station of
Yuvarúja, and placing in my hands the chief administration of affairs.

Kámapála having thus finished his story continued
to shew me the same regard: at last, time that consumes every thing summoned his royal father-in-law
to heaven. He then elevated to the Throne the
youngest son of the late King, Sinhaghosha, a child of
five years of age, his elder brother Chandaghosha
being reduced to premature decay by his debaucheries.
When the boy attained the years of puberty, the inconsiderateness of his age induced him to listen to the
insinuations of evil counsellors, and they persuaded
him that Kámapála had violently obtained the person
of the Princess, had extorted the concurrence of the
late King through his fears for his life, had taken off
the young King's elder brother by poison, and would,
no doubt, get rid of him in the same manner the
moment he should assert his claim to independent rule,
unless he were anticipated. In this way his enmity

was excited against Kámapála, but the protection of the Yakshiní defeated all schemes against her Lord.

At this time the chief Queen, Sulakshaná, said with seeming affection to Kántimatí, she was sure she was not as happy as formerly, and begged her to relate the truth. She replied, that her friend and fellow-wife Tárávalí had gone away in displeasure, because her husband had mentioned Kántimatí's name at an unsuitable season, and no entreaties had been able to pacify her, that her husband was much grieved by her disappearance, and that she herself was distressed to observe his sorrow. This Sulakshaná told the King, and he now fearlessly plotted the destruction of the minister. Accordingly whilst engaged at the palace in affairs of state, he was recently seized by men stationed for the purpose, and thrown into confinement. Charges against him have been publicly promulgated, and in consequence his eyes are to be put out, but in such a manner that death shall ensue. When I heard this news, I was overcome with grief, but at last drying my tears, I have resolved to precede my friend and patron on the road to death. This is the cause of my present affliction."

The stranger, having finished his narrative, left me no less afflicted than himself to hear of my father's peril. After checking my emotion, I told him who I was, and we concerted the possibility of effecting my father's release. Whilst thus employed, a large venomous snake thrust his head out of a hole in the wall. I immediately secured him by the power of charms,

and told my new friend that thus assisted I would
seek for my father, and privily loosing the snake
would let him bite with such restraint on the venom
that it should not be mortal; although he should drop,
as if he was dead. In the mean time he should hasten
to my mother, and apprise her of our situation: she
would come to us with all speed; but he should tell
her this, 'Let her send you fearlessly to the King, to
say to him on her part: It is a soldier's duty to suppress his foes, without regard to kindred, or alliance;
but it is a woman's duty to share the fortunes of her
husband in honor or in shame. I will therefore accompany my Lord upon the funeral pile, agreeably to
the ritual, if you will give me his body. The King
will of course assent; do you then take the body to
your house, and in a retired place inclosed with canvas
screens prepare a pile covered with a layer of Darbha
grass, as if for the wife to ascend it after her husband's
death. I will come to the spot, and you will give me
admittance; when restoring my father to perception,
we shall be all happily reunited.' When my father's
follower had received my instructions, he immediately
set off. I repaired to the place of proclamation, and
ascending a tamarind tree secreted myself among the
branches. An immense crowd soon assembled, and
presently my father, with his hands bound behind him,
and attended by a guard like a thief, appeared; when
the executioner, as usual having stopped, thrice proclaimed his imaginary crimes, charging him with
having caused the death of Chaṅdaghosha, and plotted

the destruction of the King himself by a column filled with combustibles: 'he has been sentenced therefore, he continued, to lose his eyes, and should any be wicked enough to imitate his offences, they will meet with the like reward.' When he had ceased, and the crowd began to move, I cast the snake from the tree unperceived upon my father, and then quickly descending approached him, and anticipated the fatal effect of the venom. The snake in rage and alarm bit my father, so that he immediately dropped, and to all appearance was dead. The people thought it was the act of destiny. Kántimatí, being apprised by Púrṅabhadra of what was going forward, hastened to the spot, and taking my father's head on her lap, sent word to the King: 'This is my husband; whether he has offended against you, heaven must judge, not I. This alone is my business to accompany him in death, to whom my hand, in life, was pledged, or I shall disgrace our common origin. Give permission that I may ascend the funeral pile.' The King was pleased with the application, and readily gave his assent, directing all due honors to be paid to his brother-in-law. The rest happened, as I had arranged it, and when my mother had gone through the form of assuming violent affliction, taken leave of her friends, and repeatedly refused to listen to their tears and entreaties, she entered alone the chamber, which contained the corpse; admitted by Púrṅabhadra, as agreed upon, I soon restored animation to the body by the Vainateya process, and when my mother found my father alive, she fell at his feet, and then embraced me, repeatedly expressing her joy in a flood of tears, and convulsive sobs; now congratulating herself on my recovery; now blessing my filial exertions which had saved a father; now vehemently accusing Táráválí for having so long separated us, and then in a passion of grief and joy throwing herself upon my neck; and bathing me with tears. My father in the mean time, having heard the whole story from Púrnabhadra, contemplated me with proud delight, and felt himself happier than the Lord of Heaven. When our mutual emotions had subsided, I asked my father, how we should next proceed. He replied: 'There is no occasion for secrecy; my palace is strong and well stored with arms. Many leaders of note are in my service, and most of the Chiefs of people are ill satisfied with my treatment. Let us therefore retire home, and endeavour to inflame the public resentment and dissatisfaction; when ripe for insurrection, we will assemble and arm our friends, and lead them against the abettors of the tyrant.' This was put in execution. When the King found us so secure from his power, he was vexed at what had passed, but employed all the hostile stratagems against us that he could devise: his agents however were daily cut off by our party. At last, having learned the situation of the Royal chamber, I determined to effect a subterraneous passage to it from our own palace: beginning at the angle of a turret wall, I followed it up some distance, mining below the foundation. The passage opened at last on an excavated chamber, where I was surprised to see a number of Damsels of beauty calculated to make earth a paradise. At that moment one of surpassing loveliness entered the cavern: her charms irradiated these subterraneous realms with more than mortal light: she looked like the personified earth, the abode of the flower-armed God, or the genius of the empire secreting her splendour from iniquitous monarchs under ground. As she advanced, dissipating the gloom, she resembled an image of burnished gold. When she and the other Damsels saw me, they trembled like fragrant sandal creepers agitated by the breeze of Malaya. In that assembly there was an aged woman, who resembled a tuft of white-headed Kás: she fell at my feet, and solicited my forbearance, as if I was a deity descending to battle with the denizens of the infernal shades. I replied: relinquish your fears; you see in me a mortal, the son of Kámapála and Kántimatí, who seek by these unwonted paths access to the palace. But declare, who you are, and why inhabiting a place like this. The old lady answered:

'Prince, we are fortunate in being favoured with the sight of so much dignity and grace; you shall hear. Your grandfather had by his Queen Lílávatí two children, Kántimatí your mother, and the Prince Chańdaghosha. The young Prince, when scarcely arrived at manhood, brought on a consumption by his excesses, and died before his father. He left his wife Acháravatí pregnant: she was delivered of a daughter, Mańikarńiká, whom you here behold, and died soon afterwards. The grandfather Chaṅdasinha then sent for me, and privately informed me, that he was pledged to give his grand-daughter in marriage to Darpasára, the son of his friend the King of Málava; but after the late events in which your mother Kántimatí was involved, he was apprehensive the example might have a mischievous effect, and to guard against accidents he had determined to rear Maṅikarṅiká with the greatest care and secrecy. There was a suite of rooms, he said, underground, in the heart of an artificial elevation, constructed as an asylum against the fury of a triumphant enemy; it consisted of many extensive apartments fitted up with every splendid decoration, and provided with stores for a century's consumption, and he proposed that I should bring up his granddaughter in this recess, attaching to us a suitable train. When he received my assent, he opened a trap door in the wall, fastened by a bolt, and leading from the square of his own apartments. Into the passage it opened to he made us all enter. Twelve years have since elapsed: my ward is now a woman; but the King seems to have forgotten us. It is probable that his promise of her to Darpasára will never be fulfilled, and better were it that she became the bride of one so nearly allied, and in fact betrothed to her before her birth by a secret agreement between your mother and her's, in case the latter bore a female child.' The Princess seemed nothing loth; but I interrupted them by saying, I must first accomplish what I proposed in the palace, when I should return to them.

Receiving from the matron a lamp, and following the passage from the cavern, I came to the secret entrance to the Royal chambers. At midnight I opened it, and entered the apartment where lay Sinhaghosha asleep: darting upon him, as an eagle pounces upon a snake, I seized him, and dragged him off, before he could call for succour, to the secret passage; when securing the door, I bore him to the cavern, and thence to my own dwelling. I put him in fetters, and exhibited him a captive to my own parents. I also narrated to them the adventure of the subterraneous chamber. They heard the story with great satisfaction, and detaining the King in confinement, brought the Damsels home. I married the Princess, by which I acquired a claim to the now vacant throne, and exercised the functions of royalty. In this state of things we heard of the attack upon the King of Anga, our Ally, and hastened to his assistance. The result it is unnecessary to repeat; but as we have been so fortunate as to meet with your Highness, let the unworthy Sinhaghosha share the general satisfaction, and wipe away all his offences by the penance of prostration at your feet. Rájaváhana assented; but in the mean time desired Pramati to relate his adventures. Pramati bowed and thus obeyed.

STORY OF PRAMATI.

After having wandered some time in search of your Highness, I came to a forest near the skirts of the

Vindhya mountain. There evening overtook me, and the beauty of the West was decorated with the crimson blossoms of the last rays of the sun. I refreshed myself in a limpid pool. Being unable to distinguish the irregularities of the road, levelled now by the gloom, I determined to halt, and collecting a quantity of dry leaves, I made a bed with them at the foot of a stately tree, where having recommended myself to the tutelary Dryad, I composed myself to rest. After a short interval it appeared to me, that my limbs reposed on some softer material than the ground, and sensations of exquisite delight pervaded my whole frame. I felt my right arm throb, and I thought I looked up, and beheld a white canopy, that screened me from the beams of the moon. As I cast my looks to the left, I saw the walls of a lofty apartment, along the foot to which a number of Damsels lay asleep on painted couches. I then directed my gaze to the right, and beheld a most lovely maiden, as graceful as a creeper of Indra's garden, rent from its prop by Airávata, and bowed in sleep like the Lotus when it shuts its petals on the amorous bee. She looked, as lying on the pure white couch, like the earth reclined on the ivory tusks of Ádiváráha, whilst a pearly robe, like the milky ocean, floated loosely over her well turned shoulders. The change filled me with astonishment, and I lay wondering what had become of the forest, and my leafy couch; what building was this, on whose lofty turret rose the spear-crowned figure of the martial God (Kártikeya), shaded by banners floating in the sky; how had I been transported to my present situation, and who the maidens could be, by whom I was surrounded. But the Damsel, who appeared their chief, and resembled the Goddess that bears the Lotus, was the especial object of my meditations. A mortal she certainly was, for the eyes were fast closed in sleep, like the Lotus in the lunar beams; drops of perspiration stood on her cheeks like tears of amber from the snapped branches of the mangoe, and parts of her raiment lying about were discoloured with dust*. Whilst I meditated whether I should disturb her slumbers, methought she gently opened her eyes, and surveyed me with more affection than alarm; after appearing as if she would call her attendants, she seemed to abandon the intention, and drawing herself up, and retiring to the further part of the couch, she lay watching me with half-shut eyes till again she fell asleep. I felt the same power overcome my passion, and was once more plunged into profound repose. After a time I awoke, and looking about me, found myself still at the foot of the tree, in the same place where I had lain down. It was dawn, and I arose, but recurring to the vision of the night, I could scarcely persuade myself it was a dream, and I determined to take up my residence on the spot, and spend my whole life there if necessary, until I should ascertain the truth. I had scarcely formed this determination, when a woman approached: she was of a graceful appearance, but emaciated with care,

---

* [Nalop., V, 25. Naishad., XIV, 19 ff.]

and clad in ragged attire; her eyes were red with
weeping; her hair was bound up in a plait, and her
whole semblance indicated one who had suffered the
pangs of absence and separation. She ran up to me,
and throwing her arms about my neck, expressed
every mark of maternal affection. At last, as well as
her sobs would allow her, she spoke thus:

"My dear child, behold in me the person who entrusted, as you must have heard, the infant Arthapála
to the care of the Queen of Magadha. I am the
daughter of Mańibhadra, the wife of Kámapála, the
son of Dharmapála, and your mother: having allowed
myself to feel displeasure with my husband, and having therefore quitted him in anger, I was cursed in a
dream by some one in the form of a Rákshasa, who
said: 'I take up my abode in you, oh! violent woman,
for a year.' The year, as long as a thousand years,
expired last night. I purposed, after attending the
Assembly held at the festival of Tryambaka, in the
city of Śrávastí, to reseek my Lord, and I was on my
way, when I beheld you here, and heard you solicit
the protection of the Dryad: the effects of my curse
prevented me from properly recognising you, but I
could not abandon you in the forest, and I accordingly
transported you with me: as we approached the city,
I considered that I could not take you to the meeting,
and as it chanced we were near the apartments of
the Princess Navamáliká, the daughter of Dharma-
vardkhana, King of Śrávastí, I determined to leave
you there; it was an open terrace on the roof of the

house where the Princess and her attendants were sleeping. I left you among them, whilst I repaired to the heavenly Assembly. When the ceremonies were over, and the Assembly broke up, I took my leave of my friends, and paid my homage to the Lord of the three worlds, and then offered my respects to the Goddess, to whom my heart is most devoutly attached. She smiled upon me, and said: do not fear, your period of absence is expired, go and be happy with your husband. Thus favoured, I returned to you, and being restored to my proper nature, knew you now to be my son, and the dear friend of Arthapála. I knew also the events of the night, and that you and the Princess had beheld and were enamoured of each other, and although fear and shame had withheld you from any communication, yet a feeling of love deterred the damsel from alarming her attendants. I resolved by some means to bring the event to a favourable conclusion, but was then obliged to carry you back to the forest. I must now hasten, and prostrate myself at your father's feet." So saying, she once more embraced me tenderly, and then departed, whilst I took the road to Srávastí. On the road I came to a Bunjara camp, where a great crowd was collected to behold a cock-fight. I looked on for a time, and could not suppress a smile. An old Brahman who sat near me, noticed it, and in a low tone asked the reason. I said to him: this is absurd, how could the people have thought of matching that large strong cock of the co-

coanut breed with one of the Valáka[1] tribe. He said:
you are right, but they are not up to it, so muin: and
thus saying, he offered me betel from his box, and
entered into discourse with me. The Valáka cock was
beaten, and the Brahman to whom the other belonged,
was highly pleased with his victory, and my connois-
seurship: he invited me to his house, and treated me
with every mark of attention. When I took leave of
him the next day, he begged me not to forget him,
and to depend upon his friendship, if ever I had occasion for it. I left him after due acknowledgement
of his kindness, and proceeded to Śrávastí. Being
fatigued with the length of the way, I stopped at a
garden in the suburbs, and lay down to rest at the
foot of a tree, when I was suddenly roused by the
musical clank of female anklets, and looking up beheld
a damsel approach. When she came opposite to me,
I observed that she had a picture in her hand, with
which she evidently compared my features, and having done so, appeared to express delight and surprize:
having looked at the picture, and recognised the resemblance it bore me, I begged of her to stop, and sit
down. She accepted of my invitation, and sitting
down entered into conversation with me, giving me
an account of the country; at last, perceiving, she
said, I was a traveller, and looking as if wearied by
my journey, she asked me to rest at her house. I ac-

---

[1] The Valúka, white, long-necked, long-winded, but dunghill (Skhalamána).

cepted the invitation, and followed her home, where
I was regaled in a princely manner. In the course of
conversation she enquired of me, what I considered
as the most marvellous circumstance that had befallen
me in my travels. The question inspired me with
hope, and I entertained no doubt that the picture was
the work of the Princess, to explain to her attendants
the cause of that change in her appearance, which her
passion had inflicted. I therefore replied: allow me
to look at the picture. She gave it me, and taking it
I delineated the Princess as she slept, and then said,
'I saw in a dream as I thought such a maiden as this,
as I slept once in a forest, but it was not merely a
dream.' When the Damsel saw this she was highly
delighted, and begged me to explain the whole, with
which request I complied. She then related to me the
sufferings of her friend, and we consulted by what
means our union might be effected. I told her it was
necessary for that purpose I should quit her for a few
days. I accordingly took my leave, promising to return as soon as I had matured my scheme. I went to
the old Brahman, with whom I had formed an acquaintance, who was astonished to see me back so
soon, and enquired the cause. I told him I had received a deep wound from the eyes of the Princess,
and depended upon him to extract the dart: he agreed
readily to assist me, and this was the plan we adopted.

He disguised me in female apparel, and I passed
as his daughter: then taking me with him, he went
to the King as he held public audience, and said to

him: 'Sire, this is my only daughter, her mother died, whilst she was a child, and she has been reared by my cares alone. A young Brahman, connected by marriage, went some time since to Ujjayiní to earn her dower. I have promised to give her to him: but as he delays returning, and as she is now a young woman, I purpose going myself to bring him hither, and transferring to his charge the anxious trust, thence forward lead a religious life: for the care of a full-grown daughter is at all times arduous; much more so is it, when there is no mother. In the mean time I must solicit your Majesty, the parent of your subjects, to allow her to repose in the shadow of your protection, until I return with the bridegroom.' The King complying with his petition, made me over to his daughter, and I thus obtained the means of gratifying my passion. On the ensuing Phálgun, the inmates of the female apartment celebrated a festival, when all the women repaired to bathe in the river, at an Island on which stood a Temple of Kártikeya. Here, whilst sporting heedlessly in the stream, I dived and disappeared, coming up in a retired place, where my friend awaited me with male apparel. The women thought I was drowned; the Princess exclaimed, she would not survive me, and a scene of grief and alarm ensued, which spread to the city, and excited the attention of the King. Whilst vainly searching for me, the Brahman appeared with me as his intended son-in-law, and expatiating on my acquirements, my knowledge of the four Vedas, six Angas, sixty-four Kalas, of the four branches of tactics, and the use of weapons, and of every branch of Science and Literature, demanded his daughter. The King was overwhelmed with confusion and grief, and unable to answer; the chief attendants, relating what had chanced, endeavoured to console and pacify the supposed father, but he was not to be silenced, and insisted, that in reparation for his loss, and my disappointment, the King should give me his own daughter. To this request no attention was paid, and we were at last forced out of the hall: we were not however to be so easily baffled, but collecting a quantity of wood, which we piled up at the palace gate, my friend, the Brahman, threatened to set fire to, and ascend it, unless his requests were granted: he was seemingly about to put his threats in execution, when the King attended by his chief Counsellors, entreated him to desist, and agreed to his conditions. Thus I obtained the hand of the Princess, and after a time the King finding my fitness, retired from the cares of Government, and placed it in my hands.

At this time Sinhavarmá solicited my aid, and I advanced in consequence to Champá, where I have been so fortunate as to find my Prince. Rájaváhana expressed the pleasure he had received from the account of his friend's ingenuity and fortune, and then requested Mitragupta to narrate what had befallen him.

STORY OF MITRAGUPTA.

Whilst engaged in the same object as my companions, and in quest of your Highness, I came to a city in Suhma called Dámalipta, in the skirts of which, in a stately grove, I found a crowd collected in observance apparently of some festival. I observed also in a bower of Atimukta creepers a young man sitting by himself playing on his Víńá, and approaching him I enquired what celebration was going forward, and why he sat thus apart from the rest. He replied:

Tungadhanwá, King of Suhma, had no progeny: he addressed his prayers to Vindhyavásiní, who had forgotten in her residence at this place her passion for her abode at Vindhya, and obtained from her favour two children: the Goddess appeared to him in a dream, and announced to him the birth of a son and a daughter: the former she said, should be the servant of the husband of the latter; and she directed, that the girl from the age of seven until her marriage should worship her every month on the Kŕitika Nakshatra by playing at ball in public, and further, she should be allowed to marry any one whom she should choose. The festival was to be called the Kandukotsava. In a short time the prophety of the Goddess was fulfilled, and a son and daughter were born to the King: the Damsel was named Kandukavatí, and she comes abroad to-day to play in public. Her foster sister and dear friend Chandrasená is prevented from coming with her by her wish to avoid the young Prince Bhímadhanwú, who teazes her with a suit, to which she prefers mine: her absence is the cause of my solitude and affliction.

He had scarcely ended, when we were startled by the tinkling of anklets near us, and a female entered the bower, whom as soon as the youth beheld he tenderly embraced, and making her sit down introduced her to me as his other life. After condoling with each other upon the danger and uncomfortableness of their situation, they spoke of making their escape to some other country, and the youth appealed to me, to inform him which of the places I had visited was the most fertile and civilized. I told him that there was no dearth of pleasant regions in the world, where he might find a suitable habitation, but that it was not impossible, perhaps, for them both to be happy where they were: if it was, I would show them the way. Before I could explain myself, the sound of female ornaments was distinctly heard, and the damsel sprang up in a hurry, and said to us: the Princess Kandukavatí approaches, doing honour to the Goddess in her sports. A sight of her on these occasions is allowed to all; come and behold her, and may the result be fortunate; I must attend her. So saying she departed. I followed and beheld the Princess seated in an open pavilion of great splendour. The moment I saw her my heart received the impression of her beauties. As I gazed upon her with intense love and admiration, she rose gracefully, and touched with the tips of her lovely fingers the footstool of the Goddess

as she hastily paid her devotions. She then took the
ball like the red eye of love when moved to wrath.
She first let it gently strike the ground, and as it
slowly rose beat it down with her open hand, till at
last, catching it at the rebound on the back of her
hand, she threw it up as high as she could, caught it
in its descent, and tossed it up again. As long as it
kept good time she struck it gently, but when it
slackened reiterated the blows without mercy: occasionally she kept it fluttering in the air like a bird,
hitting it up alternately with either hand, in a straight
line above her, whilst at others, when it descended
obliquely, she sprang forwards, backwards, and side-
ways to catch it. Thus sporting gracefully she attracted the gaze and applause of the people collected
around the pavilion. As I stood, leaning on the
shoulder of my new friend, lost in admiration, I drew
her notice, and then first she felt the power of Kan-
darpa, communicated by a glance, and with her sighs
repelled the bees that were attracted by the fragrance
and beauty of her Lotus cheeks. Increasing in her
speed, and driving the ball in a circle, she stood as it
were, as if abashed by my gaze, in the centre of a
flowery cage: she then followed the game in every
direction, and stooping, rising, shrinking, watching,
standing, and running pursued her sport. After this,
she united her companions in the pastime, and one
ball traversing the space between heaven and earth
seemed as if it were fifty. She then closed her exercises by repeating her homage to the Goddess, and

withdrew, followed by her attendants, and by my whole soul, darting at me as she passed sidelong looks as fatal as the chosen shafts of the flower-armed deity, and reverting as she retired her moon-like face, as if she sought to reclaim the heart she had deposited in mine. Being quite beside myself with love, I readily accepted the invitation of Koshadása to take up a temporary abode at his house: and he treated me most hospitably. In the evening Chandrasená appeared, and having saluted me inclined herself close to her lover for a little, and then sat down. Koshadása smiled and said to me: may I always find favour in your sight. I asked him what he meant: whether any unguent had been applied to the eyes of his rival, so as to induce him to cast his looks in a different direction, and regard Chandrasená as a monkey. She replied laughingly: 'your humble Servant is much obliged to you, if in this life you convert her from a human being to an ape; so be it, for thus only our desires will be gratified. The Princess was so much struck by your appearance at the festival that she immediately became the prey of the foe of Hara. This was at once perceived by me, and I shall tell my mother of it: she will inform the Queen, who will certainly communicate it to the King. He must consent to give his daughter to you, and the Prince will then become your dependant, for so the pleasure of the Goddess was announced. When the Kingdom is your's, Bhímadhanwá will no longer be able to disturb our happiness; only wait here for three or four days.'

So having said she embraced her lover and went away. Koshadāsa and I spent the night discussing what she had told us. In the morning after we were dressed, I went again to the grove where I had seen the Princess. I was there met by the Prince, who shewed me great civility, and pressing me to accompany him, took me with him to his tent, where I was treated exactly like himself: when I retired to rest, the charms of my mistress visited my slumber. I thought I was locked in her embrace, as I was awakened from my sleep by the clasp of iron fetters, and the grasp of a number of sturdy hands. The Prince thus addressed me: Hark ye, Sirrah! This old woman appointed by me to watch that hussy Chandrasenā overheard your fine discourse with her, and her impertinent swain. So, you are the object of Kandukavatī's amiable affections; I am to be your servant; am I? and you are, in my despite to give Chandrasenā to Koshadāsa. Then turning to an attendant, he said: go, toss the scoundrel into the sea. He obeyed, and I was carried off and thrown into the waves. As I had the use of my arms, I swam, as it chanced, till I came luckily across a piece of timber sent by destiny to my aid. I got upon it, and floated about till daylight, when I saw a Ship at a little distance. The crew were Yavanas; when they saw me, they made for me, and hoisting me in gave information to their Captain named Rámeshu, who ordered me to sprinkle a thousand raisins in an instant as I was strong enough. At that moment a galley surrounded by a number of vessels

bore down upon us. The Yavanas were alarmed
at seeing so many Ships advancing to assail them,
like dogs rushing upon a boar. Escape was impossible, and the crew gave themselves up for lost.
Observing their despondency, I addressed them,
and told them that, if they would take off my chains,
I would show them the way to victory. They set me
free, and I made them seize their arms, and hurl a
shower of darts and arrows at the foe: then grappling
with the foremost Ship, we sprang upon the deck,
and presently clearing it of its defenders took the
Commander alive. Who should this be but Bhima-
dhanwá. I made myself known to him, and desiring him to meditate on the vicissitudes of destiny
gave him over to my followers, by whom he was fettered with the chains which I had borne. The rest
of the enemy dispersed, and a contrary wind springing up, we were blown off to an Island in the ocean,
where we anchored. We landed in search of fresh
water, fruit and herbs, and found an abundant supply.
I came to a lofty mountain, the pleasantness of whose
brow induced me to ascend, and I held on my way,
without observing the distance, till I found myself
unexpectedly on the summit: there I discovered a
spacious reservoir, to which led steps of precious
stones, and whose waters were decorated with Lotus
flowers. I seized the opportunity of performing my
ablutions, and sipped the juice from the stalks of the
Lotuses: then throwing the flowers on my shoulders,
I proceeded, and met a Goblin of hideous aspect.—

He stood before me, and enquired in a menacing manner, who I was, and whence I came. I replied undauntedly to his enquiries, and related my adventures. He then said: answer the questions I shall put to you, or I devour you. I bid him propose them, and this conversation ensued:

Rák.—What is the most cruel of all things?

Mitr.—The heart of woman.

Rák.—What constitutes domestic happiness?

Mitr.—The attention of a wife to the gratification of her husband.

Hák.—What is love?

Mitr.—Desire.

Rák.—What overcomes difficulties?

Mitr.—Ingenuity.

I then added, 'I will give you examples of these in the anecdotes of Dkúminí, Gominí, Nimbavatí, and Natambavatí.' He desired me to narrate them, and I proceeded to

THE STORY OF DHÚMINÍ*.

In the city of Trigartta lived three brothers, Dhanaka, Dhányaka and Dhanyaka. It happened that a terrible dearth took place; there was no rain for 12 years. The grains were withered; the pools were beds of earth; the streams were dried up; religious rites fell into disuse; thieves and rogues multiplied;

---

* [Benfey, Pantschatantra, I, 436.]

the people ate one another; and the villages and towns were almost depopulated. The three brothers had consumed every thing belonging to them, even to their families, and the wife of the youngest named Dhúminí was the only eatable article left. She was accordingly devoted to the same fate as her predecessors; but as her husband Dhanyaka was too much attached to her to assent to her sacrifice, he determined to fly with her to a distance, and they set off that night into the forest, allaying their thirst with his own blood. On their way they found a miserable man deprived of nose, feet, and hands, lying by the road side. Dhanyaka, in pity of his sad plight, took him on his back, and carried him along with them, until they discovered a cave suited to their purposes. Here they halted, and finding in the vicinity a supply of roots, and some herds of deer, they took up their abode. When the party had somewhat recovered their health and strength, the evil passions of the female began to acquire activity, and as Dhanyaka was often absent in quest of game for their support, Dhúminí was left alone with the cripple, whom she compelled to comply with her desires. Hating the man she had thus injured, she next conspired her husband's death, and taking advantage of his stooping to recover a rope, which she had purposely dropped into a well, she came behind him, and pushed him over into it. She then quitted the place, carrying her mutilated lover on her back. He passed for her husband wherever they came, and the people ad-

miring her conjugal devotedness worshipped her as a
Saint. In this manner they came to Avanti, where
the circumstances being brought to the notice of the
King he gave them a comfortable maintenance as the
recompense of so much virtue. Soon after the fall of
Dhanyaka into the well, it chanced that a caravan
halted on that spot, and the merchants repairing to
the well to procure water, they extricated Dhanyaka
from his perilous situation, and took him along with
them. Amongst other places, they visited Avanti,
and Dhúminí meeting her husband, exclaimed—"that
is the wretch by whom my husband was so barbar-
ously mangled. He was in consequence immediately
seized, and ordered to be put to death. Dhanyaka
however requested, that he might be first confronted
with the cripple; admitting that, if he should confirm
the accusation, he ought to be considered guilty. The
cripple was brought, and as soon as he saw his preserver fell at his feet, acknowledging the obligations
he owed him, and revealing all the wickedness of his
wife. When the King heard this, he was highly incensed, and ordered the woman to be punished, as she
deserved. This story of Dhúminí proves my assertion
that the most cruel of all things is woman's heart. I
shall now relate to you

THE STORY OF GOMINÍ.

In Drávira is a celebrated city called Kánchí. A
young merchant of considerable wealth, named Śakti
Kumára, resided there. He was unmarried at the age

of eighteen, and considering that there was no real happiness in a single life, as also that felicity in wedlock depended upon the wife's character, he determined to set off in search of a spouse; adopting therefore the character of a fortune-teller, and carrying with him a Prastha of rice bound up in his cloth, he proceeded on his travels. Wherever he went, those who had daughters brought them to him, and when he met with a girl whose appearance pleased him, he terminated his prognostications by asking her as a favour to shew him how well she could cook his rice. Some laughed, and some were angry, but all sent him away without complying, and he went from house to house in vain. Having arrived in a town of the Śivis on the Southern side of the Káverí, he came to a house, where making his usual application, a Damsel was brought out by her nurse, her parents being both deceased. As he looked at her, he observed, that she was perfect, her limbs were neither too long nor too short, too slight nor too stout; her hands were marked with all the lucky signs, as the fish, lotus, vase, &c. her fingers were straight, and the palms ruddy; her ankles were clean and even, and her feet well turned, and fleshy, with small and scarcely visible fibres; her legs were straight and symmetrical, and well set; and her knees were small, delicate and even; her hips prominent and well rounded; her waist was slender; her body gently inclined; her breasts were protuberant, and divided by a narrow interval; her arms were long, fleshy, smooth and soft; her neck

was graceful and well turned, and surmounted by
a lovely countenance, where the pouting lips were
of a most brilliant red; the chin was elegant, and not
small; the cheeks were firm and round; the nose was
like the budding sesamum flower; the eyes were of
the darkest jet, rolling in the most crystalline white;
and the forehead as radiant as the moon, shaded by
curling locks of deep sapphire hue. Śakti Kumára
was subdued by these charms, and with an agitated
bosom proposed his ordinary test. She smiled, as she
looked archly at her attendant, and taking the rice
desired the guest to sit at the threshold, where she
washed his feet. She then steeped the grains a little
in water, dried them in the sun, and rubbing them
gently in the ground, removed the awn without breaking the grain. She then said to the nurse, 'this bran
will be acceptable to the goldsmiths to clean their je-
wellery: go, sell it to them, and purchase with the
price fuel, an earthen boiler, and two platters.' Whilst
the old woman was gone on this errand, the Damsel
brayed the grain in a mortar of arjuna wood with a
pestle of khayar headed with iron, she then winnowed
it with the basket, and having well washed it, set it to
boil in five times its quantity of water, worshipping
the chimney as she placed the boiler. When the rice
was swollen up properly, she took the boiler from the
fire, and separated the scum, then replacing it, kept
stirring it till it was quite boiled; after which she
placed the boiler with the mouth downwards, and ex-
tinguishing the fire with the cold water, sent the old

woman to dispose of the coals which were unconsumed; with the price procured for them buying vegetables, ghee, curds, oil, myrobalans, and tamarinds. These she seasoned with condiments. She then placed the scum of the rice-water in a new saucer, and cooling it with a fan, added to it perfumes evaporated on the coals. She then pealed the myrobalan, and added to it Lotus perfume, when she directed her nurse to desire Śakti Kumára to bathe. When he was bathed, and had rubbed himself with oil and myrobalan, she laid a plank on a part of the floor well swept and levelled, on which he sat down: she then placed before him on a well trimmed plantain leaf two platters. Having given him some water to drink, she served him with two spoonfuls of rice, to which she added ghee and sauce, the rest of the rice he ate with spices, curds, butter, milk, and rice gruel. She finally brought him water to drink pure, cool, and fragrant in a new jug, perfumed with agallochum. The old woman then removed the fragments, and cleaning the ground with fresh cowdung, spread her garment upon it, on which he went to sleep. When he awoke he expressed his satisfaction, and being contented to seek no further, he married the Damsel, and took her along with him, when she found herself unexpectedly a woman of wealth and consequence. She nevertheless continued to worship her husband as a God, to pay the most assiduous attention to his household affairs, and to superintend the regulation of her family. In this way she acquired the entire confidence of her spouse who, leaving all his domestic concerns to her care, tasted in his corporeal form the joys of Paradise. I shall now relate to you

THE STORY OF NIMBAVATÍ.

In the kingdom of Saurashtra, in a city called Valabhí, there dwelt Grihagupta, a Ship-owner, who was possessed of great wealth. He had a daughter named Ratnavatí, who was married by Balabhadra, a Merchant's son. Soon after their espousal the husband, finding the young bride indifferent to his endearments, conceived so violent a dislike to her, that he could not bear the sight of her; to all his friends and retainers he gave her the nickname of Nimbavatí. After some time had elapsed, and when she sorrowfully meditated on the conduct she should pursue, an old female devotee, who was like a mother to her, brought to her flowers from the idol, and noticing her distress enquired its cause. Ratnavatí informed her of her husband's aversion, and begged her to befriend her, declaring, if she could not recover that regard, which was the only happiness and honour of a woman of respectable birth and station, she would no longer suffer so hateful an existence. The old woman promised to give her whatever aid she could, and desired her to suggest a plan for the purpose. She said: "There is a neighbour, a merchant, of immense wealth and consequence; his daughter Kanakavatí is very like me in person, and of my age; she is also my particular friend. I will go to visit her, and take an opportunity of amusing myself on the terrace of her house, splendidly attired. Do you contrive to bring my husband to the place, with the assent of my friend's mother, which we will obtain. As you approach, I will let a ball fly in your direction, as if by accident; pick it up, and give it him, and tell him, 'this Damsel Kanakavatí, the daughter of Kuveradatta, is the friend of your wife, and is vehement in her abuse of you: this ball is hers, and you should not relinquish the property of an enemy?' Looking up, he will think me to be Kanakavatí, and when I descend to claim the ball, will at my request conveyed through you return it to me. From this opening his regard will be attracted, and in all probability he will become enamoured of me in the person of my friend. As he cannot expect that the haughty merchant will consent to our wedding, he will concert through your mediation measures for carrying me off, which of course I shall consent to, and we will fly together to another country." So it happened, and as the old devotee reported that Balabhadra had expressed his regret for his past neglect of his wife, her friends concluded when she disappeared that she was gone with him. On the road Ratnavatí bought a female slave, and with her they settled at a small town, where Balabhadra who was well skilled in trade soon made a large sum at a little cost, and in time became the chief man in the city, and retained a number of slaves. He now treated his first female servant with great indignity, and by his ill-behaviour to her excited her resentment,

In her rage she promulgated, as much as she thought
she knew of his secret history, as she had learnt it
from her mistress. This coming to the ears of the
mayor, he reported it to the seniors, and Balabhadra
was denounced as a disgrace to the city, having stolen
the daughter of Kuveradatta. Balabhadra when he
heard of this was excessively alarmed, but Ratnavatí
encouraged him, desiring him to say, she was not
Kanakavatí but Ratnavatí, the daughter of Gṛihagupta
of Valabhí, given him by her father in marriage, and
to desire them, if they doubted him, to send a messenger to ascertain the truth. Balabhadra said, as she
had desired him, and the elders sent to Valabhí. When
Gṛihagupta heard of his daughter's existence, he set
off with her mother to her residence, and was overjoyed
to find his Ratnavatí again. Balabhadra now perceived that he had been taken in; but Ratnavatí had
become too dear to him for him to regret the de-
ception. Therefore I say that Love is Desire. I shall
now relate to you

THE STORY OF NITAMBAVATÍ.

In Śúrasena is a city called Mathurá, where dwelt
a youth of family, who was addicted to loose pleasures,
and vicious society, and being a lad of spirit he was
so often entangled in broils, that he was called Kalaha-
kaṇṭaka. One day he saw in a painter's possession
the picture of a female, with whose charms he became
violently enamoured. After some solicitation he prevailed on the painter to tell him, who the original was,

and having learnt that she was the wife of Anantakírtti, a merchant of Ujjayiní, and her name Nitambavatí, set off in the disguise of a mendicant for that city. Having got access to the house, under pretence of soliciting alms, he obtained a sight of the lady, and found her still more fascinating than her picture. With a view to effect his projects he solicited and obtained the care of the cemetery, and with the clothes of the dead he attached to his interests a female Sramaṇiká or Bauddha devotee. This woman he employed to convey a message from him to Nitambavatí, inviting her to come and see him, to which she sent back an angry and indignant reply. He was not discouraged, but desired his messenger to return to the merchant's wife, and say to her, as from herself: 'Persons like us, who are fully acquainted with the insufficiency of life, and only desirous of final emancipation, cannot be suspected of entertaining any purpose adverse to the reputation of women of respectability. The message I lately conveyed to you I only intended to try your merit, as I was afraid such youth and beauty could scarcely be satisfied with a man so advanced in years as your husband. I was mistaken, and the result has so much pleased me, that I am anxious to confer upon you a proof of my esteem. I should wish to see you a mother, but the planet under which your husband was born, has hitherto opposed it. This evil influence however may be counteracted, if you will be content to assist. Accompany me to a grove at night, where I will bring you a seer versed in incantations; you must put your foot in his hand, whilst he conveys into it his charms. Then, as if angry, kick your husband on the breast, when the evil influence will be expelled, and you will be blessed with progeny, and your husband will venerate you as a Goddess. There is nothing to be afraid of.' Nitambavatí with some little difficulty consented, and being apprised of her intentions, the false Saint awaited her at the appointed place. She came, as was directed, and put her foot into his hand; he pretended to rub it, muttering imaginary charms all the time, until he had taken off her golden anklet, when making a sudden cut at her thigh with a knife, which he had covertly prepared, he inflicted a gash in the upper part of it, and then quickly withdrew. Nitambavatí full of pain and terror, reviling herself for her own folly, and ready to kill the Śramañiká for having exposed her to such peril, returned home, and privately dressing her wound, kept her bed for some days. The rogue in the mean time offered the anklet to Anantakírtti for sale. He knew it to be his wife's, and enquired, how the vender had come by it. He refused to tell; the merchant threatened him with punishment, on which Kalahakañṭaka professed himself ready to communicate the truth to the Guild, (or Committee of merchants). He was accordingly taken before them, when he desired the merchant to send for his wife's anklets. She replied, she had lost one of them; it was large, and had slipped off, but she forwarded the other. The anklet in the possession of the supposed mendicant being compared with this was found to correspond, and there remained no doubt of their owner. The ascetic then being questioned as to the circumstances, under which he gained possession of it, replied thus: "You are aware, Gentlemen, that I was appointed to take charge of the graves of the deceased. As some people wished to deprive me of my fees, by burning the bodies by night, I kept watch at all hours. Last night I saw a dark-complexioned female dragging the half-burnt fragments of a dead body from the funeral pile, when to punish her horrible attempt I made a cut at her with my knife, and wounded one of her thighs, as she turned to escape; she ran off however, dropping one of her anklets as she fled, and I thus became possessed of it." The account thus given inspired all the auditors with horror. Nitambavatí was unanimously pronounced a Śákiní or witch; she was turned out of his house by her husband, and rejected with abhorrence by all the citizens. In this distress she repaired to the cemetery, where she was in the act of putting a period to her life, when she was prevented by her lover. He threw himself at her feet, and told her that, unable to live without her, he had adopted this contrivance to obtain her person, and entreated her to rely upon the fervour and faithfulness of his regard. His entreaties and protestations were at last successful, combined with the consciousness of her helpless situation, and Nitambavatí rewarded his ingenuity with her affection. Therefore I say that ingenuity accomplishes the greatest difficulties.

When I had finished my narratives, the Brahma Rákshasa expressed himself highly pleased with me; but he had scarcely so spoken, when several pearls mixed with drops of water fell from the sky. I looked up, and saw a Rákshasa in the air, carrying along with him a female who struggled to free herself from his grasp. I assailed him with reproaches, but could not more actively punish his violence, as he held his course in the air. My Rákshasa friend however felt as I did, and called to the other to stop, rising at the same time to intercept him. The ravisher, obliged to defend himself, threw down his lovely burthen, intending to dash her to pieces. She dropped, like a blossom shaken from a tree of heaven, and I fortunately caught her in my arms. I held her fainting, without noticing her countenance, my gaze being quite fixed upon the conflict in the air, where the contending demons hurled vast trees, and mountain peaks against each other. To shun the falling fragments, I hastened from the spot, and carrying my gentle load to the reservoir, imagine my delight, when I found I pressed my dear life Kandukávatí to my heart. I sprinkled her with the cool wave; she recovered her senses, immediately recognised me, and suffered herself to be encouraged by my endearments. She told me that, when she heard I was drowned by

order of her cruel brother, she determined not to
survive my loss; she contrived accordingly to deceive
her attendants, and get out to the grove alone, with
an intent of there putting an end to her life. Whilst
thus engaged, she was observed by the Rákshasa who,
attracted by her person, had endeavoured to allay her
distress, and engage her regard: but finding his efforts
unavailing, he had recourse to violence, and carried
her off, when he was prevented as already narrated.
When Kandukávatí had finished her narrative, I conducted her on board-ship, and we set sail. Contrary
winds however drove us from our destined course,
and carried us again to Támaliptá. When we landed, we heard that Tungadhanwá with his Queen were
so deeply affected by the disappearance of their son,
and the loss of their daughter, that they had gone to
the banks of the Ganges, intending to abstain from all
food, and die there. As the chief citizens were
warmly attached to their King, and contemplated his
death with sincere grief, their sorrow gave place to
joy when they found that the Prince and Princess
were returned. I conducted his children to the King,
who received them with rapture, and to requite my
services bestowed on me the hand of his daughter,
and the first place in the state. The young Prince
now very willingly submitted to my superiority, and
assented to the union of Chandrasená with Koshadúsa.
We were living happily together, when our alliance
with Sinhavarmá brought us to his succour, and pro-

cured me the happiness of again beholding my honored Lord.

Mitragupta having thus concluded, Rájavábana, after expressing his admiration of the marvellous incidents his friend had encountered, requested Mantragupta to repeat his adventures: he thus obeyed.

STORY OF MANTRAGUPTA.

The direction, which I had taken in quest of your Highness, brought me to the country of the Kalingas. When I approached Kalinga the capital, I stopped at a short distance, and rested on the borders of a reservoir adjoining to the public obsequial ground. I fell asleep. When I awoke, I found it was midnight, the surrounding objects were plunged in gloom, the chilly dews fell heavily, and the cold breeze sighed sorrowfully amidst the trembling leaves. All the world was at rest, save where the imps of mischief hovered in the murky air. Whilst my eyes were scarcely open, I distinctly heard one goblin say to another: 'What orders has the parched up magician to give, what abominable desire to gratify, that he commands our attendance? I wish that some one of power adequate to the task would destroy the Añaka chief.' These words excited my curiosity, and I determined to follow them, and see the person of whom they spoke. I rose, therefore, and cautiously followed the spirits to a spot, where I beheld a man decorated with ornaments made of human bones, stained all over with the ashes of burnt wood, and bearing a

braid of hair of a lightning hue, busily feeding with
his left hand a devouring fire with Sesamum and
mustard seeds. The goblin I had followed presented
himself with joined palms before the seer, and respectfully asked, what duty he was to perform. The stern
magician replied: 'Go, bring hither Kanakalekhá, the
daughter of Kardana, King of Kalinga.' The imp vanished, and in an instant re-appeared with the Princess, half dead with terror; she called out sobbing
with low broken tones on her friends and parents, till
the magician enraged seized her by her lovely tresses
escaped from the burst fillet in one hand, whilst he
raised with the other a sharpened sword, with an intention to strike off her head. This was not to be
witnessed. I sprang upon him, and in a moment,
wresting the sword from his grasp, struck off the vil-
lain's head, and tossed it with its clotted hair-band
into the hollow of a tree. The goblin who had brought
the maiden praised the act, and rejoiced at being liberated from a master as tyrannical as savage, one,
he said, who never slept himself, and never allowed
his slaves a moment's repose. In his gratitude, he
offered to perform whatever I should order, and requested me to appoint him some task. I commanded
him to carry the Princess back to the palace whence
he had conveyed her. As he was about to execute
this commission, the Princess, who had surveyed me
sometime askance, as she stood, as if abashed, beating
the ground with her feet, and whilst the cool drops
fell from her eyes upon her bosom, and a soft sigh

like the shaft of love escaped from her lips, entreated me in most melodious accents, not to desert her, nor, after rescuing her from the hands of fate, to leave her to perish in the depths of passion. She declared, she considered herself as my slave, begged that I would regard her as an atom of the lotus dust which was allowed to rest upon my feet, and finally proposed, if I could unite my destiny to hers, that I should accompany her to the palace, where I might live with her in security, as from the faithful attachment of her attendants I might be confident that our secret would never be divulged. It needed no persuasion to gain my assent, wounded as I felt myself by the shaft of the heart-born archer, and I desired the spirit, if he was inclined to do me a service, to carry us both wherever the Princess should direct. He bore us to the palace, where I resided for some time in uninterrupted delight.

When the vernal season had set in, and the air was scented with the breezes of Malaya, and musical with the Koil's song, the King of Kalinga went with all his household and attendants, to pass a fortnight on the sea shore, where the wind cooled by the spray of the ocean attempered the fierceness of the Solar rays. Here, whilst engaged in every kind of elegant diversion, the whole party was suddenly surprised, and carried off by the King of Andhra, Jayasinha, and a body of troops, which landed unexpectedly from the flotilla, with which he scoured the coasts.

When I heard of the captivity of the Princess, I

was overcome with despair, and vainly meditated on the means of effecting her recovery. At last a Brahman who came from Andhra reported that Jayasinha, who had at first intended to put Kardana to death, was diverted from his purpose by the charms of Kanakalekhú, whom he had espoused; that the Princess, however, was possessed by a spirit, who kept at bay the King, and could not be expelled by the skill of the physicians. This account inspired me with hope, and I determined to repair to Andhra immediately. Before going thither I went to the cemetery, where I took the old conjurer's tufted locks from the tree, and his patched robe, with which I disguised my person, and collecting some disciples about me I kept them in good humour with the presents we obtained from the villagers for the tricks we practised on their credulity. In a short time we approached Andhra. I took up my abode in a grove, on the edge of a spacious lake lovely with lotus flowers, and lively with flocks of wild geese. When I was settled here, my disciples spread themselves abroad, and reported my miraculous skill and universal knowledge, and asserted also that I could answer all questions, solve all secrets, and had all the Sástras upon the tip of my tongue. Full credit was given to these reports, and my fame at last reached the King, as the only person capable of expelling the demon who had taken possession of his bride. He accordingly came to visit me, and day after day presented himself before me, treating me with the most profound

reverence, and gratifying my followers with liberal
presents. After some time he stated he had something to say to me. I appeared to be lost in a fit of
abstract meditation, and suddenly as it were recovering said, 'Son, I know what you would say, and
worthy of you is the desire to possess that damsel
the pearl of maidens, and asylum of all excellences.
There are means of obtaining for you the Goddess
Lakshmí, who wears a necklace of a thousand streams,
and a girdle of the milky sea. This Yaksha cannot
bear that one should ever look on that lotus-eyed.
Have patience therefore for three days, I will do what
is necessary.' The King departed highly pleased; in
the mean time I laboured every night to form an excavation in the bank of the lake, opening into it on
the surface of the water, taking care to avoid observation; the outer mouth of this I covered with rubbish and stones, so that it was not observable, and
worshipped daily here with prostrations and red lotus
flowers the God of the thousand rays, who wears the
planets as a gorgeous necklace, the lion that destroys
the elephant of darkness, the witness of every act of
good or ill. When three days had elapsed, and the
blaze of light was veiled by the red peak of the
Western mountain, and the sun looked like the bosom
of twilight smeared with ruddy sandal, the King came,
and stood before me, hiding his tiara in the dust at
my feet. I said: 'When fate befriends us in this world,
fortune does not take up her abode with the indolent;
prosperity is in the hands of the active. This re-

servoir must be cleaned thoroughly by your most respectable servants who are to perform the task with zeal and faith; after that, you will bathe in it to-night, and at midnight, after bathing, float on the water with suppressed breath as long as you are able; on this certain sounds will be heard by your attendants as if the bank had fallen, and as if the wild geese mourned the wounds they received from the lotus stalks; that sound having subsided, you will come forth with dripping garments, and red eyes, and in a form in which you will be the delight of all eyes; the Yaksha will not be able to stand before you, and you will instantly become the master of the maiden's heart. With regard to thy bride, the earth, when you come forth you will find a circle in your hand that shall annihilate all your foes. If you wish, you may cause the lake to be carefully examined by those in whom you confide with nets, and surround it with your troops for thirty fathoms, for who can tell what device an enemy may employ?' I was confident these precautions would not detect the hole I had made, and was sure he would attend to my instructions out of his excessive passion. I then said to him: 'King, we have tarried here too long; it is not our custom to remain any time in one place. When your purposes are attained, you will not see me more: we could not depart till we had done something to serve you, having gleaned in your kingdom: now the motive of our stay ceases. Go home, bathe in fragrant water, perfume your person, put on a white garland according to your

state, make presents to the Brahmans, and at night,
illuminating the gloom with thousands of lamps, advance to the attainment of your desires.' The King
was penetrated with gratitude, but lamented my purposed disappearance, as invalidating the favour I had
bestowed. As my will was not to be disputed, however,
he took his leave, and went to prepare for his visit to
the lake. I went forth at night alone, and entered the
hole, where I listened attentively to what was going
forward. At midnight the King, having set guards all
round, approached, and having had the pool examined was satisfied of his security, and plunged into the
water. As he floated, with his hair loose, and breath
suppressed, I cast my scarf round his neck as a noose,
and drew him down, and pummelling him to death in
an instant, thrust his body into the hole; after which
I ascended from the water. The attendants were
astonished at the surprising change of the King's
person, but suspected nothing; and ascending the royal
elephant I returned with all the pomp and splendour
of sovereignty to the palace, where in an assembly of
all the Chiefs, collected by my order, I seated myself
on a throne glittering with gems, and observing that
they were struck by my altered appearance, I thus addressed the Court: 'Observe the power of the Saint
by whose will such a transformation of our person
has been wrought. Let the heads of infidels be now
bowed down in shame. Let all honour be paid to the
shrines of the Gods, and the song and dance proclaim

their praise, and let wealth be distributed to the poor, and dissipate all their cares.'

The Ministers exclaimed: glory to the Prince! may the ten regions own his power, and his fame eclipse that of all other Kings! Repeating these wishes, they left me to obey my orders. I now noticed one of my wife's most attached servants; calling her to me I desired her to look at me, and asked her if she had ever seen me before. As soon as she looked at me, she recognized me, and while tears of transport startled from her eyes, she restrained her emotions, and replied: 'If this is not the work of magic, I know whom I behold,' and then begged me to explain to her, how I came there. I told her the story, and sent her to impart it to our friends. Having thus set the captive King at liberty, I was united without hindrance or disguise to his daughter by his consent, and in a short time communicating the truth to my father-in-law I made over to him the Kingdom, and Kardana reigned over the united dominions of Andhra and Kalinga. His ancient alliance with the King of Anga brought him hither, and led to this delightful meeting.

Rájaváhana having complimented his friend on the success with which he had sustained the saintly character, and the miracles he had wrought, seriously praised his ingenuity and courage. Then turning to Viśruta, requested him to proceed with his story. He thus complied:

STORY OF VIŚRUTA.

Whilst travelling in search of our Prince, I came to the Vindhya forest, and one day encountered by the side of a well a boy about eight years of age, who was weeping bitterly, and in great distress; as soon as he saw me, he cried to me to help him to rescue his friend, and ancient guardian, who had fallen into the well. I immediately lent my aid, and with the stalks of long creepers we succeeded in extricating from the chasm a venerable old man, after which, knocking down with stones the fruit of some tall Likucha trees, and drawing up some water in a bamboo, we recruited our strength as we sat down together at the foot of a tree. When our hunger and thirst were appeased, I asked the old man to relate his story, with which request he readily complied.

Puṅyavarmá was the king of Vidarbha; he was the ornament of the race of Bhoja, an incarnation of the God of Justice, liberal, wise and affable, the protector of his people, and the terror of his foes. When he was numbered amongst the immortals, Anantavarmá succeeded. This Prince was graced with every excellence, but held the science of Politics (Daṅdaníti) in little esteem; one of his Ministers, Vasurakshaka, reproved him for this neglect, in terms more severe than respectful: 'Sire, he said, I observe that you are not inferior to your ancestors in merit, but, unfortunately, your mind is chiefly engrossed by the trivial amusements of music, dancing, painting and poetry.

The intellect, that is not exercised in worthy studies, is like gold that has not been refined in the fire; and the Prince, whose understanding is uncultivated, is unable to anticipate how far his own elevation may be surpassed by others, or to judge of the objects to be effected, or means by which they are to be attained. Being unfit to judge of affairs, his orders are disregarded by his own servants and by strangers, and the commands of a Prince personally contemned are but of little weight, even when the purpose be public good. This contempt of authority soon leads to general demoralisation, and the corruption of public morals is ruinous to a monarch both in this world and the next. Abandon, therefore, mere external accomplishments, and study those sciences by which your authority will be respected, and your power extended throughout the sea-encircled world.' When the King had heard this address, he said, "You counsel wisely; it shall be looked to," and then withdrew to the inner apartment, and communicated what had passed to Vihárabhadra. This man was one of the Ministers, and associates of the King's pleasures: he was well skilled in singing, dancing and playing, thoroughly acquainted with the town, of witty fancy, of licentious tongue; he had a peculiar tact in finding out a person's weak side, could excite laughter, and recommend scandal; was a Pańdit in craft, a Pilot of libertinism, and a Professor of all vicious arts. Having heard the Prince's account, he smiled, and thus proceeded:

"Sire, whenever by the favor of fate a person is blessed with prosperity, there will always be found men forward to assail and teaze them, without a why or a wherefore, merely that the rogues may accomplish their own designs; thus some advise him to place his hopes on the goods of the life to come, they shave his head, gird him with straw, clothe him in skins, smear his body with butter, and send him to sleep without his supper, in return for which they consent to take all his property: nay, there are others still more heinous, who are persuaded to relinquish children, wives, and even life. If the person these men have to deal with be too cunning or too covetous to let his goods slip out of his hands, they attack him in another manner. They profess they can convert a gross of cowries to a lac of gold, they can destroy our foes without weapons, and they can make this mortal body that of an Emperor, provided those they address are ready to follow the path they will shew. If any one ask what path is that, they will reply: 'There are four branches of royal knowledge, Trayí, Várta, Anvíkshikí, (Logic) and Daṅdaníti, (or Policy); of the three first the fruits, though important, are slowly matured: let them alone therefore, and study the Daṅdaníti, as recently composed by the learned Vishṅugupta in six thousand stanzas, for the use of the King Maurya. This, though but an epitome, will require its true time, but it must be studied.' So the King sets to work, and reads and listens, till he grows old. One Sástra is connected with another; unless all are read, nothing is known; so be it, be the time long or short; still read. Well, the student is accomplished; what has he learnt? The first lesson is, never trust to wife or child. The next is, so much water is required to boil so much rice, and so much fuel to heat that water; let them be measured before they are served out. When a King has risen, and has washed his mouth, he must devote the first watch of the day to the examination of the day's receipts and expenditure; he must not let a handful, nor half a handful escape him, and yet even whilst he hears, the superintendant will cheat him twice as much as ever. Chánakya has detailed forty modes of defrauding; but servants, by the force of their own ingenuity, multiply these a thousand fold. In the second watch the Prince, whose ear is to be assailed with the squabbles of contending subjects, lives a most wretched life; on that account let judges and others, who thrive by litigation, dispose of the suits as they please, consulting their own advantage, and leaving all the sin and shame to their sovereign. In the third watch he finds leisure to bathe and eat, and until his food is digested, he lives in dread of poison. In the fourth he rises to stretch forth his hands to receive gold. In the fifth he is plagued with the schemes of his Counsellors, who like indifferent and impartial umpires are agreed amongst themselves to pervert merits and defects, misstate the reports of the spies, misrepresent possibilities and impossibilities, and confound all distinctions of place and time, confirm the friends of them-

selves and others in their appointments, excite the
King's rage in private, and allay it in public, and
leave their master not to be depended upon. In the
sixth the Prince is attended by the ministers of his
amusements, and is his own master for an hour and
a half. In the seventh watch he reviews his troops.
In the eighth he has to listen to the ambitious projects
of his friends, the Generals. Evening is now arrived;
in the first watch of the night he must receive his secret emissaries, and appoint these ferocious fellows to
their work of fire, sword, and poison. In the second,
after eating, he must begin like a Vaida Brahman to
con his book. In the third he is sent to sleep with the
sounds of the trumpet. In the fourth and fifth he may
enjoy a three hour's slumber, if his poor thought-
labouring brain will allow him to repose. In the sixth
he must begin to prepare for the duties prescribed by
the Sástras. In the seventh he must consult with the
ministers regarding the dispatch of agents and emissaries; for these fellows, who get rich by presents on
both sides, and the privileges granted to their traffic,
will make work if there be none. In the eighth the
Purohita and others assembling must relate to the
King the troubled dreams they have had, the lowering
of the planets, and the unlucky omens they have not-
ed, to avert which threatened misfortunes propitiatory
rights must be performed. So be it; the essential of
all oblations is gold. Then there are those Brahmans,
each like Brahmá himself, if they will pray for the
King's prosperity, it will be augmented. They are

poor men, have large families, are constant in devotional rites, and ascetic practices; they have yet received no bounty; whatever is given to them will be paid with long life and good fortune and happiness fit for heaven: and thus having persuaded the King to entrust them with liberal gifts, these worthy Gentlemen pocket the purchase of Paradise themselves. Thus by a life of unremitted labour and care, and without a moment's enjoyment, night or day, why should a politic Prince think of becoming an Emperor, when his own little district is with difficulty preserved? If mistrust of all is to be entertained, what is the prosperity of a state? But in those things, for which Policy provides not, the world will take care of itself: the infant needs no instructions from the Sástras to drain the maternal breast. Abandon then all absurd restraints, and follow your own inclinations. These sages, who say that the senses are to be subdued, six foes to be shunned, the expedients of pacification, &c. to be perpetually observed, questions of peace and war to be eternally discussed, and not a moment's relaxation admitted—these hypocritical counsellors only lay in wait to carry off your wealth and spend it amongst their harlots. Who are those beggarly fellows that shew such stern virtue, and lay down the laws so sagely? Your Sukra, Angiras, Visáláksha, Báhudantiputra, Parásara and others. What foes did they subdue? what Sástras did they acknowledge? did they foresee all the consequences of what they did, when they began to do any thing? Those who are deeply read are often taken in by the ignorant. Is it not the act of the Gods, that you have rank, youth, beauty and wealth? why vex your thoughts with cares of state? are all unavailing, ten thousand elephants, three lac of horse, and countless infantry, and the treasuries filled with jewels and gold beyond your utmost expenditure, even if life be lengthened to ages? is all this insufficient, that there should be occasion to labour for more? The life of Mortals lasts but three or four days, and we should therefore make the most of it. Those are fools, who whilst they are accumulating perish, and reap no benefit from what they have collected. But enough of this. Leave the load of empire to those who have your confidence, and are adequate to the task, and do you enjoy your corporeal existence, amongst the lovely damsels of the palace, in the song, the dance, and the convivial cup, whilst the season serves."

So saying, he prostrated himself on the ground, and thus remained. The denizens of the harām smiled applause; the King was also pleased, and said, 'Rise, your advice is sound, I acknowledge you to be my Guru, and who shall disobey my Preceptor's counsels?' So saying, he raised him, and resumed his amusements with greater zest than ever.

The old minister who had given such unprofitable advice, was soon sensible of an alteration in the King's behaviour: he was never entrusted with any confidential matters; he was never addressed with a courteous smile; he was never asked after his family; he never received any friendly presents, nor was he invited to the inner apartments. On the other hand, he was employed on the most disagreable duties; his suggestions were listened to in silence, or treated with ridicule; his presents, however valuable, received with contempt; and his actual enemies were always secure of the King's favor. In this dilemma he considered what was to be done: he could not abandon a Prince to whom he was attached by the ties, which had long connected their mutual ancestors, and he was yet desirous of rendering the Prince sensible of the importance of neglecting the councils he had given. He concluded that if the Kingdom were in the hands of Vasantabhánu, the ruler of Asmaka, a Prince of policy, its present ruler would suffer a heavy calamity, and determined, that it were better to support the neglect he suffered, that he might be able to serve the King more effectually, when the occasion should arrive.

In this state of affairs, it happened that Chandrapálita, the son of Indrapálita, minister of the King of Asmaka, being professedly expelled his father's palace for his profligate conduct, but, in truth, being sent by the king of Asmaka, came to Vidarbha with a numerous train of dissolute retainers. An intimate friendship was soon formed between him and Vihárabhadra, and they concerted a plot for subverting the Government by leading the King on gradually to the commission of various vices. With this view Vihárabhadra confirmed the King in every idle purpose, and eulogised

each amusement that was casually suggested. When
hunting was the theme, he recommended it as calculated
to strengthen the constitution, improve the appetite,
and render the frame strong, active, hardy: he ex-
patiated also on the utility of pursuing the deer, and
the wild cattle to punish them for the mischief they
did for the crops, and of rendering the roads safe and
free, by destroying the wolf and the tiger: he described also the pleasure of beholding various regions, and
traversing the mountains, and the forests, but above
all he argued the importance of the satisfaction thus
afforded to such a Prince's subjects, as tenanted the
wilds, and the intimidation such proofs of an active
spirit necessarily impressed upon hostile chiefs.
When gambling was spoken of, he called the loss of
wealth that of so much trash, and was warm in his
praise of unbounded munificence. Play taught persons, he said, not to be elated with success, nor
depressed by ill luck, to acquire the power of confin-
ing their thoughts to a fixed object, to exercise
determined perseverance and unremitted acuteness in
its prosecution, disregard for persons and perils, and
a noble disdain of individual danger. With respect to
sexual gratification he maintained it was the end and
recompense of wealth and virtue, a perpetual school
for eloquence and ingenuity, in gaining the damsel
loved, preserving her when acquired, enjoying her
when preserved, pleasing her when possessed, pacify-
ing her when offended; but above all in the generation
of progeny it was the source of supreme felicity both

here and hereafter. Wine, he said, was the medicament of a variety of diseases, the preserver of perpetual youth, and the dissipation of every care: it befriended love, it appeased resentment, and delighted all with the undisguised language it inspired, it prolonged enjoyment, conferred beauty, and lavished grace; as it rendered man also insensible to fear and pain, it was highly serviceable in war. He further always recommended harshness of speech, and severity of punishment, as a King, he said, was not to imitate the apathy of a Saint, if he expected to govern mankind, and keep his foes in awe.

The ascendancy of Vihárabhadra was now fully established, and the King adopted all his lessons. The people, imitating their betters, threw off all restraint, and became universally licentious; their Governors neglected their duties; the channels of the royal revenue were closed, and those of the expenditure opened to all abandoned characters. Drinking parties were publicly held by the most eminent persons, and all castes openly abandoned their observances. The women of the city, despising all reserve, intrigued with their lovers openly, even before their husbands: then affrays became frequent, the weak were assaulted by the strong, the rich were plundered by the poor, neither life nor property was secure, and general dissatisfaction and murmuring prevailed.

When this disorganization had become general, the secret enemies of the King began to carry their plots into effect: if the King went a hunting, they contrived to destroy his people in great numbers: if his men entered a cave to chace the deer, they had dry sticks and leaves collected, and setting fire to them at the only entrance, stifled both men and beasts; others were compelled to charge the tigers, to whom they fell a sacrifice; some were sent away from the places, where water was at hand, to others at a distance, so that they sank under thirst and fatigue; some were snared in pits covered over with straw and leaves; some were destroyed by poisoned knives, used to take the thorns out of their feet, and many were purposely slain with arrows, which were apparently levelled at the scattering herds of deer. In like manner, the numerous agents of the King of Aśmaka were actively employed in the capital to promote affrays in all the public meetings, foment private enmities, abet or commit assassinations, and by spreading in every way death and terror amongst the citizens to undermine the power of Anantavarmá.

Vasantabhánu now excited Bhánuvarmá, a forest Prince, to make war with Anantavarmá; the latter, therefore, having resolved to march against him, commanded his dependent Princes to meet him with their forces on the borders of the kingdom. Vasantabhánu advanced immediately to join him with his chiefs, and was admitted for his alacrity to the particular friendship of the King. The other subsidiary chiefs arrived successively on the banks of the Narmadá. It happened that a principal chief, Avantideva, ruler of Kuntala, had a female dancer in his train, of such superior accomplishments, as to be an Urvasí on earth*. This girl attracted the notice of Anantavarmá, and being pleased with her he seized her, and carried her off. The King of Asmaka excited the Chief of Kuntala to revenge this insult: 'this haughty tyrant, he said, dares to violate our females, how much longer is it to be borne? You have five hundred elephants; I have one hundred; let us unite, and we shall, I know, be joined by Vírasena, Chief of Murala, Ekavíra of Richíka, Kumáragupta of Konkaṅa, Nágapála of Sásikya, alike impatient of this tyranny. The forest monarch is my friend; whilst he encounters the despot in front, let us assail him in the rear; we shall thus master his treasures and baggage.' The Konkaṅa Chief readily entered into the plot, and with presents and persuasions induced others to associate with them. On the next day Anantavarmá was the victim of the confederacy. Vasantabhánu, who had possessed himself of the treasure and animals, then proposed to the rest, that they should share amongst them in proportion to their effects and strength, professing to be content with any thing they should be disposed to give him. This led, as he expected, to a general dispute, which ended in the ruin of all, except the crafty proposer, who consequently appropriated the whole booty to himself, presenting a small portion of the spoil to his forest ally. He then established himself in the vacant government of Anantavarmá.

---

* [or, Kahmátalorvasí by name].

The old minister, Vasurakshita, having contrived
with the aid of some ancient servants of the King, to
rescue the youth Bháskaravarmá, and his younger
sister Manjuvádiní, along with the Queen Vasundhará,
their mother, effected his retreat, but died soon after
of grief. The Queen was conveyed with her children
to Máhishmatí, and consigned to Mitravarmá, her late
husband's brother by another mother, for protection.
He soon formed improper views on his Sister-in-law,
and was repulsed with severe reproof, but apprehend-
ing that in revenge he might oppose the elevation of
the young Prince to his late father's throne, or form
designs against his life, she requested me to convey
him secretly to some place where he would be in
safety, and let her know privately where we were,
when we had secured an asylum. I set off with the
Prince, and plunged into the Vindhya forests, to keep
clear of the emissaries of the King; fatigue and thirst
having oppressed my young charge, I was endeavouring to procure him some water from this well, when
overreaching myself I fell into it, and must have
perished but for your timely succour."

After repeating his thanks to me, I enquired the
family of the Princess, and found that she was the
daughter of Kusumadhanwá, King of Kośala, by Sá-
garadattá, daughter of Vaiśravaña, a merchant of
Pátaliputra: his mother and my father were therefore
descended from a common maternal grandfather;
Suśruta, my father, being the son of Sindhudatta.
Having, therefore, an additional motive to interest

myself in my young kinsman's behalf, I vowed I would
not be satisfied until I had replaced him on his throne
and overturned the usurpation of the King of Asmaka.
In the meanwhile it was a consideration, how we were
to appease our hunger.

At this moment appeared two deer, chased by a
huntsman, who expended three shafts on them in vain.
I made him give me the bow, and two remaining arrows, and presently shot the animals. One I gave to
the hunter, the other I skinned and cleaned, remov-
ing the entrails, and cutting off the feet, and spitting
it with a stake I roasted it at a fire. We made a
hearty meal upon the flesh. The forester was highly
pleased with my skill, and kept us company. I asked
him if he had heard any news from Máhishmatí. He replied, he was just come from thence, having been there
to sell a tiger-skin, and that great preparations were
making for the marriage of Prachaṅḍavarmá, the
younger brother of Chaṅḍavarmá with Manjuvádiní,
the daughter of Mitravarmá. On hearing this, I took
the old man aside, and thus spoke: 'I understand the
plot; by treating the daughter as his own child Mitravarmá wishes to gain the confidence of the mother,
and the person of the Prince, whom he may then put
to death. This must be prevented: go back to the
Queen, and tell her, what has chanced, in private.
Then in concert with her give out that the Prince has
been killed by a tiger: news that will be highly
pleasing to Mitravarmá, although he may assume the
outward semblance of distress. After this let the

Queen appear to be disposed to listen to his addresses, and so give a fresh impulse to his affections. Then let her rub her necklace with this poison, Vatsanága, and taking an opportunity strike him on the breast with it, saying, If I am faithful to my Lord, may this necklace be as a sword to thee. Let her then wash the necklace well with water and present it to the Princess, who by wearing in safety what was fatal to her uncle will prove the purity of the Queen. The Queen may then promise to give her daughter and the kingdom to Prachańdavarmá, and invite him for that purpose: in the mean time we will arrive in the disguise of Kápálika mendicants, receive alms from the Queen, and take our station in the cemetery. Let the Queen call the old ministers and chief citizens together, and tell them in private, the Goddess Vindhyavásiní has appeared to her in a dream, and assured her, that the Prince is still alive, having been carried off by the Goddess herself in the form of a tigress, in order more effectually to protect him; that in four days Prachańdavarmá will die. On the fifth her son will be found in company with another youth in a lonely temple of the Goddess on the bank of the Revá river, when his companion shall re-establish him in the Sovereignty, and you shall give him in recompense the hand of the Princess, but let her add this is to be a profound secret till we see what chances.'

The old Courtier approved of my plans, and leaving his charge to me set off to his mistress. In a few days the general rumour spread, that the marvellous faculty of conjugal fidelity had converted a necklace into a sword fatal to Mitravarmá, but otherwise innocuous, being actually worn by the young Princess. Upon this we presented ourselves, disguised as mendicants, to the Queen. When the Queen saw us, although she was prepared for our visit, she could scarcely suppress her emotions, as she spoke to us; she said, she had had a vision, the result of which was yet to be proved; but if her fate was favourable, she was no longer destitute.

Having made Manjuvádiní, whose looks evinced the interest she felt in me, pay her obeisance, she continued smilingly: "If your appearance is assumed, I shall lay my hands on this youth and detain him to-morrow." I cast an expressive glance on Manjuvádiní, and said, 'so may it be!' We then received alms, and went, having previously given a sign to Nálíjangha to follow us. When alone, I asked him where Prachańdavarmá was. He told me, that, being quite sure of the Sovereignty, he occupied the royal palace, where he amused himself with the company of dancers. The Prince I left in an empty temple, not far from the wall, and told him to keep close. I then entered the throng, and exhibiting as a dancer attracted the notice of Prachańdavarmá. When it was sun-set, I performed in various styles of dancing and singing, imitated different voices, and assumed different postures, as those of a scorpion, Makara, and fish. I then borrowed the daggers of the standers by, and fixing them in my body displayed

feats not easily described. Whilst thus engaged I
struck Prachańdavarmá, although he was at the
distance of twenty yards, on the breast with a knife,
exclaiming, May Vasantabhánu live a thousand years!
One of the attendants attempted to seize me, but I
shook him off senseless; then looking disdainfully on
the frightened crowd I leaped over a wall of the
height of two men, and then plunged into a neighbouring grove, whilst Nálíjangha following me levelled
the marks of my footsteps. I continued my flight so
as to beguile pursuit, and at last leaping the ditch, got
safe out of the palace, and came to the temple where
I had left my young charge, resuming my mendicant
garb. We then set out again, and having passed
through the crowds collected about the palace gate,
with difficulty reached the cemetery. In the temple
of Durgá, which stood there, I had formerly practised
a small cavity leading from the outside to below the
pedestal of the image, and concealed the outer entrance with a large slab of stone, which I had taken
out of a part of the wall where it was loose. At midnight, having put on suitable dresses gorgeous with
costly gems, brought us by a confidential messenger
from the Queen, we entered the chasm. The Queen
having caused the funeral ceremonies for Prachańdavarmá to be performed, and spread the report that
his death had been contrived by the ruler of Aśmaka,
came the next day, as had been concerted, to the
temple and worshipped the Goddess, throwing open

the shrine to all people, that they might satisfy themselves it was occupied. After which they retired, closing the door, but keeping near the building, and on the outside awaited the results, whilst the drums beat loudly. On this I lifted up the image, and its iron base upon my head (no easy labour), and setting it on one side, issued forth with the Prince. I then replaced the image as before, and the doors being again opened, we were accordingly found in the temple to the great delight and astonishment of the people. I immediately addressed them and said, 'Hear and believe what the Goddess declares to you through me. The tiger that bore off the Prince was myself, and I have adopted him as my son; receive him, and dread my power; respect me as his protector, and acknowledge my protection by giving me his sister.' They all exclaimed with delight: The offspring of the race of Bhoja is given us by the Goddess for a ruler! No words could express the joy of the Queen, who made me happy that day with the hand of her daughter. I took care to fill our hiding place in the temple, and as no trace of our contrivance was discovered, the people believed me to be some superhuman personage, and were not therefore to be diverted from respect to me by any malignant divinations or underhand contrivances. The Prince was generally known as Áryáputra, or the son of the Goddess. In order to enable him to complete his political studies, I conducted the affairs of state. Government is an arduous

matter; it has three principles, Council, Authority
and Activity. These mutually assisting each other
dispatch all affairs; Council determines objects,
Authority commences, and Activity effects their
attainment. Policy is a tree, of which Council is
the root, Authority the stem, and Activity the
main branch, the seventy-two Prakŕitis are the
leaves, the six qualities of royalty the blossoms,
Power and Success the flowers and the fruit. Let
this shade protect the King. There was a person at
Court, named Áryaketu, who had been the minister of
Mitravarmá; he was a skilful counsellor, and well-
disposed to the Queen, being from the same country,
Kośala. It was very desirable to secure his attachment, and I therefore taught Nálíjangha to say to him
thus, as it were, in confidence: 'Tell me, wise Sir,
who is this man of marvel that appropriates the prosperity of the state? shall this snake be suffered to
swallow the Prince, or compelled to re-gorge him?'
The answer of Áryaketu my agent was to bring to
me, and this and similar conversations he held with
him, but in vain. The other replied, "Speak not in
this manner. The qualities of this person are most
admirable, and I equally venerate his prudence and
amenity, his prowess and skill. When the kingdom
shall be in a state of security, and its inveterate foes
appeased or eradicated, I have no doubt we shall see
the young Prince duly installed in his father's throne,
and the Prince of Aśmaka, wise as he thinks himself,

deprived of his possessions." Having thus ascertained the friendly disposition of Áryaketu, I entered into an intimate confederacy with him, and attached to myself him, and all his friends, men of fidelity and skill, by whose assistance I governed all the Kingdom, and maintained justice and religion within its boundaries.

IX.

ON THE ART OF WAR AS KNOWN TO THE HINDUS.

(Read before the R. As. Society, June 17, 1849.)

However unsuccessful in their contests with foreign invaders, the inferiority of the Hindus in the art of war arose from no want of cultivation of it as a science, and in theory, though not in practice, they were probably superior to those by whom they were overcome.

A supplementary portion of the sacred institutes of the Hindus, or the Vedas, was appropriated to the subject of military science under the appellation of *Dhanur-veda*, the Veda or institutes of Archery. The original treatise so termed is not known to exist, and is probably lost. A short tract entitled Dhanur-veda in Mr. Colebrooke's collection is a modern composition, and is of little value: a more detailed treatise and one much more ancient occupies several chapters of the *Agni Purána*, as that Purána is met with in some parts of Upper India. The chapters do not occur in either of two copies of the Purána in the India House Library. They have a place in a copy in my possession*; but unfortunately the MS. is mutilated and incorrect in many passages of the chapters on the military art, and the information derivable from the work is in most respects fragmentary and uncertain: from these two sources however, from original Lexicons, and from incidental notices in the heroic poems, especially the Mahábhárata, a variety of interesting particulars of the ancient art of war amongst the Hindus may be gleaned.

The use of the term *Dhanush*, or in composition Dhanur (as Dhanur Veda), as synonymous with arms in general is at once characteristic of Hindu warfare. The *bow* was the weapon on which they principally depended. So also the words Dhánushka and Dhanwin, signifying literally a bowman, are always used to denote a warrior or soldier. Hence perhaps one of the elements of Indian inferiority in the field, as the arrow, however formidable as a missile, was but a feeble instrument in close combat, and its use was calculated to impair the courage of the combatant by habituating him to shun rather than to seek the contiguity of his foeman. Although the favourite weapon however, it was by no means exclusively employed, and other missiles, as the discus, short iron clubs and javelins, were in general use. The troops were armed also with swords, maces, battle-axes and spears, and

* (Aufrecht, Catal. Codd. MSS., I. p. 7.)

were defended from the weapons of the enemy by shields, helmets, quilted jackets or iron armour, and coats of mail.

According to the best authorities, the component parts of an Indian army were four: Elephants, chariots, cavalry, and infantry.

These were arranged in bodies of various strength, but theoretically at least in always the same proportion. The smallest division was termed a *Patti* and consisted of one elephant, one chariot, three horse and five foot. The next, the *Senámukha*, was formed of three elephants, three cars, nine horse and fifteen foot. The larger bodies, companies, regiments, brigades, and armies, were made up in the same ratio, each component part becoming successively of thrice the strength of that which belonged to the preceding aggregate. The whole of the specifications are the following:

	Elephant.	Chariot.	Horse.	Foot.
Patti	1	1	3	5
Senámukha	3	3	9	15
Gulma	9	9	27	45
Gaṅa	27	27	81	135
Váhiní	81	81	243	405
Pritaná	243	243	729	1215
Chamú	729	729	2187	3645
Anikiní	2187	2187	6561	10935

An *Akshauhiní*, or complete army, comprised ten Anikinis, or 21,870 elephants, as many chariots, 65,610 horse and 109,350 foot. It is asserted in the

Mahábhárata that eighteen Akshauhinís were destroyed in the series of battles fought in the country between Hástinapura and Indraprastha, or the upper part of the Doáb near Delhi, between the sons of Pándu and their kinsmen of the race of Kuru for the sovereignty of India.

Independently of the extravagant numbers assigned to the larger divisions, it is obvious that armies so composed can have existed only in imagination, and that thousands and tens of thousands of elephants could never have been brought at one time into action. In smaller bodies the proportion may have been observed, and three horsemen and five footmen may have been the complement of a single elephant or chariot as long as the corps did not exceed the strength of the *Gulma*. As the companies increased, the proportion must have been altered. In one place in the Agni Puráña it is enjoined that fifteen foot soldiers should be attached to each elephant, and this is a more likely proportion than five. Even then we cannot admit the possibility of the ratio, as the numbers of cars and elephants augmented, or in fact of the numbers themselves. No army was ever accompanied by 20000 elephants, and even a twentieth part were questionable, although, as we know from the Greek historians of Alexander's expedition, the Indian armies did present a formidable array of these powerful animals: according to one account there were two hundred in the army of Porus. The enumeration however is valuable as presenting characteristic features of Hindu warfare and expressing the importance in their system of elephants and chariots as the most essential portions of the army.

Notwithstanding the prominence thus given to these two arms, there is a great and characteristic distinction in their application. It is remarkable that in the heroic poems a hero is very rarely represented riding on an elephant, and never on a horse: his appropriate station is the chariot, and hence a leader and a warrior of note is most commonly designated as a *Rathin*, a rider in a car, or an *Atiratha* or a *Mahárathá*, a rider in a great car. There are however some instances of a chieftain's moving through the army upon an elephant or even going to battle so mounted, and the Grecian accounts of Porus on his elephant are therefore not without warrant. Thus Duryodhana in the first encounter with the Pāṅdavas rides through his own ranks on an elephant[*]. Bhagadatta, Vinda and Anuvinda, three of his allies, are described in the review of his army as riding on elephants. Bhíshma, praising his grandnephews Duryodhana and the rest, says of them that they are able to fight equally well on an elephant's shoulders or the floor of a chariot: and in the first day's battle Uttara, the son of Virāṭa, mounted on an elephant, attacks king Śalya in his chariot. The elephant kills the horses, but Śalya launches a javelin at Uttara and kills him. It would seem as if the warrior who fought on an elephant also guided him: for it is said by the poet that, as Uttara

---

[*] (Mahābhārata, Bhīshma Parva [v. 747]).

fell, he quitted hold of both javelin and goad,—he fell pramuktánkuśatomara. The *ankuśa* is the instrument still used to direct the elephant's course.

The more usual riders on elephants were soldiers of a lower grade, several of whom were placed on the animal's back in a kind of chair or howdah, and were armed with bows and arrows and other missiles. According to Megasthenes, as quoted by Strabo*, each Indian elephant carried three archers besides the driver, and his account agrees well enough with what may be inferred from the incidental notices of Sanskrit writers. Besides the detriment inflicted by the archers on the enemy, the especial service of the elephants was to act as pioneers upon a march, clearing away such impediments as small trees and shrubs, and in battle to oppose the elephants of the enemy and break in upon and scatter his array.

The *chariot* was in a still greater degree than the elephant characteristic of Indian warfare; but, as above observed, it was the especial vehicle of the chiefs and leaders. That it bore a large proportion to the whole force is confirmed by *classical* authority, as according to Curtius** there were three hundred chariots in the first line of Porus's battle. He says that each chariot held six men, two bearing shields, two bowmen, and two armed drivers. This however does not seem to be correct. Other classical authorities state the

---

* [XV, 1, 52. Lassen, Ind. Alt., III, 332.]
** [XIII, 13. Lassen, I. I., II. 147.]

number of persons carried by the war-car at three, or two warriors and the driver. This may have been occasionally the case, but in general, according to the heroic poems, there were in the Hindu chariot as in the Grecian at the siege of Troy but two individuals, the combatant and his charioteer. The latter also as amongst the Greeks was no ordinary person: he was a warrior and at least the confidential attendant and friend of the chief. On particular occasions heroes of renown did not disdain to take the reins in company with an equal. Thus Karńa, the prince of Anga, drives the car of Śalya, king of Madra, and Kŕishńa acts as the charioteer of his friend Arjuna. The car was drawn by two horses in general, but sometimes by four, and one object of attack seems to have been the destruction of the horses, compelling the rider to quit his car and fight on foot. This however he frequently did without being so compelled, whenever apparently his arrows and darts failed, and he had recourse to his sword, axe or mace. The facility with which this is effected shews that the chariot was open either all round or behind and at no great elevation above the ground. There is otherwise no description of its form, although many of its parts are specified in lexicons. One part of its decorations was the banner of the chief, a flag with a device peculiar to the individual. Thus Arjuna's banner bore the monkey Hanumán, Bhíshma's a palm tree, Duryodhana's a serpent, Kŕipa's a bull.—The car was not armed in any way, as were those of the Persians and

Scythians with scythes. The use of war chariots and the mode of employing them seems to have been common to the Asiatic Greeks, the Egyptians and the Hindus, and in early times at least neither of these nations was equestrian. The chariot, if ever employed by the European Greeks, amongst whom it would have been of little advantage owing to the nature of the country, soon fell into disuse. On the level plain of Egypt it continued much later, and in this as well as in the importance attached to the bow there is an evident resemblance between the Egyptians and Hindus. At the same time it is obvious that no intercourse could have subsisted between them, or the former would have learnt from the latter the management of the elephant. The animal was close at hand in the wilds of Africa, but no delineation of it, tame or wild, in peace or war, appears in the numerous representations which have been discovered of battles, sieges or processions. As with the Greeks so with the Hindus the horse came to supersede the chariot. There is no mention of the latter in the accounts given by Mohammedan writers of their first engagements with the Hindus. Its use is characteristic of antiquity, and its exchange for the horse may not improbably be ascribed in some degree to the infusion of Scythian tribes and manners from the west about the commencement of our era.

Whatever was the distribution of the combatants, it does not appear that there was much difference in the weapons which they wielded. The bow and arrow, the mace, the javelin, a club either made of iron altogether or in part, the sword and shield seem to have been the principal arms of the chiefs, whilst in addition to these spears and axes of different forms and missiles of various kinds were employed by their followers and occasionally by themselves. Detailed descriptions of some of these weapons are given in the Dhanur-veda, Agni Puráńa and commentaries on the Amarakosha and Mahábhárata. They do not always agree, but they sometimes afford curious particulars.

Thus of *Bows* it is said that they may be made of metal, horn or wood, the bowstring of cord made from hemp, flax, the pát or lute plant, from the fibres of bark, or from animal membrane, especially of the deer, buffalo or ox. The kinds of horn preferred are those of the buffalo and Rauhisha, a sort of deer. Different kinds of wood, whether of trees or twining plants, are used; but the best bows are constructed of the Bambu, cut at the end of autumn. The length of a bow varies from one as long as a man's arm to one of four cubits or six feet: the latter is declared to be the best. The *arrows* also vary in length from three feet to five or six: they should be smooth and tough, be made of wood or of bambus, feathered at the bulk and tipped at the head with steel points variously shaped, needle or lance-pointed, semicircular, dentiform, double-edged or jagged like a saw: they should be greased or anointed with various substances to facilitate their action, but no notice of poisoned arrows as used in battle occurs. Such arrows were sometimes employed in the chase. Besides the arrows commonly used the Dhanur-veda describes two other kinds, the Náracha entirely of iron, and the Nálika made of a reed. The latter was intended for a long flight and is therefore said to be most appropriately used for sieges. Curtius perhaps alludes to the Náracha when he says, some of the Indian archers shot with arrows which were too heavy to be very manageable. The arrows were carried in a quiver on the right hip. Part of the archery practice of the Hindus consisted in shooting a number of arrows at once, from four to nine at a time.

Swords were of various shapes and sizes. The best are said to be brought from countries with which we are unacquainted, that is, if the names be rightly given, from Kháli Vattara and Súryavaka. Those made in Bengal and Behar are commended as tough and capable of taking a fine edge. Those are fabricated of the best steel which ring sharply on being struck. The best-sized sword is one fifty fingers long, having the handle guarded by an iron netting: this must have been a two-handed weapon.

The technical classification of weapons is most usually fivefold,—or 1. Missiles thrown with an instrument or engine, *Yantramukta*, as arrows from bows; 2. Missiles hurled by hand, *Hasta-mukta*,— stones, clubs, darts, discuses; 3. Weapons which may be thrown or not, *Muktámukta*, javelins, tridents, spears, clubs; 4. Those which are not thrown, *Amukta*, swords, axes, maces;—and 5. Natural weapons, as the fists. In the commentaries on Lexicons and Poems we have explanations of a variety of the individual weapons composing these classes; but their descriptions do not always agree. Thus the commentators on Amara call the *Bhindipála* a short arrow either cast with the hand or blown through a tube, or it is a short club hurled by the hand; the commentator on the Mahábhárata says, it is the instrument called by the Mahrattas Gophan, which is interpreted a sling. The former identify the *Tomara* with the Savali, which in Hindi and Bengali is the name of an iron bar or crow; the latter says it is a dart with a long stick or a javelin, and its use, as noticed in the text, is most in accordance with his explanation. According to him also the *Náracha* is a large arrow with a broad blade, but the others agree in asserting that it is an arrow entirely of iron. One of the commentators on Amara calls the *Prása* a Chákí, a sort of quoit or discus still thrown by the Sikhs; the rest generally explain it by the terms konch, kunta and neza, which imply a lance or spear; the commentator on the Mahábhárata calls it the Saintí, a javelin with a string fastened to it, so as to recover it after it has been cast. These differences indicate the imperfect acquaintance possessed by later writers amongst the Hindus with the weapons familiar to their forefathers, and the same inference may be drawn from their vague and imperfect notices of other implements mentioned in the heroic poems, as the *Rishti* said to be a short dart thrown by the hand, the

Paṭṭiśa, which appears to have been a kind of bill or halberd; the *Kṛipáṇa* and *Kshepaṇi* are missiles, but of what nature has not been ascertained. The *Páśa*, which is specified in the Agni Puráṇa amongst military weapons, is any sort of noose or binding, and the *Yantra*, which has also a place in the same enumeration, denotes any sort of machine, implement or engine.

A question of great historical interest is the knowledge possessed by the Hindus in early ages of any such combustible as gunpowder or of its application to military purposes. It is one to which no satisfactory answer can be yet given: our research into Hindu antiquity is yet too superficial, our acquaintance with Hindu literature and science too imperfect to warrant our replying in the negative, because we have not yet found any positive mention of such an article in the passages which have been consulted. The Hindus, as we find from their medical writings, were perfectly well acquainted with the constituents of gunpowder—sulphur, charcoal and saltpetre,—and had them all at hand in great abundance. It is very unlikely that they should not have discovered their inflammability either singly or in combination. To this inference a priori may be added that drawn from positive proofs, that the use of fire as a weapon of combat was a familiar idea, as it is constantly described in the heroic poems. The *Agni-astra* or Fire-arm is, it is true, the element itself wielded by some superhuman hero or demigod, who exercises a miraculous command over fire; but the notion might have originated in some mere mortal device for the production of flame and smoke. *Rockets* appear to be of Indian invention and had long been used in native armies when Europeans came first in contact with them: whether they are mentioned by Sanskrit authorities, has yet to be determined. It is commonly said by the Paṇḍits that the Rocket is intended by the *Śataghnī*, a weapon named by the poets. The term means the destroyer of hundreds; according to some explanations it was a ball of stone or metal studded with spikes; but if so, it could scarcely have been thrown by hand[*]. Amongst ordinary weapons again one is named the *Vajra*, the thunderbolt, and these specifications seem to denote the employment of some explosive projectile, which could not have been in use except by the agency of something like gunpowder in its properties. That the Hindus had something like Greek fire is also rendered probable by Ctesias who describes their employing a particular kind of inflammable oil for the purpose of setting hostile towns and forts on fire[**].

The subject of *Tactics* was not omitted in Hindu military science, and a great variety of modes of array are mentioned in the Agni Purāṇa and the heroic poems. They are not described however sufficiently in detail to give us very precise ideas of their several dispositions.

---

[*] [Cf. Śabdakalpadruma s. v., and Note II. "On the early use of gunpowder in India", in Sir H. Elliot's Index to the Historians of Muhammedan India. Calcutta: 1849, especially p. 358 ff.]

[**] [Sir H. Elliot. l. l., p. 370 ff. Lassen, Ind. Alt., II, 641 f.]

The component divisions of an army in array are variously enumerated as three, four, or seven. In the first we have the *Uras*, the breast or centre, the *Kakshas*, the flanks, and the *Pakshas*, literally as with ourselves—the wings. The second classification adds to these the *Pratigraha*, the reserve. In the larger number* we have also the *Koti*, a van or body in advance, the *Madhya* or middle, a second line or centre behind the breast, and the *Prishtha*, the back, a third line between the Madhya and the reserve. These divisions however are considered to be more than ordinarily necessary, and Vrihaspati, an old authority on all matters of regal administration, civil or military, whose works are no longer extant, is quoted in the Agni Puráńa as holding the four-fold disposition to be sufficient for all useful purposes.

Of the *order of march* we have these particulars in the Agni Puráńa: "After due deliberation with his council the king or general should set forth with his elephants, chariots, cavalry, infantry, and treasure. Whenever unusual danger is apprehended in consequence of having to traverse rivers, mountains or forests, or to pass by fortified posts, the army should proceed in order of battle. The scouts with a strong vanguard should lead the way. The king with his women, his baggage and his treasure should be stationed in the centre, supported immediately by the elephants; on the right and left of them should move

---

* [Kámandaki, XIX. 30.]

the chariots, and the horse should cover the extreme flanks. The forest or irregular bands and auxiliaries should bring up the rear. The order is to be diversified according to the direction from which an attack may be anticipated."

"When the contending parties are fairly matched, hostilities should be carried on openly and honourably. If one be much weaker than the other, he may allowably have recourse to stratagems, such as making a show of battle in the front of the enemy whilst the real assault is covertly directed against his rear, or as falling upon the rear of an enemy with one part of the army whilst another previously placed in ambuscade assails the van during the confusion. It is also permitted to take advantage of the ground, and to attack hostile troops whilst embarrassed in a defile or in a broken country, or to commence an action with inferior troops, so as to exhaust the enemy's strength, and then to fall upon him with fresh forces of the best description, or to surprise the enemy's camp when the troops are unprepared or asleep."

"The especial offices of the elephants are, on a march to make way through thickets in an attack on fortified places, to force open the gateways or pull down palisades, and in action to lead the charge, especially against compact divisions. The drivers of the chariots are also to head a charge and penetrate through the enemy's line, so that the horse and foot may follow. They are also intended to bear off the wounded from the field and to afford means of escape to the chiefs if defeated. They bear the bravest and most illustrious warriors to every part of the field, where their presence is most needed, and they are to drive through and disorder the enemy's ranks in every direction."

"A *commander in chief* should be careful to select his position according to the composition of his forces. Plains of considerable extent and of tolerably level surface are best adapted for the evolutions of both infantry and cavalry. If intersected by hills, it is not material, provided they be of no great elevation and inequality. Level ground free from trees, bricks, stones and mud is best suited to chariots. Elephants act to advantage in a similar situation, but brushwood and thicket, if consisting of only small trees and creepers, are no obstructions to them. In every case care should be taken to provide ample space for the movements of the different bodies, and that neither en masse nor individually the troops be inconveniently crowded."

"The general of an army is to remain in rear of his forces, attended by his chief officers and guarded by a strong reserve. He is never to expose himself to personal danger, for the general is the soul of the army, and deprived of him it cannot escape destruction."

The array of forces in action is termed generally *Vyúha*. The different kinds of array are sufficiently numerous: they are designated by appellations having reference to their supposed figures; but the terms are for the most part too fanciful to express any very definite signification. In the Amara Kosha* it is said, the Vyúhas are the Daṅda and others. Daṅda, literally a stick or staff, is explained to signify the army in line. The commentator Ráya Mukuṭa particularises three of the other Vyúhas, the *Bhoga* or column, the *Mańdala* or hollow circle, and the *Asanhata* or detached arrangement of the different parts of the force, the elephants, cars, horse and foot severally by themselves. Each of these Vyúhas is subdivided into many modifications: there are seventeen varieties of the Daṅda, five of the Bhoga, and several of both the Mańdala and Asanhata. Their names are enumerated in the Agni Puráṅa, and an attempt is made to describe a few of them, but the description is rarely intelligible without plans or diagrams; indeed details of this nature must almost always be indistinct, even when minutely particularised. In the authority referred to however the particulars are few and by no means precise. Some Vyúhas are named from their object. Thus the *Madhyabhedi* is intended to break the centre of the enemy's array, the *Antarbhedi* to penetrate between its divisions. Most commonly however the nomenclature is derived from a supposed resemblance of the array to some real or imaginary figure. Thus the *Makaravyúha* is the army drawn up like the Makara, a fabulous marine monster; the *Śyenavyúha*

---

* [II, 8, 2, 47; and Kámandaki XIX, 41--43, with the commentary.]

is the array in the form of a hawk or eagle with its wings spread. In the *Sakatavyúha* the army is arranged in the shape of a waggon, and in the *Arddhachandra* in that of a half moon; *Sarvatobhadra* is the hollow square or disposition of the troops facing every way outwards, and *Gomútrika* is said to be a diagonal disposition, a sort of arrangement in echellon*. In short, as the original observes, the Vyúha should assume every possible shape which may be best fitted to oppose the disposition and strength of the hostile force. Some further and perhaps more particular illustration of this subject may be derived from the heroic poems in their descriptions of battles. Thus in the Mahábhárata** in the first encounter of the opposing armies Yudhishthira, in consequence of finding himself very inferior in numbers to the Kurus, suggests to his brother Arjuna the adoption of the *Súchímukha*, the needle-pointed array. Arjuna recommends the *Vajra* or thunderbolt array for the same reason. It is easy to conceive what is meant by either, especially as the purport of the Pándavas is offensive rather than defensive: a narrow front or close column is to be formed with a view to break the enemy's line. Accordingly Duryodhana, the commander of the Kurus, is apprehensive of being attacked, and arranges his army in the *Abhedya*—the impenetrable— array, in which the different parts of the army, or the

---

* [See the commentary on Kámand. XIX, 48 ff.]
** [VI, 599, 729.]

foot, horse, cars and elephants, are so intermingled as to support each other. There are many such incidental notices in the Mahábhárata, but in a work of such extent it would be a task of much time and trouble to collect them.

Nothing is said in the Agni Puráṅa of the *encampment* of an army, but that this subject received due attention appears from various passages in the heroic poems. With one of these this imperfect notice of Hindu military science may be concluded. It is taken from the Udyoga Parva of the Mahábhárata*.

"Then Yudhishthira led the army to a level and fertile spot abounding with fodder and fuel, taking care not to trespass in the march upon funeral grounds, temples, places of pilgrimage or the hermitages of holy men, and commanded his troops to halt on a place that was commodious, agreeable and well watered. After a short interval of repose the prince went forth, followed by many of his leaders and attended by a strong detachment, and having driven back the hostile squadrons of Dhritaráshtra, examined the ground in every direction carefully, assisted by Krishńa. In obedience to his orders Dhrishṭadyumna, the son of Parvata, Sátyaki, the skilled in chariots, and the hero Yuyudhána caused the ground to be measured for the site of the encampment, and carrying it on one side along the sacred river of Kurukshetra, the Hiranvatí, which was flowing with

---

* [vv. 5170—87. See also Kámandakíya nítis., ch. 16.]

pure and salubrious waters undefiled by mud and sand, Keśava directed a deep ditch to be dug on the other sides for the greater security of the camp. The army was then marched into the inclosed space and arranged agreeably to the precepts which regulate the practice of encampment. Whatever it was proper to do on such occasion Keśava commanded to be executed. Store of fire-wood and of all necessaries for eating and drinking was provided. Large and handsome huts like the spacious vehicles of the gods were erected severally for the chiefs. Artificers dexterous in various handicrafts were there in numbers, and skilful Surgeons were in attendance, well furnished with the means of healing wounds. Quantities of honey and ghee and resin and fuel and piles of bows and arrows and armour were heaped up like mountains, and Yudhishthira took care that in every tent fodder, fuel and water should be abundantly provided. Great engines of war, iron shafts, spears, axes, bows, arrows, quivers and elephants like mountains armed with spikes and covered with housings of iron mail were beheld in the camp by hundreds and thousands. When the Páńdavas knew that their friends had taken up their respective quarters, they moved with their own divisions to their several stations; and the Kings their allies, in order to secure their triumph observed in their encampment the strict rules of self-denial, liberality and religion."

X.

THE MEGHA DÚTA

OR

CLOUD MESSENGER:

A Poem in the Sanskrit language, by Kálidása.

Translated into English verse, with notes and Illustrations.

Preface to the second edition. London: 1843.

THE Translation of the Megha Dúta was the first attempt made by me to interest European readers in the results of my Sanskrit studies. It has the imperfections of a juvenile work; and the Translator has no doubt sometimes not only departed from his original further than was necessary, but further than was justifiable; and has occasionally mistaken its meaning. Some of the mistakes I have corrected; and in some instances have altered the arrangement of the lines, so as to adhere more nearly to the order of the original. I have not cared, however, to render the version much closer or more faithful; as even had I been inclined to take the trouble, the circumstance of the book becoming a class-book would have deterred me from the attempt: but it is very possible, that whatever poetical fidelity the version may possess, might have been injured by verbal approximation, and that the attempt to give a more literal likeness of the poem of Kálidása would only have impaired the similitude of its expression.

I have gone over the Notes with more attention, and have continued the information they convey to the present time. I have added some, and omitted some, especially those which were designed to place the parallel passages of European poets in contiguity with the language and sentiments of the Indian bard. Such analogies will readily suggest themselves to well-educated minds; and it cannot be necessary to endeavour to prove to them, that Imagination, Feeling, and Taste, are not exclusively the products of the Western Hemisphere.

The Megha Dúta, or Cloud Messenger, is recommended to a Student of Sanskrit by its style and by its subject. The style is somewhat difficult, but the difficulty arises from no faults of conception or construction. There must, of course, be some unfamiliar imagery, some figures of purely local associations, in every foreign—in every Oriental composition; but, with a few possible exceptions, the Megha Dúta contains no ideas that may not be readily apprehended by European intellect. It has no miserable conceits, no enigmatical puzzles, which bewilder a poetic reader, and overwhelm a prosaic one with despair; and which, when the riddle is solved, offer no compensation for the labour of solution. The language, although remarkable for the richness of its compounds, is not disfigured by their extravagance: the order of the sentences is in general the natural one, with no more violent inversion than is indispensable for the convenience of the rhythm. The metre combines melody and dignity in a very extraordinary manner; and will bear an advantageous comparison, in both respects, with the best specimens of uniform verse in the poetry of any language, living or dead.

The subject of the poem is simple and ingenious: a Yaksha, a divinity of an inferior order, an attendant upon the god of riches, Kuvera, and one of a class which, as it appears from the poem, is characterized by a benevolent spirit, a gentle temper, and an affectionate disposition, has incurred the displeasure of his sovereign, and has been condemned by him to a twelvemonths' exile from his home. In the solitary but sacred forest in which he spends the period of his banishment, the Yaksha's most urgent care is to find an opportunity of conveying intelligence and consolation to his wife; and, in the wildness of his grief, he fancies that he discovers a friendly messenger in a cloud*—one of those noble masses which seem almost

---

* [Wilson's transl. of Málatímádhava, Calc. ed., p. 110 f., Sanskrit text, p. 150 f.]

instinct with life, as they traverse a tropical sky in the commencement of the Monsoon, and move with slow and solemn progression from the equatorial ocean to the snows of the Himálaya. In the spirit of this bold but not unnatural personification, the Yaksha addresses the Cloud, and entrusts to it the message he yearns to despatch to the absent object of his attachment. He describes the direction in which the Cloud is to travel—one marked out for it, indeed, by the eternal laws of nature; and takes this opportunity of alluding to the most important scenes of Hindu mythology and tradition;—not with the dulness of prosaic detail, but with that true poetic pencil which, by a few happy touches, brings the subject of the description vividly before the mind's eye. Arrived at the end of the journey, the condition of his beloved wife is the theme of the exile's anticipations, and is dwelt upon with equal delicacy and truth; and the poem terminates with the message that is intended to assuage her grief and animate her hopes. The whole of this part of the composition is distinguished by the graceful expression of natural and amiable feelings, and cannot fail to leave a favourable impression of the national character; whilst the merely descriptive portion introduces the student to a knowledge of a variety of objects of local, traditional, and mythological value, with which it is his duty to become familiar; and which he will when in India contemplate with additional interest and pleasure, from his previous acquaintance with the verses of Kálidása.

Little is known of the literary history of the Megha Dúta. It is, by common assent, attributed to Kálidása, a celebrated poet, who is reputed to have been one of the ornaments of the Court of Vikramáditya, king of Ujjayiní, whose reign, used as a chronological epoch by the Hindus, is placed 56 years before the Christian æra. There is no reason to dispute the truth of these traditions[*]. The poem undoubtedly belongs to a classical period of Hindu Literature; and that period, there is reason to believe, did not long survive the first centuries of Christianity. At a later date, the Poets were men of more scholarship than imagination, and substituted an overwrought display of the powers of the language for the unforced utterance of the dictates of the feeling or the fancy. This is not the case with the Megha Dúta; and although it is rather of a more sustained elevation of language than other works attributed to the same author, particularly his dramatic compositions, Śakuntalá, and Vikrama and Urvaśí, yet there is a community of character in them, a similar fidelity to nature, a like delicacy and tenderness of feeling, and the same felicity of description, gracefulness of imagery, and elegance of expression,

---

[*] [Lassen (Ind. Alt. II, 1158 ff.) places the age of Kálidása about the commencement of the 3rd century a. D.; Weber (Málaviká und Agnimitra. Berlin: 1856, p. XXVI—XL.) between the second & fourth; and Bháo Dáji (Journal Bombay Br. R. As. Soc., VI, 19 ff. & 207 ff.) about the middle of the sixth.]

which leave it sufficiently probable that they are the works of the same master-hand. There are, indeed, in the Vikrama and Urvaśí especially, passages which call the Megha Dúta to recollection; and in one place, where the deserted monarch inquires of the passing Cloud whither Urvaśí has fled*, we have the germ of the perhaps later poem, the Cloud Messenger. Of the other works attributed to Kálidása, the Ritu-sanhára, Raghuvanśa, Málavikágnimitra, Kumára-sambhava, Śringára-tilaka, Praśnottara-málá, Hásyárnava, and Śruta-bodha, some of them are certainly not of his composition.

WHERE Rámagíri's cool, dark woods extend,
And those pure streams, where Sítá bathed, descend; 2

---

* [IV, atr. 74.]

Verse 1. Rámagiri] Is a compound term signifying The mountain of Ráma, and may be applied to any of those hills in which the hero resided during his exile or peregrinations. His first and most celebrated residence was the mountain Chitrakúta in Bundelcund, now known by the name of Comptah, and still a place of sanctity and pilgrimage. We find that tradition has assigned to another mountain, a part of the Kimoor range, the honour of affording him, and his companions, Sítá and Lakshmańa, a temporary asylum, upon his progress to the south; and it is consequently held in veneration by the neighbouring villagers: see Capt. Blunt's journey from Chunarghur to Yertnagoodum, Asiatic Researches, vii. 60. An account of a journey from Mirzapore to Nagpore, however, in the Asiatic Annual Register for 1806, has determined the situation of the scene of the present poem to be in the vicinity of the latter city. The modern name of the mountain is there stated to be Ramtéc: it is marked in the maps, Ramtego; but I understand that

Spoiled of his glories, severed from his wife,
A banished Yaksha passed his lonely life: 4
Doomed, by his lord's stern sentence, to sustain
Twelve tedious months of solitude and pain.

---

the proper word is Rámienka, which, in the Mahratta language, has probably the same import as Rámagiri, The hill of Ráma. It is situated but a short distance to the north of Nagpore, and is covered with buildings consecrated to Ráma and his associates, which receive the periodical visits of numerous and devout pilgrims.

Verse 2. Where Sitá bathed.] In his exile Ráma was accompanied by his younger brother, Lakshmaṇa, and his faithful consort Sitá, or, as she is called in the original, the daughter of Janaka, until the latter was carried off by the demon or giant Rávaṇa: see the Rámáyaṇa. The performance of her ablutions in the springs of the mountain is here stated to have rendered their water the object of religious veneration.

Verse 4. A Yaksha] Is a demigod, of which there exists a Gaṇa or class. They have few peculiar attributes, and are regarded only as the companions or attendants of Kuvera, the god of wealth. The word is derived from यज् 'to worship'; either, because they minister to Kuvera, are reverenced themselves by men, or are beloved by the Apsaras, the courtezans of Indra's heaven. They have, however, their own female companions, or wives; as appears by the poem. One writer, cited and censured by a Commentator on the Amara Kosha, derives the name from अद् 'to eat,' because he says they devour children. [For another etymology proposed by Weber see his "Indische Studien", II, 185, and "Omina and Portenta". Berlin: 1859, p. 326.] Occasionally, indeed, the Yakshas appear as Imps of evil; but, in general, their character is perfectly inoffensive.

Verse 5.] The lord of the Yakshas is Kuvera, who, in Hindu mythology, performs the functions of the Grecian Plutos. He is the god of wealth, and master of nine inestimable treasures. His capital is situated on mount Kailása, and inhabited by Yakshas, Kinnaras,

To these drear hills through circling days confined,
In dull unvaried grief, the god repined;
And sorrow, withering every youthful charm,
Had slipped the golden bracelet from his arm;
When with Áshádha's glooms the air was hung,
And one dark Cloud around the mountain clung;

---

and other inferior deities. He has a variety of appellations alluding to these circumstances, but is most commonly designated by the one here employed. The term is expressive of his deformity, being derived from कु 'vile', and वेर 'body'; and he is described as having three legs, and but eight teeth. No images of him occur, nor is any particular worship paid to him; and in these respects there is a considerable analogy between him and his Grecian parallel. Plutus is described as blind, malignant, and cowardly; and seems to have received but very slender homage from Greek or Roman devotion. The term "sentence", here used, is, more literally, 'curse.' The text also states that it was incurred by a neglect of duty, the Yaksha having been heedless in his office, स्वाधिकारप्रमत्तः. According to the Commentators, he was the warder of the gate of Kuvera's garden: and, quitting his post for a season, allowed Indra's elephant to commit a trespass, and trample down the flower-beds.

Verse 10. Had slipped the golden bracelet from his arm.] This is a favourite idea with Hindu poets, and repeatedly occurs: thus, in the elegant drama of Śakuntalá, [Str. 61 D., 66 W.] Dushmanta says:

एतदपिधुरिरत्नकांतांपातिविवर्णमेव्रीकृतं
लिपि लिपि भुजमनुतापानुसारिभिरयुभिः ।
स्वमभियुक्तिमञ्चातानाडुं मुद्रमेविश्वप्रवनात्
जलबस्रजयं खर्वं खर्वं मया प्रतिषाह्यते ॥

or, in Sir William Jones's version, "This golden bracelet, sullied by the flame which preys on me, and which no dew mitigates, but the tears gushing nightly from my eyes, has fallen again and again on my wrist, and has been replaced on my emaciated arm."

In form some elephant, whose sportive rage
Ramparts, scarce equal to his might, engage.
Long on the mass of mead-reviving dew
The heavenly exile fixed his eager view;   16
And still the melancholy tear suppressed,
Though bitterest sorrow wrung his heaving breast.
For e'en the happy husband, as he folds
His cherished partner in his arms, beholds   20

Verse 11. *When with Ashádha's glooms.*] The month Ashádha or Ashárha comprehends the latter part of June and the commencement of July, and is the period about which the south-west monsoon, or rainy season, usually sets in.

Verse 13. *In form some elephant.*] Thus, in the Purāṇa Sarvaswa, clouds are described as महिषाव वराहाव मत्तमातङ्गरूपिण: 'Shaped like buffaloes, boars, and wild elephants.' In Chapman's Bussy D'Ambois they are said to assume

> In our faulty apprehensions
> The forms of dragons, lions, elephants.

And Shakspeare, although he omits the elephant, gives them, with his usual overflow of imagery, a great variety of shapes:—

> Sometime we see a cloud that's dragonish,
> A vapour sometime like a bear or lion,
> A tower'd citadel, a pendant rock,
> A forked mountain, or blue promontory,
> With trees upon 't, that nod unto the world,
> And mock our eyes with air.
>
> ANTHONY & CLEOPATRA [IV, 12.].

Verse 20. *For e'en the happy husband.*] The commencement of the rainy season being peculiarly delightful in Hindustan, from the contrast it affords to the sultry weather immediately preceding it, and the refreshing sensations it excites, becomes, to the lover and the poet, the same source of love and tenderness, as the season of Spring is to the young and poetical in Europe.

This gathering darkness with a troubled heart:
What must they feel, whom fate and distance part!
Such were the Yaksha's thoughts; but fancy found
Some solace in the glooms that deepened round: 24
And bade him hail amidst the labouring air
A friendly envoy to his distant fair;
Who, charged with grateful tidings, might impart
New life and pleasure to her drooping heart. 28

Cheered with the thought, he culled each budding
          flower,
And wildly wooed the fertilizing power;
(For who, a prey to agonizing grief,
Explores not idlest sources for relief: 32
And, as to creatures sensible of pain,
To lifeless nature loves not to complain?)
Due homage offered, and oblations made,
The Yaksha thus the Cloud majestic prayed:— 36

Verse 35. And oblations made.] The oblation of the blossoms of the Kuṭaja, 'a small tree'', (Wrightea antidysenterica) is called Argha (अर्घ) in the original, a religious rite, which seems to be analogous to the libation of the earlier periods of the Grecian ritual. अर्घ, in the Amara Kosha [III, 4, 27], is described as a species of worship, and is perhaps more properly the act of offering a libation to a venerable person, or to a deity; although it also implies the oblation itself, otherwise denominated अर्घ्य. This oblation, of which water forms the basis, is presented in a cup, a shell, or any metallic oblong and boat-shaped vessel. [See Mrs. Belnos' "The Sandhya", pl. XIII.] The vessel in the spoken dialects is called by a similar name اَرْغَى,' 'Arghā'. Indeed, Mr. Wilford states, Asiatic Researches, iii. 364, and viii. 274, that Argha, in Sanskrit, means 'a boat'; whence he deduces the ship Argo, &c.; and whence, with Mr.

Hail, friend of Indra, counsellor divine,
Illustrious offspring of a glorious line!

Bryant's assistance, we may deduce the Ark of Scripture. The Sanskrit word, however, has not been found in any of the vocabularies of the language with the import Mr. Wilford has assigned to it.

The oblation called Argha or Arghya, generally considered, comprises eight articles, thus enumerated:

आप: क्षीरं कुशायानि दधि सर्पिष्य तथुल्ला: ।
यवा: सिद्धार्थकं चैव अष्टाङ्गार्घ्यं प्रकीर्तितम् ॥

"The eight-fold Arghya is formed of water, milk, the points of Kuśa-grass, curds, clarified butter, rice, barley, and white mustard." In the Áchárádarśa of Srídatta [Benares edition p. 91], in a passage quoted from the Devi Purána, they are stated somewhat differently; thus,

रक्तविन्यासी: पुष्पैर्दूर्व्वांकुशैर्विषी: ।
सामान्य: सर्व्वदेवानामर्घो'यं परिकीर्तित: ॥

"The general Argha, proper for any of the gods, consists of saffron, "the Bel, unbroken grain, flowers, curds, Dúrba-grass, Kuśa-grass, "and Sesamum." Water is not mentioned here, being considered as the vehicle of the whole: the same author adds, that should any of these not be procurable, they may be supplied by the imagination:

अभावे दधिदूर्व्वादीनामर्घं वा प्रकल्पयेत् ॥

Besides the Argha common to all the gods, there are peculiar ones for separate deities: thus we find a few new-blown buds are sufficient for a cloud; and in the Sarvaswa Purána the Argha for the Sun is thus enumerated,

सचन्दनोदकस्निग्धं रत्नार्घ्यं कुसुमं रवे: ॥

"Having presented an Arghya to the Sun, of water mixed with "sandal, and flowers": and an oblation to the same planet, as given by Mr. Colebrooke, Asiatic Researches, ch. v, 357 [Essays. 1858, p. 84.] is said to consist of Tila, flowers, barley, water and red sanders. Water alone is also sufficient to constitute the Argha. In the articles which form the Argha of the Hindus, as well as in the mode of presentation, that of pouring it out, or libating, we trace

Wearer of shapes at will, thy worth I know,
And bold entrust thee with my fated woe: 40

---

its analogy with the ancient libation. Of course, wine could never enter into Hindu offerings of this kind; but we find that the Greeks had their νηφάλια ἱερά or 'sober sacrifices,' from which wine was excluded. These were of four kinds: τὰ ὑδρόσπονδα, 'libations of water,' τὰ μελίσπονδα, 'of honey,' τὰ γαλακτόσπονδα 'of milk,' and τὰ ἐλαιόσπονδα 'of oil;' which liquors were sometimes mixed with one another. According to Porphyry [Abstin. II, 20.] most of the libations in the primitive times were νηφάλιοι. See Potter's Antiquities of Greece. We have here, then, three of the four fluid substances of an Argha, as first enumerated above, if we may compare the clarified butter with the oil: honey would, of course, be omitted on the same account as wine, being a prohibited article in Hindu law. With respect to the solid parts of the offering, a reference to the same authority will shew that they consisted of green herbs, grains, fruits, flowers, and frankincense; analogous to the grasses, rice, barley, flowers, sandal, &c. of the Sanskrit formulæ.

Verse 87. *Hail, friend of Indra!*] Indra is the sovereign deity of Swarga, or the Hindu Olympus. The cloud is here considered as his friend or counsellor, in allusion to his functions as regent of the atmosphere, where he appears in the character of the Jupiter Tonans or Νεφεληγερέτα Ζεύς. The appellative सुसुद, used in the original, is considered, by Etymologists, as irregularly derived from the passive form of सु, 'to adore,' 'to worship'.

Verse 88. *Illustrious offspring of a glorious line.*] According to the original, "Descended from the celebrated line of the Pushkarávarttakas," translated, in a prose version of this passage, "Diluvian Clouds:" see Colebrooke on Sanskrit and Prakrit Prosody, Asiatic Researches, Vol. X. Clouds, agreeably to the Brahmánda Purána, are divided into three classes, according to their origin from fire, the breath of Brahmá, or the wings of the mountains, which were cut off by Indra (पक्ष). These latter are also called पुष्करावर्तक, being especially the receptacles of water. Thus, in the Purána Sarvaswa,

For better far, solicitation fail
With high desert, than with the base prevail.

Thou art the wretch's aid, affliction's friend;
To me, unfortunate, thy succour lend: 44
My lonely state compassionate behold,
Who mourn the vengeance of the god of gold;

पुष्करा नाम ये मेघा वृहतवीचमत्सरा:
पुष्करावर्त्तकाखेन वार्वन्ते ह्यविद्मा: ॥

"The clouds called Pushkara are those large clouds which are in-"satiable of water; and, on that account, they are called in this "world, Pushkaravarttakas." So also it is said, upon the authority of the Váyu, Linga, and Matsya Puránas, "The third class of clouds "is that of the Pakshaja, or those, which were originally the wings "of the mountains that were cut off by Indra. These are also term-"ed Pushkaravarttakas, from their including water in their vortices. "They are the largest and most formidable of all; and those which, "at the end of the Yugas and Kalpas, pour down the waters of the "Deluge." Vishnu Purána, p. 231, note.

Verse 39. Wearer of shapes at will;] Or Kámarúpa; from काम 'desire,' and रूप 'form,' 'shape': thus Socrates, In the "Clouds:"

Σω. Γίνονται παν' ότι αν βώλωνται.
Soc. Why, then,
Clouds can assume what shapes they will, believe me!
CUMBERLAND's Translation.

Verse 40. For, better far, solicitation fail &c.] This is a senti-ment of rather an original strain, and indicates considerable eleva-tion of mind. Something of the same kind occurs in Massinger's play of the "Bondman;" where Lisander says,

I'd rather fall under so just a judge,
Than be acquitted by a judge corrupt
And partial in his censure.

Verse 46. The god of gold,] Kuvera. See above.

Condemned amidst these dreary rocks to pine,
And all I wish, and all I love resign.

Where dwell the Yakshas in their sparkling fields,
And Śiva's crescent groves surrounding gilds,
Direct thy licensed journey, and relate
To her who mourns in Alaká, my fate.
There shalt thou find the partner of my woes,
True to her faith, and stranger to repose;
Her task to weep our destiny severe,
And count the moments of the lingering year:
A painful life she leads, but still she lives,
While hope its aid invigorating gives;
For female hearts, though fragile as the flower,
Are firm, when closed by hope's investing power.

Verse 50. *Where Śiva's crescent realms surrounding gilds.*] The crest of Śiva is the new moon, which is sometimes described as forming a third eye in his forehead. The Himálaya mountains, amongst which we shall hereafter find Kailása to be situated, are Śiva's favourite haunts. He also resides occasionally on that mountain, and is represented as the particular friend and frequent guest of Kuvera.

Verse 52. I have here taken a liberty with the order of the original, and brought the description of the Yaksha's wife a little in advance, in order to preserve the description which follows, of the Cloud's progress, more connected. The Hindu poets are not very solicitous in general about arrangement; but it is possible that in this case I may not have improved upon that of Kálidása. The 10th stanza of the Sanskrit corresponds with these lines.

Verse 53. Alaká is the capital of Kuvera, and the residence of his dependent deities.

Still, as thou mountest on thine airy flight,
Shall widowed wives behold thee with delight,
With eager gaze, their long locks drawn apart,
Whilst hope re-animates each drooping heart: 64
Nor less shall husbands, as thy course they trace,
Expect at hand a faithful wife's embrace;
Unless, like me, in servitude they bend,
And on another's lordly will depend. 68
The gentle breeze shall fan thy stately way,
In sportive wreathes the Cranes around thee play;

Verse 70. Valáká (वलाका) is said, in Mr. Colebrooke's Amara Kosha, to mean a 'small crane.' The word is always feminine, and perhaps therefore means the female bird only. Indeed, some of the Commentators on this poem call it the female of the Vaka (वक), Ardea Torra and Putea. The rainy season is that of their gestation; which explains their attachment to the Cloud, and the allusion to its impregnating faculty mentioned in the text of the original, गर्भाधानक्षणपरिचयात्.—The periodical journeys and orderly flight of this kind of bird have long furnished classical poetry with embellishments: they are frequently alluded to by Homer, as are the wild geese, of which mention is also made below:—thus, in the Iliad, Book ii. 459:

Τῶν δ', ὥστ' ὀρνίθων πετεηνῶν ἔθνεα πολλὰ,
Χηνῶν, ἢ γεράνων, ἢ κύκνων δουλιχοδείρων,
Ἀσίῳ ἐν λειμῶνι, Καϋστρίου ἀμφὶ ῥέεθρα.

Not less their number than th' embodied cranes,
Or milk-white swans in Asia's watery plains,
That o'er the windings of Cayster's springs
Stretch their long necks and clap their rustling wings. POPE.

The translator has omitted the geese. Milton also describes the flight of these birds:

Pleased on thy left the Chátaka along
Pursue thy path, and cheer it with his song;
And when thy thunders soothe the parching earth,
And showers, expected, raise her mushroom birth,

> So steers the prudent Crane
> Her annual voyage, borne on winds.
> PARADISE LOST, vii, 430.

And again, line 442:

> Others on silver lakes and rivers bathed
> Their downy breast.——
> ——Yet oft they quit
> The dank, and, rising on stiff pennons, tower
> The mid aërial sky.

Verse 71. The Chátaka is a bird supposed to drink no water but rain-water: of course he always makes a prominent figure in the description of wet or cloudy weather. Thus in the rainy season [II, 5.] of our author's (ऋतुसंहार) 'Ritu Sanhára,' or Assemblage of Seasons:

तृषाकुलैश्चातकपक्षिभिः कृतः
मयाचिताधोवमरावलम्बिनः ।
प्रयान्ति मन्दं जयवारिवारिणो
बलाहकाः श्रीवनमीदूरसनाः ॥

> The thirsty Chátaka impatient eyes
> The promised waters of the labouring skies,
> Where heavy Clouds, with low but pleasing song,
> In slow procession murmuring move along.

The Chátaka is the Cuculus Melanoleucus. The term वाम is rendered by the Commentators in general 'left,' on the left side; but Rámanátha Tarkálankára interprets it 'beautiful'; and maintains that the cry of birds, to be auspicious, should be upon the right side, not upon the left. Bharata Mallika, however, cites astrological writers to prove that the Chátaka is one of the exceptions to this rule:

वर्षिष्यत्सलभावाचा ये च पुंस्त्रिङ्गाः खगाः ।
तूला वा बालना हृद्याः चैवमन्यमुदाहृताः ॥

72

The Swans for mount Kailása shall prepare,
And track thy course attendant through the air.   76
Short be thy farewell to this hill addressed,
This hill with Ráma's holy feet imprest;

"Peacocks, Chátakas, Cháshas (blue jays), and other male birds, oc-
"casionally also antelopes, going cheerfully along the left, give good
"fortune to the host." The Greek notions agreed with those of
Rámanátha, and considered the flight of birds upon the right side to
be auspicious: the Romans made it the left; but this difference arose
from the situation of the observer, as in both cases the auspicious
quarter was the east; the οἰωνοπόλος facing the north, and Aruspex
the south. In general, according to the Hindus, those omens which
occur upon the left side are unpropitious.

Verse 75. "The Rájahansas, desirous of going to the lake Má-
"nasa, shall accompany thee as far as Kailása, having laid in their
"provisions from the new shoots of the filaments of the stalk of the
"lotus." This is the closer reading of the text. Kailása is, properly
speaking, a mythological mountain; but the name is also applied to
the lofty range that runs parallel with the Himálaya, on the north
of that chain. The lake Mánasa lies between the two ranges: and
it is quite true, that it is the especial resort of the wild grey goose
at the beginning of the rainy season; "Those birds finding in the
"rocks bordering on the lake an agreeable and safe asylum, when
"the swell of the rivers in the rains and the inundation of the plains
"conceal their usual food." Moorcroft's Journey to Mánasarovara:
Asiatic Researches, xii. 466. The Rájahansa is described as a kind
of goose with white body and red legs and bill; whence Mr. Ellis
affirms that it is properly applicable to the Phoenicopteros or fla-
mingo. Asiatic Researches, xiv. 28, note.

Verse 76. With Ráma's holy feet imprest.] In the original text
we have, "marked with the steps of Raghupati, venerated of men."
This appellation is given to Ráma, as the most distinguished, the
lord or master as it were, of the line of Raghu, an ancestor of that
warrior, and himself a celebrated hero and sovereign. Ráma is

Thine ancient friend, whose scorching sorrows mourn
Thy frequent absence and delayed return. 80

Yet ere thine ear can drink what love inspires,
The lengthened way my guiding aid requires:
Oft on whose path full many a lofty hill
Shall ease thy toils, and many a cooling rill. 84
Rise from these streams, and seek the upper sky;
Then to the north with daring pinions fly.
The beauteous Sylphs shall mark thee with amaze,
As backward bent thou strik'st their upward gaze, 88
In doubt if by the gale abruptly torn
Some mountain-peak along the air is borne.

---

hence also termed Rághava (राघव), a regular derivative from Raghu, implying family descent. The exploits of the two heroes form the chief subject of another poem by our author, entitled Raghuvansa (रघुवंश), or The race of Raghu.

Verse 85. We now begin the geographical part of the poem; which, as far as it can be made out through the difference of ancient and modern appellations, seems to be very accurately conceived. The two extreme points of the Cloud's progress are the vicinity of Nagpore, as mentioned in the note on Verse 1, and the mountain Kailása, or rather the Himálaya range. During this course, the poet notices some of the most celebrated places, with the greater number of which we are still acquainted. In the first instance, we have here his direction due north from the mountain of Rámagiri; and we shall notice the other points as they occur.

Verse 87. Literally, the wives of the Siddhas. The Siddhas are originally human beings, but who, by devout abstraction, have attained superhuman powers, and a station apparently intermediate between men and gods. They tenant the upper regions of the air.

The ponderous Elephants, who prop the skies,
Shall view thy form expansive with surprise; 92
Now first their arrogance exchanged for shame,
Lost in thy bulk their long unrivalled fame.

Eastward, where various gems, with blending ray,
In Indra's bow o'er yonder hillock play, 96
And on thy shadowy form such radiance shed,
As Peacocks' plumes around a Krishńa spread,
Direct thy course: to Mála's smiling ground,
Where fragrant tillage breathes the field around; 100

Verse 91. Each of the four quarters, and the four intermediate points of the compass, has, according to the Hindus, a regent or presiding deity. Each of these deities also has his male and female elephant. The names of them all are enumerated in the following verse of the Amara Kosha [1, 1, 2, 8.]:

ऐरावत: पुखरीको वामन: कुमुदो-ञ्जन: ।
पुष्पदन्त: सार्वभौम: सुप्रतीकच दिग्गजा: ॥

Airávata, Púndaríka, Vámana, Kumuda, Anjana, Pushpadanta, Sárvvabhauma, and Supratíka, (are) the elephants of the sky.

Verse 95. A reference to the map will shew that it was necessary for the Cloud to begin the tour by travelling towards the east, in order to get round the lofty hills which in a manner form the eastern boundary of the Viudhya chain. It would otherwise have been requisite to have taken it across the most inaccessible part of those mountains, where the poet could not have accompanied it; and which would also have offended some peculiar notions entertained by the Hindus of the Vindhya hills, as we shall again have occasion to remark.

Verse 96. Indra's bow is the rainbow.

Verse 97. The body of Krishńa is represented of a dark blue colour; and the plumes of the peacock are frequently arranged upon the images of this deity. Allusion is especially made to Krishńa in his juvenile character, as a cow-herd in the groves of Vrindávana.

Thy fertile gifts, which looks of love reward,
Where bright-eyed peasants tread the verdant sward.

Thence sailing north, and veering to the west,
On Ámrakúta's lofty ridges rest; 104

Verse 99. It is not easy, after the lapse of ages, to ascertain precisely the site of several places enumerated in the poem before us. The easterly progress of the Cloud, and the subsequent direction by which he is to reach the mountain Ámrakúta, prove that the place here mentioned must be somewhere in the immediate vicinity of Ruttunpoor, the chief town of the northern half of the province of Cheteesgarh, and described in Captain Blunt's tour, Asiatic Researches, Vol. vii., and also in that of Mr. Colebrooke, published in the Asiatic Annual Register for 1806. The only modern traces that can be found of it are in a place called Múldá, a little to the north of Ruttunpoor. In Ptolemy's map there is a town called Maleta, and situated, with respect to the Vindhya mountains, similarly with the Mála of our poet. I should have supposed that the Mála mentioned from the geography of the Puránas by Mr. Wilford (Asiatic Researches, viii. 336) was the same with the place alluded to in the text of Kálidása: if, however, that gentleman is correct in applying the name to the Malbhoom of Midnapoor, it will be much further to the east than will do for our present purpose, and must be an entirely different place. There is little reason to think that either of these Málas are the country of the Malli, who are mentioned by Pliny; and who are more probably the same with the *Malloi* of Arrian, and the inhabitants, as is stated by Major Rennell, of the province of Multan.

Verse 104. The course pointed out to the Cloud, and an allusion which follows to the vicinity of the Narmadá river, furnish us with reasons for supposing that the mountain here mentioned is that more commonly designated by the name of Omerkuntuk. The change of sound is not more violent than it is in a number of evident corruptions from the Sanskrit language, now current in the dialects of India. The term Ámrakúta means the Mango Peak, and refers to

Oft have thy showers the mountain's flames allayed,
Then fear not wearied to demand its aid.
Not e'en the basest, when a falling friend
Solicits help it once was his to lend,   108
The aid that gratitude exacts denies:
Much less shall noble minds the claim despise.
When o'er the wooded mountain's towering head
Thy hovering shades like flowing tresses spread, 112
Its form shall shine with charms unknown before,

---

the abundance of mango-trees in the incumbent and surrounding forests. Should this conjecture be correct, it will invalidate the derivation assigned with some ingenuity to the word Omerkantak, in a prefatory note to a pleasing little oriental poem published in England, called the Metamorphosis of Sona. The author of that note imagines the proper name to be Omer Khandaka; and he is happy in the affinity of the sound, though not in his definition of the sense, as "the district of Omer" is exceedingly unmeaning, and erroneous. Amara Khandaka might mean the "immortal portion," but I do not know of any reason for assigning such an epithet to the mountain in question.

Verse 107. The Hindus have been the object of much idle panegyric, and equally idle detraction. Some writers have invested them with every amiable attribute, and they have been deprived by others of the common virtues of humanity. Amongst the excellencies denied to them, gratitude has been always particularized; and there are many of the European residents in India who scarcely imagine that the natives of the country ever heard of such a sentiment. To them, and to all detractors on this head, the above verse is a satisfactory reply; and that no doubt of its tenor may remain, I add the literal translation of the original passage. "Even a low man, when his friend comes to him for assistance, will not turn away his face, in consideration of former kindness;—how, therefore, should the exalted act thus?"

That heavenly hosts may gaze at, and adore,
This earth's round breast, bright swelling from the
                                        ground,
And with thy orb as with a nipple crowned.   116

Next bending downwards from thy lofty flight,
On Chitrakúta's humbler peak alight;
O'er the tall hill thy weariness forego,
And quenching rain-drops on its flames bestow;   120
For speedy fruits are certain to await
Assistance yielded to the good and great.
Thence journeying onwards, Vindhya's ridgy chain,
And Revá's rill, that bathes its foot, attain;   124

Verse 117. The mountain here mentioned must be in the vicinity of Omerkuntuk, and part of the same range: the name signifies, "the variegated or wonderful peak," and is applied to a number of hills: the most famous hill of this name, as was mentioned in the first note, is situated in Bundelkand.

Verse 123. The Vindhya range of mountains holds a very distinguished station both in the mythology and geography of Hindustan: these points are both discussed at some length in the tour from Mirzapore to Nagpore, already cited; and, as in those passages which I have been able to investigate I find a perfectly accurate statement, I shall here transcribe the words of its author.

"Bindh, in Sanskrit named Vindhya, constitutes the limit between Hindustan and the Deccan. The most ancient Hindu authors assign it as the southern boundary of the region which they denominate Áryabhúmi or Áryávarta. Modern authors, in like manner, make this the line which discriminates the northern from the southern nations of India. It reaches almost from the eastern to the western sea; and the highest part of the range deviates little from the line of the tropic. The mountainous tract, however, which retains the appellation, spreads much more widely: it meets the Ganges in sev-

Whose slender streams upon the brown hill's side,
Like painted streaks upon the dusky hide

---

eral places towards the north; and the Godávari is held to be its southern limit.

"Sanskrit etymologists deduce its name from a circumstance to which I have just now alluded: it is called Bindhya, says the author of a Commentary on the Amarakosha, because people think (वारयति) the progress of the sun is obstructed (वेध) by it. Suitably to this notion, the most elevated ridge of this tropical range of mountains is found to run from a point that lies between Chhota Nagpore and Palamo, to another that is situated in the vicinity of Oogein. But the course of the Narmadá river better indicates the direction of the principal range of the Vindh hills. From Amrakúta, where this river has its source, on the same spot with the Sone and the Hateo, to the gulf of Cambaya, where it disembogues itself into the sea, the channel of the Narmadá is confined by a range of hills, or by a tract of elevated ground, in which numerous rivers take their rise; and by their subsequent course towards the Sone and Jamoná on one side, and towards the Taptí and Oodaver on the other, sufficiently indicate the superior elevation of that tract through which the Nermadá has forced its way." [For a better etymology compare Lassen, I. l., I, 81.]

"The vast extent of this mountainous tract, contrasted with the small elevation of these hills, viewed from the plains of Hindustan, has furnished grounds for a legend to which the mythological writings of the Hindus often allude. Vindhya having once prostrated himself before his spiritual guide, Agastya, still remains in that posture, by command of the holy personage. This humiliation is the punishment of his presumption, in emulating the lofty height of Himálaya and Meru. According to this legend, Vindhya has one foot at Chunar; and hence the real name of that fortress is said to be Charanádri (चरणाद्रि): his other foot is, I think, placed by the same legend in the vicinity of Gayá: the vulgar, very inconsistently, suppose the head of the prostrate mountain near the temple of Vindhya Vásini, four miles from Mirzapore."

Of the tall Elephant—in bright display,
Through stones and rocks wind slow their arduous
                                                way.   128

Here the soft dews thy path has lost resume,
And sip the gelid current's rich perfume,
Where the wild Elephant delights to shed
The juice exuding fragrant from his head.   132

Verse 124. The Revá is a name of the Narmadá river, which, as we have seen in the preceding note, rises from the mountain Ámrakúṭa or Omerkuntuk. It may be here observed, that the rivers are always personified by the Hindus, and are, in general, female personifications. Thus we have Gangá, the daughter of Jahnu; Yamuná, the daughter of the Sun; and Revá, or Narmadá, the daughter of Himála, as is said in the hymn translated from the Váyu Puráńa, and given by Captain Blunt, Asiatic Researches vii. 103. The names of the Narmadá river are thus stated in the Amara Kosha. [1, 2, 3, 52]:

रेवा तु नर्मदा सोमोद्भवा मेकलकन्यका

"Revá, Narmadá, Somodbhavá, and Mekala-Kanyaká;" which are explained by the best Commentators [e. g. Dhanudikshita] thus, "who flows, who delights, who is descended from the line of the moon, and who is the daughter of Mekala." The last term is applied either to the Vindhya mountain, or is considered to be the name of a Rishi or saint, and progenitor of the river-goddess. Tradition has assigned to this river a very Ovidian kind of tale; which is related in Captain Blunt's tour, and which has been repeated in verse, with much elegance and spirit, by the author of the Metamorphosis of Soña.

Verse 131. The juice exuding fragrant from his head.] It is rather extraordinary that this juice which exudes from the temples of the elephant, especially in the season of rut, should have been unnoticed by modern writers on natural history, until the time of Cuvier (Règne animal), although mention of it is made by Strabo

Then swift proceed, nor shall the blast have force
To check with empty gusts thy ponderous course.
Reviving nature bounteous shall dispense,
To cheer thy journey, every charm of sense;　136
Blossoms, with blended green and russet hue,
And opening buds, shall smile upon thy view.
Earth's blazing woods in incense shall arise,
And warbling birds with music fill the skies.　140

Respectful Demigods shall curious count
The chattering Storks, in lengthening order mount;
Shall mark the Chátakas, who in thy train
Expect impatiently the dropping rain:　144
And, when thy muttering thunders speak thee near,
Shall clasp their brides, half ecstasy, half fear.

Ah! much I dread the long-protracted way,
Where charms so numerous spring to tempt delay:　148
Will not the frequent hill retard thy flight,
Nor flowery plain persuade prolonged delight?

---

from Megasthenes. The author of the Wild Sports of the East states, that "on each side of the elephant's temples there is an aperture about the size of a pin's head, whence an ichor exudes;" but he does not appear to have been aware of its nature. Indeed his descriptions, though entertaining, are frequently defective, owing to his extreme ignorance of the languages, the literature of which he so liberally devotes to the flames. In the Amara Kosha [II, 8, 37], this fluid is termed मद्: and दानम्; and the elephant, while it flows, is distinguished by the terms प्रभिन्न:, वर्षित:, मत्त: from the animal out of rut, or after the juice has ceased to exude, and which is then called उद्रान्त: or निर्मद्:. All these names are expressive

Or can the Peacock's animated hail,
The bird with lucid eyes, to lure thee fail?   152

---

of the circumstances. The exudation and fragrance of this fluid is frequently alluded to in Sanskrit poetry. Its scent is commonly compared to the odour of the sweetest flowers, and is then supposed to deceive and attract the bees. These circumstances occur in this passage from a work already referred to, the Ritu Sanhára [II, 15]:—

मदद्विपानां नवतोयदघर्मनिन्दान्वितानां समता मुञ्चुञ्जः ।
कपोलदेश्य विमलीत्कषप्रभास्भृङ्गदूषर्मदवारिभिः चिताः ॥

> Roars the wild Elephant inflamed with love,
> And the deep sound reverberates from above;
> His ample front, like some rich lotus, shews
> Where sport the bees, and fragrant moisture flows.

Verse 151. *Or can the Peacock's animated hail?*) The wild peacock is exceedingly abundant in many parts of Hindustan, and is especially found in marshy places. The habits of this bird are, in a great measure, aquatic; and the setting in of the rains is the season in which they pair. The peacock is therefore always introduced in the description of cloudy or rainy weather, together with the Cranes and Chátakas, whom we have already had occasion to notice. Thus, in a little poem descriptive of the rainy season &c., entitled Ghaṭakarpara (घटकर्पर), [v. 2] the author says, addressing his mistress—

यदानुमसाः द्विखिनो नद्रति मेघागमे कुब्जसमानदुगति ॥

> O thou, whose teeth enamelled vie
> With smiling Kunda's pearly ray,
> Hear how the Peacock's amorous cry
> Salutes the dark and cloudy day!

And again, in one of the Śatakas or Centos of Bhartṛi Hari, [I, 42] where he is describing the same season—

द्विखिजुलकषवेका रावरम्या यमाभाः ।
सुखिनमसुखिनं वा सर्वमुत्कण्ठयन्ति ।

> When smiling forests, whence the tuneful cries
> Of clustering pea-fowls shrill and frequent rise,

Lo! where awhile the Swans reluctant cower,
Daśárńa's fields await the coming shower.
Then shall their groves diffuse profounder gloom,
And brighter buds the deepening shade illume; 156
Then shall the ancient tree, whose branches wear
The marks of village reverence and care,

Teach tender feelings to each human breast,
And charm alike the happy or distrest.

Verse 154. *Daśárńa's fields await the coming shower.*] No traces of this name are to be found in modern maps: [according to Lassen (I, 117), however, it corresponds to the modern Dossan; cf. also III, 160 f.] It is enumerated in Major Wilford's lists from the Puráńas, Asiatic Researches, vol viii. amongst the countries situated behind the Vindhya mountains; and corresponds, according to him, with the Dosarene of Ptolemy and the Periplus. Ptolemy's map has also a Dosara and Dosaronis Fluvium; and in the Pauráńik list of rivers, there is also a Daśárńá river, which is said to rise from the mountain Chitrakúťa. It may possibly correspond, at least in part, with the modern district of Cheteesgerh, as the etymology of both words refers to similar circumstances. [According to Dr. F. E. Hall (Journal Am. Or. Soc. VI, 521) It was situated to the east of Chandeyree.] Cheteesgerh is so named from its being supposed to comprise Thirty-six forts; and according to Bharata, the Commentator on our text, Daśárńa is derived from Daśa (दश) Ten, and Ŕińa (ऋण), a strong hold or Durga, the Droog of the Peninsula, and thence means the district of the Ten citadels. [See the Petersburg Dictionary, s. v., and Weber's Ind. Stud., I. 209.]

Verse 157. *Then shall the ancient tree, &c.*} A number of trees receive particular veneration from the Hindus; as the Indian fig, the Holy fig tree, the Myrobalan trees, &c. In most villages there is at least one of these, which is considered particularly sacred, and is carefully kept and watered by the villagers, is hung occasionally with garlands, and receives the Prańám or veneratory inclination of the head, or even offerings and libations. The birds mentioned in

Shake through each leaf, as birds profanely wrest
The reverend boughs to form the rising nest. 162

Where royal Vidiśá confers renown
Thy warmest wish shall fruit delightful crown:
There Vetravatí's stream ambrosial laves
A gentle bank with mildly murmuring waves; 164
And there her rippling brow and polished face
Invite thy smiles, and sue for thy embrace.

Next o'er the lesser hills thy flight suspend,
And growth erect to drooping flowerets lend; 168

---

the text by the epithet गृहविभुक् are the Vakas or Cranes. The term signifies, "who eats the food of his female"; गृह commonly a house, meaning, in this compound, a wife. At the season of pairing, it is said that the female of this bird assists in feeding the male; and the same circumstance is stated with respect to the crow and the sparrow, whence the same epithet is applied to them also.

Verse 161. Where royal Vidiśá confers renown.] Vidiśá is described as the capital of the district of Daśárńa. It appears to be the modern Bhilsá, in the province of Málwa. It is still a place of some note; and is well known in India for the superior quality of the tobacco raised in its vicinity. [Another etymology is proposed by F. E. Hall in the Journal As. Soc. Bengal for 1862, p. 112.]

Verse 103. The Vetravatí is the modern Betwah. It rises on the north side of the Vindhya chain; and, pursuing a north-easterly course of 340 miles, traverses the province of Málwa and the south-west corner of Allahabad, and falls into the Jamná below Kalpee. In the early part of its course, it passes through Bhilsá or Vidiśá.

Verse 167. Next o'er the lesser hills thy flight suspend.] The term in the text, नीचैराख्यं गिरिं, is explained by the Commentators to signify either the hill named Nichais, a mountainous range, of little note, or of little elevation. It is of no great moment; but perhaps the latter, which meaning we select, is the most satisfactory.

While sweeter fragrance breathes from each recess,
Than rich perfumes the hireling wanton's dress.

On Naga Nadí's banks thy waters shed,
And raise the feeble jasmin's languid head; 172
Grant for a while thy interposing shroud
To where those damsels woo the friendly Cloud;
As, while the garland's flowery stores they seek,
The scorching sunbeams singe the tender cheek, 176

Verse 168. *And growth erect to drooping flowerets lend.*] This passage, more literally rendered, is, "That hill which with upright flowers is like the body with its hair on end." The erection of the hairs of the body is, with the Hindus, constantly supposed to be the effect of pleasure or delight.

Verse 171. *On Naga Nadí's banks.*] Some of the Commentators notice various readings of the name of this river, which occurs, as given in the translation, Naga Nadí (नगनदी), 'the mountain stream'; Nava Nadí (नवनदी), 'the new river;' and Vana Nadí (वननदी), 'the forest river.' It is probably one amongst a number of small streams falling from the Vindhya range of hills; and, indeed, the whole province of Málwa abounds in water; so that, as is stated in the Ayeen Akbery, "you cannot travel two or three coss without meeting with streams of good water, whose banks are shaded by the wild willow and other trees, and decorated with the hyacinth and other beautiful and odoriferous flowers." Gladwin's Translation, vol. ii.—I have given the preference to the Naga Nadí as above, from finding a river west of the Betwah, which we have crossed, named the Parbatty; and which, rising in the Vindhya chain, runs north-west, till it joins another called, in Arrowsmith's Map, the Seprá; and the two together fall into the Chambal. The word Parbatty, or Parvati, means, 'sprung from the mountains'; and Naga Nadí, as I have mentioned, bears a similar import; so that they possibly are synonyms of the same stream.

Verse 175. *As, while the garland's flowery stores they seek.*]

The ear-hung lotus fades: and vain they chase,
Fatigued and faint, the drops that dew the face.

What though to northern climes thy journey lay,
Consent to track a shortly devious way;
To fair Ujjayinī's palaces and pride,
And beauteous daughters, turn awhile aside.
Those glancing eyes, those lightning looks unseen,
Dark are thy days, and thou in vain hast been.

The use of garlands in the decoration of the houses and temples of the Hindus, and of flowers in their offerings and festivals, furnishes employment to a particular tribe or caste, the Mâlakâras or wreath-makers. The females of this class are here alluded to.

Verse 181. Ujjayinī, or the modern Oujein, is supposed to have been the residence of our poet, and the capital of his celebrated patron, Vikramâditya. Few cities, perhaps, can boast of a more continuous reputation; as it has been a place of great note from the earliest periods of Hindu tradition down to the present day. It is now in the possession of the family of Scindiah, and is the capital of his territories. A full and highly-interesting account of it is to be found in the Sixth Volume of the Asiatic Researches, in the Narrative of a Journey from Agra to this city, by the late Dr. Hunter,—a gentleman, the activity of whose mind was only equalled by the accuracy of his judgment, and the extensiveness of whose acquirements was only paralleled by the unwearied continuance of his exertions.

Verse 184. Dark are the days.] The expression of the poet is simply, "If you do not enjoy the glances, &c., you are defrauded" (वञ्चितो ऽसि), and the Commentators explain it by adding, "of the "object of your life." That is, if you have not seen these beauties, you might as well have been blind, or not have existed at all. This compliment is rather hyperbolical; but we are acquainted with it in Europe: and the Italian proverb, "He who has not seen Rome has not seen any thing", conveys a similar idea.

Diverging thither now the road proceeds,
Where eddying waters fair Nirvindhyá leads,
Who speaks the language amorous maids devise,
The lore of signs, the eloquence of eyes;   188
And seeks, with lavish beauty, to arrest
Thy course, and woo thee to her bridal breast.

The torrent passed, behold the Sindhu glide,
As though the hair-band bound the slender tide;   192
Bleached with the withered foliage, that the breeze
Has showered rude from overhanging trees:

Verse 186. *Fair Nirvindhyá leads.*] This stream has not been found by name in the maps; but a number of small rivers occur between the Parbatty and the river mentioned below, the Siprá, one of which must be the Nirvindhyá of the poet. The four following lines, descriptive of the female personification of the current, are englished rather with respect to the sense than the words, the plainness of which might perhaps offend European fastidiousness. There is not, however, any one of Kálidása's river-ladies who behaves so indecorously as several of Drayton's similar personifications; and there is not one of them possessed of speech at all, to say nothing of such speech as is made use of by the Hayle, and other like "lusty nymphs," of that author's Poly-olbion.

Verse 191. *Behold the Sindhu glide.*] This is a stream also, with which the maps are not acquainted by name. As, however, it is the nearest river to Oujein, it may probably be the same with that now called Ságurmuttee. The river having been diminished by the preceding hot weather, the poet compares it to a long single braid of hair; and, conformably to the personification of it as a female, he supposes the braid to have been bound, in consequence of the absence of the Cloud, after the fashion in which the hair is worn by those women whose husbands are absent;—a custom we shall again be called upon to notice.

To thee she looks for succour, to restore
Her lagging waters, and her leafy shore. 196

Behold the city whose immortal fame
Glows in Avanti's or Visálá's name!
Renowned for deeds that worth and love inspire,
And bards to paint them with poetic fire; 200

Verse 197. The synonyms of Oujein are thus enumerated in the Vocabulary of Hemachandra [976]:

उज्जयिनी क्षितिपाला ऽवन्ती पुष्पकरण्डिनी ।

Ujjayiní, Visálá, Avanti, and Pushpakarandiní.

Verse 199. Renowned for deeds &c.] I have here taken some liberty with the text, the literal translation of which is "famous for the story of Udayana, and the number of its learned men." The story of Udayana, or Vatsarája, as he is also named, is thus told concisely by the Commentators on the poem:—Pradyota was a sovereign of Oujein, who had a daughter named Vásavadattá, and whom he intended to bestow in marriage upon a king of the name of Sanjaya. In the mean time, the princess sees the figure of Vatsarája, sovereign of Kusha Dwipa, in a dream, and becomes enamoured of him. She contrives to inform him of her love, and he carries her off from her father and his rival. The same story is alluded to in the Málatí Mádhava [p. 38.], a drama by Bhavabhúti; but neither in that, nor in the Commentary on the Megha Dúta, is mention made of the author, or of the work in which it is related. Mr. Colebrooke, in his learned Essay on Sanskrit and Prákrit Prosody, in the Tenth Volume of the Asiatic Researches, has stated, that the allusion by Bhavabhúti was unsupported by other authority; not having, perhaps, noticed the similar allusion in this poem. [Comp. however, Hindu Theatre, Vol. I, 89, Vol. II, Mál. Mádh. p. 32, F. E. Hall's Vásavad., p. 2 ff., and A. Weber in "Zeitschrift der D. Morg. Ges.", VIII, 530 f.] He has also given an abstract of the Vásavadattá of Subandhu; a tale which corresponds, in many points, with that of Udayana, as here explained. Udayana is also

The fairest portion of celestial birth,
Of Indra's paradise transferred to earth;
The last reward to acts of virtue given;
The only recompence then left to Heaven. 204

the hero of part of the Kathá Sarit Ságara; and his marriage with Vásavadattá is there related in nearly a similar manner as that just described. The story was evidently popular; and the text might be rendered Ujjayini, "great or illustrious by the number of those skilled in the tale of Udayana."

Verse 204. *The only recompence then left to Heaven.*] To understand this properly, it is necessary to be acquainted with some of the Hindu notions regarding a future state. The highest kind of happiness is absorption into the divine essence, or the return of that portion of spirit which is combined with the attributes of humanity to its original source. This happiness, according to the philosopher, is to be attained only by the most perfect abstraction from the world, and freedom from passion, even while in a state of terrestrial existence: but there are certain places, which, in the popular creed, are invested with so much sanctity, as to entitle all who die within their precincts to final absorption or annihilation. One of these is Oujein, or Avantí; and they are all enumerated in this verse:

अयोध्या मथुरा माया काशी कांची अवन्तिका ।
पुरी द्वारावती चैव सप्तैता मोक्षदायिकाः ॥

"Ayodhyá, Mathurá, Máyá, Káśí, Kánchí, Avantiká, and the city "Dwárávatí, are the seven places which grant eternal happiness." [Cf. Káśíkańḍa. c. 7.]

Besides this ultimate felicity, the Hindus have several minor degrees of happiness; amongst which is the enjoyment of Indra's Swarga, or, in fact, of a Muhammedan paradise. The degree and duration of the pleasures of this paradise are proportioned to the merits of those admitted to it; and "they, who have enjoyed this lofty region of Swarga, but whose virtue is exhausted, revisit the habitation of mortals." The case now alluded to seems, however,

Here, as the early Zephyrs waft along,
In swelling harmony, the woodland song,
They scatter sweetness from the fragrant flower
That joyful opens to the morning hour.
With friendly zeal they sport around the maid
Who early courts their vivifying aid;
And, cool from Siprá's gelid waves, embrace
Each languid limb and enervated grace. 212

Here should thy spirit with thy toils decay,
Rest from the labours of the wearying way:
Round every house the flowery fragrance spreads;
O'er every floor the painted footstep treads; 216

---

to be something different from that so described by Sir William Jones. It appears, by the explanation of the Commentators, that the exhausted pleasures of Swarga had proved insufficient for the recompence of certain acts of austerity, which however, were not such as to merit final emancipation: the divine persons had therefore to seek elsewhere for the balance of their reward; and for that purpose they returned to Earth, bringing with them the fairest portion of Swarga, in which they continued to live in the discharge of pious duties till the whole account was settled, and their liberated spirits were re-united with the great, uniform, and primeval essence. The portion of Swarga thus brought to Earth was the city Avanti; whose superior sanctity and divine privileges are here alluded to, and thus explained by the poet.

Verse 211. The Siprá is the river upon the banks of which Oujein stands, and which is called Sipparah in the maps. In Arrowsmith, however, there is another stream with a similar name, the Siprá, which appears to be a continuation of the Sagarmuttee, considerably to the north-east of Oujein. There can be no doubt of the position of the river mentioned by the poet.

Breathed through each casement, swell the scented air,
Soft odours shaken from dishevelled hair;
Pleased on each terrace, dancing with delight,
The friendly Peacock hails thy grateful flight: 220
Delay then! certain in Ujjayin to find
All that restores the frame, or cheers the mind.

Hence, with new zeal, to Śiva homage pay,
The god whom earth and hell and heaven obey: 224
The choir who tend his holy fane shall view
With awe, in thee, his neck's celestial blue:

Verse 216. *The painted footstep.*] Staining the soles of the feet with a red colour, derived from the Mehndee, the Lac, &c., is a favourite practice of the Hindu toilet. It is thus elegantly alluded to in the Ode to one of the Female Personifications of Music, the Rāginī Asaveree:

> The rose hath humbly bowed to meet,
> With glowing lips, her hallowed feet,
> And lent them all its bloom.

Hindu Odes, by John David Paterson, Esq., published in the New Series of Gladwin's Oriental Miscellany, Calcutta.

Verse 223. The Commentators have thought proper, in explaining this verse and the preceding, to transpose the order of the explanations;—I do not see for what reason, and have therefore conformed to the text.

Verse 224. *The god whom earth and hell and heaven obey.*] "Lord of the three worlds" in the expression of the original text: the worlds are, Swarga or heaven, Pātāla or hell, and Bhūmi or the earth.

Verse 226. *With awe, in thee, his neck's celestial blue.*] The dark blue of the Cloud is compared to the colour of the neck of Śiva, which became of this hue upon his swallowing the poison

Soft through the rustling grove the fragrant gale
Shall sweets from Gandhavatí's fount exhale: 228
Where with rich dust the lotus-blossoms teem,
And youthful beauties frolic in the stream.

Here, till the sun has vanished in the west,
Till evening brings its sacred ritual, rest;— 232
Then reap the recompence of holy prayer,
Like drums thy thunders echoing in the air.
They who, with burning feet and aching arms,
With wanton gestures and emblazoned charms, 236

---

produced at the churning of the ocean. The story is thus related in Wilkins's Translation of an Episode of the Mahábhárata, affixed to his Bhagavad Gítá:—"As they continued to churn the ocean more than enough, that deadly poison issued from its bed, burning like a raging fire; whose dreadful fumes in a moment spread throughout the world, confounding the three regions of the universe with its mortal stench, until Seev, at the word of Brahmá, swallowed the fatal drug, to save mankind; which remaining in the throat of that sovereign Dew of magic form, from that time he was called Neel-kant, because his throat was stained blue."

Verse 232. *Till evening brings its sacred ritual, rest.*] There are three daily and essential ceremonies performed by the Brahmans, termed Sandhyás (सन्ध्या), either from the word Sandhi (सन्धि), 'junction', because they take place at the joinings of the day as it were, that is, at dawn, noon, and twilight; or as the term is otherwise derived from सम् 'with,' and धी, 'to meditate religiously'. When the ceremonies of the Sandhyá are of a public nature, they comprehend the ringing of bells, blowing the conch, beating a tabor, &c.; and this kind of sound the Cloud is directed by the Yaksha to excite, as an act of devotion.

Verse 235. *They who, with burning feet and aching arms.*] The female attendants upon the idol.

In Mahádeva's fane the measure tread,
Or wave the gorgeous chowrie o'er his head;
Shall turn on thee the grateful-speaking eye,
Whose glances gleam, like bees, along the sky, 240
As from thy presence showers benign and sweet
Cool the parched earth, and soothe their tender feet.
Nay, more,—Bhaváni shall herself approve,
And pay thy services with looks of love; 244

Verse 238. *The gorgeous chowrie.*] The Chowrie, or more properly Chounri (چَوری), is a brush of Peacock's feathers, or the tail of a particular kind of cow, &c., set in a handle of such materials as suit the fancy or the means of the proprietor. It is used for a fan, or to whisk off flies and other insects; and this piece of attention is always paid by the Hindus to the figures of their gods.

Verse 240. *Whose glances gleam, like bees, along the sky.*] Although this allusion may be new to European imagery, it is just and pleasing. The consequence of the glance is well conveyed by the sting of the bee, while its poetically radiating nature is not unaptly compared to the long flight of a line of these insects. The lengthened light of a glance is familiar to us; for Shakspeare speaks of "eyes streaming through the airy region": and the continuous flight of bees was noticed so long back as the time of Homer, who describes them as proceeding in branches, a circumstance which his translator, Pope, has omitted:—

Βοτρυδὸν δὲ πέτονται ἐπ' ἄνθεσιν εἰαρινοῖσιν. [Il. II, 89.]

Branching, they fly abroad o'er vernal flowers;
Or, as in Pope,

Clust'ring, in heaps on heaps, the driving bees &c.

Verse 242. *And soothe their tender feet.*] It is to be recollected that these ladies are dancing bare-footed: divesting the feet of the shoes is a mark of reverence or respect paid to sacred places, such as the interior or vestibule of a temple, which has been from the remotest times practised in the East, as we know from the authority of Scripture.

When, as her Śiva's twilight rites begin,
And he would clothe him in the reeking skin,

Verse 343. *Bhaváni shall herself approve.*] Bhaváni is one of the many names of the consort of Śiva. The reason of her satisfaction, and indeed the whole of this passage, although familiar to a Hindu, and although much amplified in the translation, requires a little explanation to be rendered intelligible to the English reader. Śiva is supposed to be dancing at the performance of the evening Sandhyá, and to have assumed as his cloak the bloody skin of an elephant formerly belonging to an Asura destroyed by him. As this is no very seemly ornament, Bhaváni is delighted to find it supplied by the Cloud; which being of a dusky red, through the reflexion of the China roses now abundant, and being skirted, as it overhangs a forest, by the projecting branches of trees, resembles the elephant hide in colour, and its dangling limbs as well as in its bulk, and is mistaken for it by Śiva in his religious enthusiasm. The office performed by the Cloud has often been assigned to it in the West: thus, Horace, Ode II. Book I.:

>Nube candentes humeros amictus
>Augur Apollo.——

Or come Apollo, versed in fate, and shroud
Thy shining shoulders with a veiling cloud.

So Milton, in his Penseroso, speaking of the Morning, describes it as

>Kerchief'd in a comely cloud.

Lee invests sentiments of the mind with a similar garb, and has—

>For true Repentance never comes too late;
>As soon as born, she makes herself a shroud,
>The weeping mantle of a fleecy cloud.

And a Poet of later day, but of no inferior name, has made a very fine use of this figure:

>I've known her long, of worth most excellent;
>But in the day of woe she ever rose
>Upon the mind with added majesty;

He deems thy form the sanguinary hide,
And casts his elephant attire aside;   248
For at his shoulders, like a dusky robe,
Mantling, impends thy vast and shadowy globe;
Where ample forests, stretched its skirts below,
Projecting trees like dangling limbs bestow;   252
And vermil roses, fiercely blooming, shed
Their rich reflected glow, their blood-resembling red.
Amidst the darkness palpable, that shrouds,
Deep as the touchstone's gloom, the night with clouds,   256

> As the dark mountain more sublimely towers,
> Mantled in clouds and storm.
>
> Miss Baillie's De Montfort.

The action, the elephant skin, and other attributes of Śiva, are well described in a passage cited by Mr. Colebrooke, in his Essay on Sanskrit Prosody, from the Drama of Bhavabhúti, though there assigned to a form of his consort Durgá:

प्रचलितकरिचर्मपर्यन्तचञ्चत्कराघातनिर्भिन्नचुम्बिक्षमामुकुट-
स्रोतोजीवत्कपालावलीमुग्रचण्डाट्टहासैरवदूरिभूतमचुतर्हसति:

> The elephant hide that robes thee, to thy steps
> Swings to and fro; the whirling talons rend
> The crescent on thy brow; from the torn orb
> The trickling nectar falls; and every scull
> That gems thy necklace laughs with horrid life.
> Attendant spirits tremble and applaud.
>
> [Málatímádh., p. 81. Calc. ed.]

Verse 255. Amidst the darkness palpable, that shrouds.] So Milton's celebrated expression,

> And through the palpable obscure find out
> His uncouth way.—

The literal interpretation of the original passage is, "the darkness that may be pierced with a needle."

With glittering lines of yellow lightning break,
And frequent trace in heaven the golden streak:
To those fond fair who tread the royal way,
The path their doubtful feet explore betray: 260
Those thunders hushed, whose shower-foreboding
sound
Would check their ardour, and their hopes confound.

On some cool terrace, where the turtle-dove
In gentlest accents breathes connubial love, 264
Repose awhile; or plead your amorous vows
Through the long night, the lightning for your
spouse.
Your path retraced, resume your promised flight,
When in the east the sun restores the light, 268
And shun his course; for with the dawning sky
The sorrowing wife dispels the tearful eye,
Her lord returned:—so comes the sun, to chase
The dewy tears that stain the Padma's face; 272
And ill his eager penitence will bear,
That thou shouldst check his progress through the
air.

Now to Gambhírá's wave thy shadow flies,
And on the stream's pellucid surface lies, 276

Verse 275. *Now to Gambhírá's wave.*] This river, and the Gandhavati in the vicinity of the temple of Siva, which lately occurred, are probably amongst the numerous and nameless brooks with which the province of Málwa abounds.

Like some loved image faithfully imprest
Deep in the maiden's pure unsullied breast:
And vain thy struggles to escape her wiles,
Or disappoint those sweetly treacherous smiles, 280
Which glistening Sapharas insidious dart,
Bright as the lotus, at thy vanquished heart.

Verse 281. *Which glistening Sapharas.*] The Saphara is described as a small white glistening fish; which darting rapidly through the water, is not unaptly compared to the twinkling glances of a sparkling eye. Assigning the attributes of female beauty to a stream, ceases to be incongruous when we advert to its constant personification by the Hindus: and it is as philosophical as it is poetical, to affiance a River and a Cloud. The smiles of rivers, nay, of the Ocean itself, have often been distributed by poetical imagination: thus Lucretius, invoking Venus, says,

  Tibi rident æquora ponti.
  The ocean waves laugh on you:

for his late translator, Mr. Good, is very angry at the conversion of this laugh into a smile, as effected by less daring of his predecessors. Milton again gives to the Ocean nose as well as dimples:

  Cheered with the grateful smell, old Ocean smiles,

And Metastasio, in his beautiful Ode to Venus, has,

   E i flutti ridono
   Nel mar placati.
  The waves now placid play,
  And laugh amidst the deep.

All these, however, as well as our author, are far surpassed by Drayton, in his Poly-olbion; where hill and dale, forest and river, are constantly described with male or female attributes. With respect to the streams, he is not satisfied with wedding them to various objects, but fairly subjects them to the pains of parturition. The instances are frequent; but we may be content with the follow-

What breast so firm unmoved by female charms?
Not thine, my friend: for now her waving arms, 284
O'erhanging Bayas, in thy grasp enclosed,
Rent her cerulean vest, and charms exposed,
Prove how successfully she tempts delay,
And wins thee loitering from the lengthening way. 288

Thence, satiate, lead along the gentle breeze
That bows the lofty summits of the trees;
And pure with fragrance, that the earth in flowers
Repays profuse to fertilizing showers; 292
Vocal with sounds the elephants excite,
To Devagiri wings its welcome flight.

---

ing, especially as it is explained and defended by his very learned illustrator:—

> When Pool, quoth she, was young, a lusty sea-born lass,
> Great Albion to this nymph an earnest suitor was,
> And bare himself so well, and so in favour came,
> That he in little time upon this lovely dame
> Begot three maiden Isles, his darlings and delight.

"As Albion (son of Neptune), from whom that first name of this Britain was supposed, is well fitted to the fruitful bed of this Pool, thus personated as a sea-nymph, the plain truth (as words may certify your eyes, saving all impropriety of object) is, that in the Pool are seated three isles, Bruntsey, Fursey, and St. Helen's, in situation and magnitude as I name them. Nor is the fiction of begetting the Isles improper, seeing Greek antiquities tell us of, divers in the Mediterranean and the Archipelagus; as, Rhodes, Delus, Hiera, the Echinadra, and others which have been, as it were, brought forth out of the salt womb of Amphitrite." Selden's Illustrations.

Verse 294. Devagiri is the mountain of the deity, and may perhaps be the same with a place called in the map Dewagor, situated

There change thy form, and showering roses shed,
Bathed in the dews of heaven, on Skanda's head;   296
Son of the Crescent's god, whom holy ire
Called from the flame of all-devouring fire,

---

south of the Chumbul, in the centre of the province of Málwa, and precisely in the line of the Cloud's progress; which, as we shall hereafter find, has been continued nearly due north from Oujein. This hill is the site of a temple of Kártikeya; which, as well as that of Śiva described above, we must suppose to have enjoyed, in the days of antiquity, considerable reputation, or they would not have been so particularly specified in the poem.

Verse 296. Bathed in the dews of heaven.] "Moistened with the waters of the Mandákiní", the celestial Ganges. Skanda, or Kártikeya, is the son of Śiva and Párvati, and the Mars of Hindu mythology. There are various legends respecting his birth, one of which is presently noticed by the poet.

Verse 297. Several instances of the solitary production of offspring occur in the Hindu as well as in the Grecian mythology. Thus, as Pallas sprang from the brow of Jupiter, we have Skanda generated solely by the deity Śiva: Gangá springs from the head of the same deity, and Ganeśa is the self-born son of the goddess Párvati. The miraculous birth of the warrior deity, Skanda, was for the purpose of destroying Táraka, an Asura or demon, who, by the performance of continued and severe austerities, had acquired powers formidable to the gods. [Váráha Pur. 25, Vámana Pur. 57 ff. Kálika Pur. 66.] The excentric genius of Southey has rendered it unnecessary, by his poem, 'The Curse of Kehama,' for me to explain the nature or results of these acts of devotion. The germ of Skanda was cast by Śiva into the flame of Agni, the god of fire; who, being unable to sustain the increasing burden, transferred it to the goddess Gangá: she accordingly was delivered of the deity, Skanda; who was afterwards received and reared, among thickets of the Śara reed (Saccharum Sara), by the six daughters of a king, named Kŕittiká; or according to other legends, by the wives of

To snatch the Lord of Swarga from despair,
And timely save the trembling hosts of air. 300

Next bid thy thunders o'er the mountain float,
And echoing caves repeat the pealing note;
Fit music for the bird, whose lucid eye
Gleams like the horned beauty of the sky; 304
Whose moulting plumes, to love maternal dear,
Lend brilliant pendants to Bhavání's car.
To him whose youth in Śara thickets strayed,
Reared by the nymphs, thy adoration paid, 308
Resume thy road, and to the world proclaim
The glorious tale of Rantideva's fame,
Sprung from the blood of countless oxen shed,
And a fair river through the regions spread. 312

---

seven great Rishis or Saints. In either case, they form in astronomy the asterism of the Pleiades. Upon his coming to maturity, Skanda encountered and killed the demon, who had filled the region of Indra with dismay:—

> Emissomque imâ de sede Typhoëa terrâ,
> Cœlitibus fecisse metum.

Verse 305 &c. *Whose moulting plumes, to love maternal dear.*] Skanda, or Kártikeya, is represented mounted upon a peacock; and Bhavání we have already seen is the wife of Śiva, and half-mother to this deity. We have also noticed the frequency of the allusion to the delight the peacock is supposed to feel upon the appearance of cloudy and rainy weather.

Verse 310. Rantideva is the son of Sankriti, and sixth in descent from Bharata. Vishńu Puráńa, p. 450 [IV, 19, 9.].

Verse 311. *Sprung from the blood of countless oxen shed.*] The sacrifice of the horse or of the cow, the गोमेधा or चवमेधा, appears to have been common in the earliest periods of the Hindu

Each lute-armed spirit from thy path retires,
Lest drops ungenial damp the tuneful wires.

---

ritual. It has been conceived that the sacrifice was not real, but typical; and that the form of sacrificing only was performed upon the victim, after which it was set at liberty. The text of this passage, however, is unfavourable to such a notion, as the metamorphosis of the blood of the kine into a river certainly implies that blood was diffused. The expression of the original, literally rendered, is, "sprung from the blood of the daughters of Surabhi", that is, 'kine'; Surabhi being a celebrated cow produced at the churning of the ocean, and famed for granting to her votaries whatever they desired. "Daughter of Surabhi" is an expression of common occurrence, to denote the cow.

Verse 312. *And a fair river through the regions spread.*] The name of this river is not mentioned in the text of the poem, but is said by the Commentators to be the Charmanvati; and such a name occurs in Major Wilford's lists, from the Puránas, amongst those streams which seem to arise from the north-west portion of the Vindhya mountains. The modern appellation of the Charmanvati is generally conceived to be the Chumbul, which corresponds with it in source and situation; and which, as it must have been traversed by the Cloud in its northerly course, would most probably have been described by the poet. It may be curious to trace the change of Charmanvati into Chumbul; which seems very practicable, notwithstanding their present dissimilarity. Tavernier, describing the route from Surat to Agra by way of Brampore, calls this river the Chanmelnadi; the possessive termination Vatí (वती) having been confounded with the Nadi (नदी) 'a river': Chanmelnadi is, therefore, the Chanmel river. Again, the addition Nadi being regarded as superfluous, it has been dropped altogether, and we have the Chanmel, or Chambel. The word Chanmel may readily be deduced from Charman; as, in the dialects of Hindustan, the letters N and L are constantly interchangeable, and careless pronunciation may easily convert Charmel into Chanmel, or Chambel. (Lassen, I, 116.)

Celestial couples, bending from the skies
Turn on thy distant course their downward eyes, 316
And watch thee lessening in thy long descent,
To rob the river's scanty stores intent;
As clothed in sacred darkness not thine own,
Thine is the azure of the costly stone, 320
A central sapphire in the loosened girth
Of scattering pearls, that strung the blooming earth.

The streamlet traversed, to the eager sight
Of Daśapura's fair import delight; 324
Welcomed with looks that sparkling eyes bestow,
Whose arching brows like graceful creepers glow,

Verse 314. These two lines occur a little earlier in the Sanskrit; but as they seemed more connected with the two following, and to be rather awkward in their original position, they have been introduced here.

Verse 319. In sacred darkness not thine own.] Being of the same dark blue colour as Krishńa; a hue the poet charges the Cloud with having stolen.

Verse 321. A central sapphire &c.] This comparison, when understood, is happily imagined; but to understand it, we must suppose ourselves above the Cloud, and to be looking obliquely downwards upon its dark body; as shining drops of rain form a continuous line on either side of it, and connect it with the earth.

Verse 324. Daśapura, according to its etymology, should mean a district, that of the ten cities. It is said however by the Commentators to be the name of a city; and by one of them, Mallinátha, to be that of the city of Rantideva: if he is correct, it may possibly be the modern Rintimpore or Rantampore; especially as that town, lying a little to the north of the Chambul, and in the line from Oujein to Tahurasr, is consequently in the course of the Cloud's progress, and the probable position of Daśapura.

Whose upturned lashes to thy lofty way
The pearly ball and pupil dark display; 329
Such contrast as the lovely Kunda shows,
When the black bee sits pleased amidst her snows.
Hence to the land of Brahmá's favoured sons,
O'er Kuru's fatal field, thy journey runs. 332
With deepest glooms hung o'er the deadly plain,
Dewed with the blood of mighty warriors slain.
There Arjun's wrath opposing armies felt,
And countless arrows strong Gáńdíva dealt, 336

Verse 329. *Such contrast as the lovely Kunda shews.*] The Kunda (Jasminum pubescens) bears a beautiful white flower; and the large black bee being seated in the centre of its cup, they afford a very delicate and truly poetical resemblance to the dark iris, and white ball of a full black eye. [Sakunt. 120. W.]

Verse 331. *Hence to the land of Brahmá's favoured sons.*] Brahmávartta (ब्रह्मावर्त) is the abode of Brahmá, or the holy land of the Hindus. It is thus described by Manu, ii. 17:

सरस्वतीदृषद्वत्योर्देवनद्योर्यदन्तरम् ।
तं देवनिर्मितं देशं ब्रह्मावर्तं प्रचक्षते ॥

"Between the two divine rivers, Saraswati and Dŕishadwati, lies the tract of the land which the sages have named Brahmávarta, because it was created by the gods." [Lassen, I. I., I, 91. 126.]

Verse 332. Kuru-Kshetra (कुरुक्षेत्र), the Field of the Kurus, is the scene of the celebrated battle between them and the Páńdus, which forms the subject of the Mahábhárata. It lies a little to the south-east of Tahnesar, and is still a place of note and pilgrimage. It is not far from Panniput, the seat of another celebrated engagement, that between the assembled Princes of Hindustan, and the combined strength of the Mahrattas. This part of the country, indeed, presenting few obstacles to the movement of large armies, has in every period of the history of Hindustan been the theatre of contention.

Thick as thy drops, that, in the pelting shower,
Incessant hurtle round the shrinking flower.

O'er Saraswatí's waters wing thy course,
And inward prove their purifying force;
Most holy, since, oppressed with heaviest grief,
The ploughshare's mighty Lord here sought relief;

Verse 335. Arjuna was the friend and pupil of Kŕishńa, and the third of the Pándava Princes. He has been long ago introduced to European readers, especially in Sir Charles Wilkins' able translation of the Bhagavad-Gítá; and appears, in the opening of that poem, in a very amiable light:

अहोवत महत्पापं कर्तुं व्यवसिता वयम् ।
यद्राज्यसुखलोभेन हन्तुं स्वजनमुद्यताः ॥ ४४ ॥
यदि मामप्रतीकारमशस्त्रं शस्त्रपाणयः ।
धार्तराष्ट्रा रणे हन्युस्तन्मे क्षेमतरं भवेत् ॥ ४५ ॥

"Alas! that for the lust of the enjoyments of dominion we stand "here ready to murder the kindred of our own blood. I would "rather patiently suffer that the sons of Dhŕitaráshtra, with their "weapons in their hands, should come upon me, and, unopposed, kill "me unguarded in the field."

Verse 336. As the horses and swords of chivalry received particular names, so the weapons of the Hindu knights have been similarly honoured. Gándíva is the bow of Arjuna.

Verse 339. The Saraswatí, or, as it is corruptedly called, the Sursooty, falls from the southern portion of the Himálaya mountains, and runs into the great desert, where it is lost in the sands. It flows a little to the north-west of Kuru-kshetra; and though rather out of the line of the Cloud's progress, not sufficiently so to prevent the introduction into the poem of a stream so celebrated and so holy.

Verse 342. We have here the reason why the waters of the Saraswatí are objects of religious veneration. Balaráma is the eldest brother of Kŕishńa. He is called (लांगली) Lángali, (हलभृत्) Ha-

No longer quaffed the wine cup with his wife,
But mourned in solitude o'er kindred strife. 344

Thy journey next o'er Kanakhala bends,
Where Jahnu's daughter from the hills descends;

---

labhŕit, &c., from his being armed with a ploughshare; which he is said to have employed as bills were formerly used, for pulling his enemies down from their horses, &c., which enabled him then to dispatch them with his club. Although Kŕishńa took an active part in the warfare between the Kurus and Páńdus, Balaráma refused to join either party; and retired into voluntary seclusion, filled with grief at the nature of the contest: 'deserting', the poet says, 'his favourite liquor marked by the eyes of Revatí';—that is, emulating their brightness as she shared the revels of her husband. Vishńu Puráńa, p. 510, 604.

Verse 345. The name is Kalakhala in the original, but it more properly is as given above. The meaning of the word, agreeably to a forced etymology, is thus explained in the Gangádwára Máhátmya section of the Skanda Puráńa:

कः को नाम मुक्तिं न भजते तव मज्जनात्
यतः कनखलं तीर्थं नाम्ना बहुर्मुनीश्वराः ॥

"What man (क:) so wicked (खल) as not to obtain (न) future happiness from bathing there? Thence the holy sages have called this Tirtha by the name of Kanakhala."

It also occurs in this passage of the Hari Vansa portion of the Mahábhárata:

गङ्गाद्वारे कनखलं नीलं च यत्र संज्ञितः ॥

"Gangádwára, Kanakhala, and where the moon impends";
and, in both instances, is applied to the place where the Ganges descends into the low ground of Hindustán. The name is still retained; as appears from the testimony of an impartial witness, Lieut. Webb, in his Survey of the Sources of the Ganges; a survey which has essentially improved the geography of those regions:—
"The party arrived at Haridwára, and encamped at the village of

Whose sacred waters, to Bhagirath given,
Conveyed the sons of Sagara to heaven.   348

Kanakhala" (Kankhal), on the west bank of the Ganges, at the distance of about two miles from the fair." Asiatic Researches, xi. 449. The Ganges does not now descend at Kankhal; and it is a question for geologists to solve, whether the Ganges has, in the course of nineteen centuries, so corroded the skirts of the mountain, as to have thrown back the gorge through which she passes, a distance of two miles. See note on a view of Kankhal, Oriental Portfolio.

Verse 346. *Where Jahnu's daughter from the hills descends.*] Jahnu's daughter is Gangá, or the Ganges; which river, "after forcing its way through an extensive tract of mountainous country, here first enters on the plains." It is rather extraordinary that Kálidása should have omitted the name of Haridwára (Hurdwár), and preferred Kanakhala, especially as the former occurs in the Puránas, in the Skanda Puráńa, as mentioned in the note, page 450, vol. xi. of the Researches; and in this passage from the Matsya Puráńa, cited in the Puráńa Sarvaswa:

सर्वत्र सुलभा गङ्गा त्रिषु स्थानेषु दुर्लभा ।
हरिद्वारे प्रयागे च गङ्गासागरसङ्गमे ॥

"The Ganges is everywhere easy of access, except in three places, Haridwára, Prayága, and her junction with the sea." Jahnu is the name of a sage, who, upon being disturbed in his devotions by the passage of the river, drank up its waters. Upon relenting, however, he allowed the stream to re-issue from his ear; and the affinity of Gangá to the saint arises from this second birth.

Verse 348. *Conveyed the sons of Sagara to heaven.*] The Ganges, according to the legend, was brought from heaven, by the religious rites of Bhagiratha, the great-grandson of Sagara; who, as well as that king, had engaged in a long series of acts of austerity, for the purpose of procuring the descent of the river to wash the ashes of Sagara's 60,000 sons. The youths had been reduced to this state by the indignation of Kapila, a saint, whose devotions they had disturbed in their eager quest of the horse that was to be the victim

She, who with smiling waves disportive strayed
Through Sambhu's locks, and with his tresses
                                       played;
Unheeding, as she flowed delighted down,
The gathering storm of Gauri's jealous frown.   352

Should her clear current tempt thy thirsty lip,
And thou inclining bend the stream to sip;
Thy form, like Indra's Elephant, displayed,
Shall clothe the crystal waves with deepest shade;   356

---

of an Aśwamedha by their father. Their misfortunes did not, however, cease with their existence, as their admission to Swarga depended, according to the instructions of Garuda, upon the use of the water of the Ganges in the administration of their funeral rites. At this period the Ganges watered the plains of heaven alone; and it was no easy undertaking to induce her to resign those for an humble and earthly course. Sagara, his son Anśumán, and grandson Dilípa, died without being able to effect the descent of the heavenly stream: but his great-grandson, Bhagíratha, was more fortunate; and his long-continued austerities were rewarded by the fall of the Ganges, the bathing of the ashes of his ancestors with the holy water, and the establishment of them in the enjoyments of Swarga. The whole story is told in the First Book of the Rámáyaña, [from the 41st to the 44th section S., 42-45 G., 40-44 Madras ed.]

Verse 349. She, who with smiling waves disportive strayed.] The earth being unable to bear the sudden descent of so great a river as the Ganges, Śiva was induced, at the intercession of Bhagíratha, to interpose his sacred head. Accordingly, Gangá first alighted on the head of the deity, and remained for a considerable period wandering amongst the tresses of his long and entangled hair, to the extreme jealousy and displeasure, according to Kálidása, of the goddess Gaurí or Párvatí, Śiva's consort.

Verse 355. Thy form, like Indra's Elephant.] We have already

With sacred glooms the darkening waves shall glide,
As where the Jamná mixes with the tide.

As Śiva's Bull upon his sacred neck,
Amidst his ermine, owns some sable speck; 360
So shall thy shade upon the mountain show,
Whose sides are silvered with eternal snow;
Where Gangá leads her purifying waves,
And the Musk Deer spring frequent from the caves. 364

---

noticed that presiding deities are attached to the various points of the compass, and that each of these deities is furnished with a male and female Elephant. Amongst these, the most distinguished is Airávata, the Elephant of Indra, in his capacity of Regent of the East.

Verse 358. *As where the Jamná mingles with the tide.*] The waters of the Jamná, or Yamuná, are described as much darker than those of the Ganges at the point of their confluence, from the circumstances of the stream being less shallow and less discoloured with clay or sand. Occasionally, indeed, the waters of the Ganges there are so white from the diffusion of earthy particles, that, according to the creed of the natives, the river flows with milk. The confluence of rivers always forms a sacred spot in India: but the meeting of the Ganges and Jamná at Prayága or Allahabad, from the sanctity of both the currents, and from the supposed subterraneous addition of the Saraswatí, is a place of distinguished holiness.

Verse 359. *As Śiva's Bull upon his sacred neck.*] The Bull is the vehicle of Śiva, and the animal of the god is always painted of a milk-white colour.

Verse 864. *And the Musk Deer spring frequent from the caves.*] This animal is what is called the Thibet Musk; "but its favourite residence is among the lofty Himalley (Himálaya) mountains, which divide Tartary from Hindustán." See the best account of the Musk Deer yet published, in Gladwin's Oriental Miscellany, Calcutta 1798,

From writhing boughs should forest flames arise,
Whose breath the air, and brand the Yak supplies; 366

accompanied with accurate drawings by Mr. Home, of the figure, teeth, hoofs, &c.

Verse 365. *Should forest flames arise.*] The conflagration of the woods in India is of frequent occurrence; and the causes of it are here described by the poet. The intertwining branches of the Saral (Pinus longifolia), of the Bambu, and other trees, being set in motion by the wind, their mutual friction engenders flame. This spread abroad by the air, and, according to the poet, by the thick tails of the Yak of Tartary or Bos Grunniens (from which Chowries are made), readily communicates to the surrounding foliage, dried up by the heat of the sun, and exceedingly inflammable. The burning of a forest is so well described in the 1st book of the Ritu Sanhára, that I cannot avoid citing the passage, although its length perhaps requires an apology:

पटुतरवेगहतानां मुहुरभ्यमरीहाः पवनपवनवेगात् विप्रसर्पमुखपर्वाः ।
दिनकरपरितापात् शीघतोया: सम्मादू विदूधति भवमुर्धिरीक्षमाखा
वनानां ॥ २२ ॥

विकचनवयुसुमसदृशिष्टुरभासा पवनपवनवेगोन्नतवेगेन पूर्वम् ।
तर्द्विटपसंताघाशिर्घनवाकुलेन दिशि दिशि परिदग्धा भूभव: पाव-
केन ॥ २४ ॥

अमति पवनविद्धः पर्वतानां हरीषु स्फुरति पटुनिनादः गुल्मषण्जकलीषु ।
भवति गहनमध्ये भस्मवृष्टि: क्वचन पयपति भूजवर्मं शाखषटो द्रुमा-
णिम् ॥ २५ ॥

वञ्चतर एव आतः शाखजीनां वनेषु स्फुरति कनकजीर्णः कोटरेषु द्रुमाणाम् ।
परिवदहरूबाखादुत्यतानाम्‌ पूषाद् धमति पवनभूत: सर्वतो अग्निर्न-
नायो ॥ २६ ॥

Which, omitting a few repetitions and excrescences, may be thus translated:

The forest flames—the foliage, sear and dry,
Bursts in a blaze beneath the torrid sky.
Fanned by the gale, the fires resplendent grow,
Brighter than blooming Safflower's vermil glow,

Instant afford the aid 'tis thine to lend,
And with a thousand friendly streams descend. 368
Of all the fruits that fortune yields, the best
Is still the power to succour the distrest.

Shame is the fruit of actions indiscreet,
And vain presumption ends but in defeat. 372
So shall the Śarabhas, who thee oppose,
Themselves to pain and infamy expose;
When round their heads, amidst the lowering sky,
White as a brilliant smile, thy hailstones fly. 376

Next to the mountain, with the foot imprest
Of him who wears the crescent for his crest,

    Brighter than Minium's fierceness, as they wind
Around the branch, or shoot athwart the rind:
Play through the leaves, along the trunk ascend,
And o'er the top in tapering radiance end.
The crackling Damba rushing flames surround,
Roar through the rocks, and through the caves resound.
The dry blade fuel to their rage supplies,
And instant flame along the herbage flies,
Involves the forest tenants in its sphere,
And in its rapid course outstrips the deer.
Like palest gold the towering ray aspires,
And wafting gusts diffuse the wasting fires:
Wide fly the sparks, the burning branches fall,
And one relentless blaze envelopes all.

  Verse 373. The Śarabha is a fabulous animal, described as possessing eight legs, and of a fierce untractable nature. It is supposed to haunt these mountains especially.

  Verse 376. White as a brilliant smile.] It is remarkable that a laugh or smile is always compared to objects of a white colour by Hindu writers.

Devoutly pass, and with religious glow
Around the spot in pious circles go: 380

Verse 377. *Next to the mountain, with the foot imprest.*] The fancied or artificial print of some saint or deity on hills or detached stones is a common occurrence in the creeds of the East. The idea is not confined to the inhabitants of Hindustán; but is asserted similarly by those of Nepal, Ceylon, and Ava; as may be seen in Turner's Journey to Nepal, Symes's Embassy to Ava, &c. The Mussulmans also have the same notion with respect to many of the Prophets; for they believe that the marks of Adam's feet remain on a mountain in the centre of Ceylon; and that those of Abraham were impressed upon a stone which was formerly at Mecca, and which he had used as a temporary scaffold in constructing the upper part of the primary Kaaba. A number of similar stories may be found in Mirkhond, and other Mohammedan authors. The Himálaya mountains are the scene of most of Śiva's adventures, his religious abstraction, his love, marriage &c.; and the place here mentioned may have some connexion with the Ghát, and neighbouring hill at Haridwára, mentioned in Capt. Raper's account of the survey of the Ganges, by the name of Haraká Pairi, 'the foot of Hara or Śiva.'

Verse 380. *Around the spot in pious circles go.*] Circumambulating a venerable object, or person, is a usual mark of profound respect. Thus, in Śakuntalá [p. 160 W.], Kaṇwa thus addresses his foster-daughter, on the eve of her departure:

यासि एतः सखी प्रतापीत्प्रदक्षिणीकुरुष्व ।

"My best beloved, come and walk with me round the
sacrificial fire."

And again, in the Rámáyaṇa, we have the same ceremony described thus:

जनकस्य वचः श्रुत्वा राघवीम्यापिभिस्सुतम् ।
पवादे चतसृणां महिषप भने चिता: ॥
चर्चि मङ्गिवे कृत्वा वेदिं राजानमेव च ।
चवीचापि महाबाज: सहभार्या रघूद्वहः ॥

"Hearing the words of Janaka, the four supporters of Raghu's race,

For there have Saints the sacred altar raised,
And there eternal offerings have blazed,
And blest the faithful worshippers; for they
The stain of sin with life shall cast away, 384
And after death a glad admittance gain
To Śiva's glorious and immortal train.
Here wake the chorus:—bid the thunder's sound,
Deep and reiterated, roll around, 388
Loud as a hundred drums;—while softer strains
The swelling gale breathes sweetly through the
                                        canes;
And from the lovely songsters of the skies
Hymns to the victor of Tripura rise. 392

"previously placed according to the direction of Vaśishṭha, took the
"hands of the four damsels within theirs, and, with their spouses,
"circumambulated the fire, the altar, the king, and the sages."
                Rámáyaṇa, with Translation, I, 60, 37. [I, 73, 32 f.
                        S. 75, 24 f. G. 73, 34 f. Madras ed.]

A somewhat similar practice seems to have been in use amongst
the Celtic nations. The Highland leech, who is called to the aid
of Waverley, "would not proceed to any operation until he had
perambulated his couch three times, moving from east to west, according to the course of the sun." And Sir Walter Scott observes,
in a Note, that "the Highlanders will still make the 'deasil'" (the
circumambulation, or 'pra-dakshiṇa') "around those whom they
wish well to." [Comp. also J. F. Campbell's Tales of the West
Highlands, IV, 314 ff.]

Verse 391. The lovely songsters of the skies] are the females of
the Kinnaras, or demigods, attendant upon Kuvera, and the musicians of Swarga.

Verse 392. Hymns to the victor of Tripura rise.] Tripura is the
name of a city, or rather, as its etymology implies, three cities col-

Thence to the snow-clad hills thy course direct,
And Krauncha's celebrated pass select;
That pass the swans in annual flight explore:
And erst a Hero's mighty arrows tore.   396

---

lectively: these formed the domain of a celebrated Demon, or Asura, destroyed by Śiva, and were reduced to ashes by that Deity. [See the quotations in Weber's Ind. Stud., II, 310.] According to the Commentators, we have here a full and complete concert in honour of Mahádeva.

Verse 394. And Krauncha's celebrated pass select.] I have not been able to make any thing of this pass or hole (क्रौञ्चरन्ध्र). The original text states it to be on the very skirt (उपान्त) of the snowy mountain; and calls it also हंसद्वार, 'The gate of the geese', who fly annually this way to the Mánasarovara lake. Krauncha is described as a mountain, in the Mahábhárata [Hariv. 942]; and, being personified, is there called the son of Maináka. A mountain also called Krauncha Meru occurs in Mr. Wilford's lists, amongst those mountains situated in the north. It must lie at some distance from the plains; and perhaps the Poet, by using the term उपान्त, implies its relative situation with the loftiest part of the range or proper snow-clad mountains.

Verse 396. And erst a Hero's mighty arrows tore.] The Krauncha pass, or defile, in the Krauncha mountain, is said to have been made by the arrows of Bhrigupati, or Paraśuráma, who was educated by Śiva on Mount Kailása, and who thus opened himself a passage from the mountains upon the occasion of his travelling southwards to destroy the Kshatriya or military race. Paraśuráma is an Avatár, or descent of Vishńu, in the person of the son of the Saint Jamadagni; and this Saint being also descended from the celebrated sage Bhrigu, his son is named Bhrigupati, or, Chief of that race. See Legend of Paraśuráma, Vishńu Puráńa, p. 401 [transl. from Mahábh. III, 11071—12010]. The fissure in the Krauncha mountain is, in the Váyu and Vámana [57 ff.] Puráńas, ascribed to Kártikeya. Ibid, p. 109, note 10.

Winding thy way due north through the defile,
Thy form compressed, with borrowed grace shall
smile:
The sable foot that Bali marked with dread,
A god triumphant o'er creation spread. 400
Ascended thence, a transient period rest,
Renowned Kailása's venerated guest;

Verse 399. *The sable foot that Bali marked with dread.*] The story of Bali and the Vámana, or dwarf Avatár, was first told by Sonnerat, and has since been frequently repeated. As the former is a good specimen of the style in which Hindu legends were narrated by European travellers in the last century, it may be here inserted. "The fifth incarnation was in a Bramin dwarf, under the name of Vamen: it was wrought to restrain the pride of the giant Bely. The latter, after having conquered the gods, expelled them from Sorgon: he was generous, true to his word, compassionate, and charitable. Vichenou, under the form of a very little Bramin, presented himself before him while he was sacrificing, and asked him for three paces of land to build a hut. Bely ridiculed the apparent imbecility of the dwarf, in telling him that he ought not to limit his demand to a bequest so trifling;—that his generosity could bestow a much larger donation of land. Vamen answerd, that being of so small a stature, what he asked was more than sufficient. The prince immediately granted his request; and, to ratify his donation, poured water into his right hand; which was no sooner done, than the dwarf grew so prodigiously, that his body filled the universe! He measured the earth with one pace, and the heavens with another; and then summoned Bely to give him his word for the third. The prince then recognised Vichenou, adored him, and presented his head to him: but the god, satisfied with his submission, sent him to govern the Pandalon; and permitted him to return every year to the earth, the day of the full moon, in the month of November."
Sonnerat's Voyages in the East Indies, Calcutta edition,
vol. 1, p. 22.

That mount, whose sides with brightest lustre shine,
A polished mirror, worthy charms divine;   404

Verse 402. *Kailása's venerated guest*] Kailása, as it here appears, a part of the Himálaya range, is in fable a mountain of costly gems or of crystal, the site of Kuvera's capital, and the favourite haunt of Śiva. I shall borrow, from the notes to Southey's 'Curse of Kehama', a description of it from Baldæus, curious enough in itself, but still more so for its strange medley of accuracy and incorrectness, and its uncouth transformation and commixture of the Sanskrit names, "The residence of Isora (Iswara or ईश्वर) is upon the silver mount Kalaja (Kailása or कैलास), to the south of the famous mountain Mahameru, being a most delicious place, planted with all sorts of trees, that bear fruit all the year round. The roses and other flowers send forth a most odoriferous scent; and the pond at the foot of the mount is enclosed with pleasant walks of trees, that afford an agreeable shade; whilst the peacocks and divers other birds entertain the ear with their harmonious noise, as the beautiful women do the eyes. The circumjacent woods are inhabited by a certain people called Munis or Rixis (Rishis or ऋषि), who, avoiding the conversation of others, spend their time in offering daily sacrifices to their god.

"It is observable, that though these Pagans are generally black themselves, they do represent these Rixis to be of a fair complexion, with long white beards, and long garments hanging cross-ways, from about the neck down over the breast. They are in such high esteem among them, that they believe whom they bless are blessed, and whom they curse are cursed.

"Within the mountain lives another generation, called Jexaquinnera (Yaksha or यक्ष, and Kinnara or किन्नर), and Quendra (Indra or इन्द्र), who are free from all trouble, and spend their days in continual contemplation, praises, and prayers to god. Round about the mountain stand seven ladders, by which you ascend to a spacious plain, in the middle whereof is a bell of silver and a square table, surrounded with nine precious stones of divers colours: upon this table lies a silver rose, called Tamarapua (?[तामरपुष्प]), which contains two

Whose base a Rávan from its centre wrung,
Shaken, not sundered, stable though unstrung;
Whose lofty peaks to distant realms in sight
Present a Siva's smile, a lotus white.   408
And lo! those peaks, than ivory more clear,
When yet unstained the parted tusks appear,

---

women as bright and fair as a pearl: one is called Drigasiri(?), *i. e.* 'The lady of the mouth;' the other Tarasiri(?), *i. e.* 'The lady of the tongue:' because they praise God with the mouth and tongue. In the centre of this rose is the triangle of Quivelinga (Siva-lingn); which, they say, is the permanent residence of God." BALDAEUS. The latter part of this description is quite new to the Pandits, and I suspect is rather Mohammedan than Hindu. Little is said of Kailása in authentic Hindu legend. See Vishnu Puráńa, p. 172.

Verse 406. Shaken, not sundered, stable though unstrung.] This alludes to a legend of Rávana's having attempted to remove the mountain from its situation; although he did not succeed as well as Satan and his compeers, when,

"From their foundations loosening to and fro,
They plucked the seated hills."

He considerably unhinged its foundations. The story perhaps originates with the curious vibrating rock at Mahábalipuram; of which it may be said, as is observed by Selden of Mainamber, *i. e.* Ambrose's stone in Cornwall, not far from Penzance, that "it is so great, that many men's united strength cannot remove it, yet with one finger you may wag it."

Verse 407. Whose lofty peaks to distant realms in sight.] The lofty peaks of the Himálaya range of mountains are very justly stated by the poet to be visible to surrounding regions (परिदृश्यम्). They are seen, in the south, from situations more remote than those in which any other peaks have been discerned; and the supposition of their exceeding even the Andes in elevation has been confirmed by recent inquiries.

Beam with new lustre, as around their head
Thy glossy glooms metallic darkness spread; 412
As shews a Halabhrita's sable vest
More fair the pallid beauty of his breast.
Haply across thy long and mountain way
In sport may Gauri with her Śiva stray; 416

Verse 412. *Thy glossy glooms metallic darkness spread.*] The expression in the original (चिरचभिन्नाञ्जनामि) may be rendered, "shining like glossy powdered antimony", a preparation used for darkening the eye-lashes or the edges of the eye-lids, a practice common to the females of the East. It is also explained to mean merely, "black divided antimony"; and the shining greyish-blue of the sulphuret of antimony, the substance alluded to, may often be observed in the hue of heavy clouds. ["Antimony mixed with oil." Schütz.]

Verse 413. Halabhrita is a name of Balarama; and implies, as has been before explained, his use of a ploughshare as a weapon. He is represented of a white colour, clothed in a darkblue vest; and is thus alluded to in the introduction [v. 12] to the Gita Govinda of Jayadeva:

वहसि वपुषि विशदे वसनं जलदाभं हलहतिभीतिमिलितयमुनाभम् ॥
केशव धृतहलधररूप जय जगदीश हरे ॥

Thus translated by Sir William Jones, in his Essay on the Chronology of the Hindus: "Thou bearest on thy bright body a mantle "shining like a blue Cloud, or like the water of the Yamuna trip-"ping towards thee through fear of thy furrowing ploughshare, O "Cesava! assuming the form of Balarama, be victorious O Heri! "Lord of the Universe."

Verse 416. *In sport may Gauri with her Śiva stray.*] I have already noticed that these mountains are the scene of Śiva's loves and sports: they may still be considered as his favourite haunts, for some traces of him seem to start up in every direction amongst them. See the late Travels to the Source of the Ganges, and Col. Hardwicke's Tour to Sirinagur.

Her serpent bracelet from her wrist displaced,
And in her arms the mighty god embraced.
Should thus it fortune, be it thine to lend
A path their holy footsteps may ascend; 420
Close in thy hollow form thy stores comprest,
While by the touch of feet celestial blest.

Then shall the nymphs of heaven, a giddy train,
Thy form an instrument of sport detain: 424
And with the lightning, round each wrist that gleams,
Shall set at liberty thy cooling streams.
But should they seek thy journey to delay—
A grateful solace in the sultry day— 428
Speak harsh in thunder, and the nymphs shall fly
Alarmed, nor check thy progress through the sky.

Where bright the mountain's crystal glories break,
Explore the golden lotus-covered lake; 432

Verse 424. *Thy form an instrument of sport.*] Literally, "They shall take thee as being the abode of an artificial water-work"—a jet-d'eau, or shower-bath; or, according to some of the Commentators, a vessel for sprinkling water, either a common syringe or squirt, or the more elegant Asiatic apparatus in use for sprinkling perfumed waters, especially rose-water—a Guláb-pásh.

Verse 425. *And with the lightning, round each wrist that gleams.*] The diamond and thunderbolt, according to Hindu notions, are of one substance, and are called by the same appellation (वज्र). As the fall of the thunderbolt is usually followed by rain, and may thus be considered as its cause; the propinquity and the mutual friction of the same substance upon the wrists of our young ladies is, in like manner, supposed to occasion the dispersion of the fluid treasures of the Cloud.

Imbibe the dews of Mánasa, and spread
A friendly veil round Airavata's head;
Or, life dispensing, with the Zephyrs go,
Where heavenly trees with fainting blossoms blow. 436

Now on the mountain's side, like some dear friend,
Behold the city of the gods impend;
Thy goal behold, where Gangá's winding rill
Skirts like a costly train the sacred hill; 440

Verse 433. Mánasa, Mánasarovara, or commonly Man-sarour, is a celebrated lake situated in the centre of the Himálaya mountains, and was long said to be the source of the Ganges and Brahmaputra rivers: with respect to the first of these, the statement has been found to be erroneous; and we have no positive proofs of its accuracy with regard to the latter. When the passage in the text was translated, the chief information regarding the latter was derived from the vague reports of Hindu Pilgrims. Since then, Mánasarovara was visited by that enterprising traveller, Moorcroft. He has not yet had a successor. [A. Gerard, Journal of the A. Soc. of Bengal, XI, 363—88.]

We here take leave of the geographical part of the poem, which is highly creditable to Kálidása's accuracy; and now come to the region of unmixed fable, the residence of Kuvera and his attendant demigods.

Verse 434. A friendly veil round Airavata's head.] Indra's Elephant, at supra, verse 365.

Verse 436. Where heavenly trees with fainting blossoms blow.] Literally, the Kalpa trees, one of the five kinds which flourish in Indra's heaven. They are thus enumerated in the Amara Kosha [I, 1, 50]:

पञ्चैते देवतरवो मन्दारः पारिजातकः ।
सन्तानः कल्पवृक्षच पुंसि वा हरिचन्दनम् ॥

Verse 438. The city of the gods impend.] Alaká, the capital of Kuvera.

Where brilliant pearls descend in lucid showers,
And Clouds, like tresses, clothe her lofty towers.

There every palace with thy glory vies,
Whose soaring summits kiss the lofty skies; 444
Whose beauteous inmates bright as lightning glare,
And tabors mock the thunders of the air;
The rainbow flickering gleams along the walls,
And glittering rain in sparkling diamonds falls. 448

There lovely triflers wanton through the day,
Dress all their care, and all their labour play;

Verse 149. I have availed myself of the aid of the Commentators to make out this passage rather more fully than it occurs in the original, and consequently more intelligibly to the English reader. The poet describes the toilet of the Yakshiṇis, or female Yakshas, through the six seasons of the year, by mentioning as the selected flowers those peculiar to each period. Thus the Lotos blooms in Sarat or the sultry season, two months of our autumn; the Kunda (Jasminum pubescens) in Sisira or the dewy season; the Lodh, a species of tree (Symplocos recemosa, Rox.), is in blossom in Hemanta or winter; the Kuravaka (Gomphræna globosa) in Vasanta or spring; the Sirisha (Mimosa Sirisha) in the hot months, or Grishma; and the Nipa or Kadamba (Nauclea Kadamba) at the setting in of the rains. It is to the Commentators also that I am indebted for the sole occupation of the goddesses being pleasure and dress. The fact is,
——To sing, to dance,
To dress, and troll the tongue, and roll the eye.
constitutes a very well-educated female, according to the customs of Hindustan. We cannot help, however, being pleased with the simplicity and propriety of taste which gives to the graceful ornaments of nature so prominent a part in the decoration of feminine beauty.

One while, the fluttering Lotus fans the fair,
Or Kunda top-knots crown the jetty hair.   452
Now, o'er the cheek the Lodh's pale pollen shines,
Now midst their curls the Amaranth entwines.
These graces varying with the varying year,
Sirísha-blossoms deck the tender ear;   456
Or new Kadambas, with thy coming born,
The parted locks and polished front adorn.

Thus graced, they woo the Yakshas to their arms,
And gems, and wine, and music, aid their charms.   460
The strains divine with art celestial thrill,
And wines from grapes of heavenly growth distil.
The gems bestrew each terrace of delight,
Like stars that glitter through the shades of night.   464
There, when the Sun restores the rising day,
What deeds of love his tell-tale beams display!
The withered garlands on the pathway found;
The faded lotus prostrate on the ground;   468
The pearls, that bursting zones have taught to roam,
Speak of fond maids, and wanderers from home.

Verse 462. *And wines from grapes of heavenly growth distil.*]
So MILTON, Paradise Lost, v. 426:

——In heaven, the trees
Of life ambrosial fruitage bear, and vines yield nectar.

And again, line 635:

——Rubined nectar flows,
Fruit of delicious vines, the growth of heaven.

Verse 464. *Like stars that glitter through the shades of night.*]
Thus B. JONSON:

The starres that are the jewels of the night.

Here filled with modest fears, the Yaksha's bride
Her charms from passion's eagerness would hide; 472
The bold presumption of her lover's hands
To cast aside the loosened vest, withstands;
And, feeble to resist, bewildered turns
Where the rich lamp with lofty radiance burns; 476
And vainly whelms it with a fragrant cloud
Of scented dust, in hope the light to shroud.

The gale that blows, eternally their guide,
High over Alaká the clouds divide 480
In parted masses, like the issuing smoke
Of incense by the lattice-meshes broke:

Verse 470. *Speak of fond maids, and wanderers from home.*] I have already mentioned that the Hindus always send the lady to seek her lover, and they usually add a very reasonable degree of ardour and impatience. Our poet, in another place, compares the female so engaged to a rapid current. Thus, in the Rítu Sanhára [II, 7]:

नियातवक्त्र: परिसर्पदुर्गमाः । द्रुतद्वेगैर्लसितसीत्करनिनदैः ॥
स्त्रियः प्रकामा एव जातविभ्रमाः । नयन्ति नदस्सरितं पयोनिधिम् ॥

    Fast flow the turbid torrents, as they sweep
    The shelving valleys to rejoin the deep:
    Impetuous as the maid whom passion warms,
    And drives impatient to her lover's arms,
    Along they bound with unresisted force,
    And banks and trees demolish in their course.

Verse 478. *Of scented dust.*] She casts upon it a handful of *Chúrńa:* which means not only any powdered or pounded substance, but especially aromatic powders; which we may suppose to constitute part of an Indian lady's toilet, as they did in the last century of those of Europe, when the toilet of a belle was equipped

    With patches, powder-box, pulvil, perfumes.

Scattered they float, as if dispersed by fear,
Or conscious guilt spoke retribution near;   484
Their just award for showers that lately soiled
Some painted floor, or gilded roof despoiled.

Ere yet thy coming yields opposing gloom,
The moon's white rays the smiling night illume,   488
And on the moon-gem concentrated full,
That hangs in woven nets in every hall;
Whence cooling dews upon the fair descend,
And life renewed to languid nature lend.   492

What though while Śiva with the god of gold
Delights a friendly intercourse to hold;
The Lord of Love, remembering former woe,
Wields not in Alaká his bee-strung bow: 496

Verse 486. *Some painted floor.*] It is customary amongst the Hindus, upon festival occasions, to smooth and paint the ground on which worship is to be performed, or the assembly to be held. As this spot is generally in an open area within the walls of the house, a shower of rain is of course very hostile to such decoration.

Verse 489. The moon-gem, or Chandrakánta (चन्द्रकान्त), which is supposed to absorb the rays of the moon, and to emit them again in the form of pure and cool moisture. [St. Julien Mémoires sur les contrées occidentales. Paris: 1858, II, p. 145.]

Verse 495. *The Lord of Love, remembering former woe.*] This alludes to the fate which befel the Hindu Cupid upon his assailing Śiva, whom, at the desire of the gods, he inflamed with the love of Párvati. Śiva, in his wrath, reduced the little deity to ashes, by a flame from the eye in his forehead; and, although he was subsequently restored to animation, he is here supposed to remain in dread of his former enemy. The whole story is spiritedly told in Sir William Jones's Hymns to Camdeo and to Durgá.

Yet still he triumphs: for each maid supplies
The fatal bow with love-inspiring eyes;
And wanton glances emulate the dart,
That speeds unerring to the beating heart. 500

Northward from where Kuvera holds his state,
Where Indra's bow surmounts the arching gate;
Where on rich boughs the clustering flower depends,
And low to earth the tall Mandára bends; 501
Pride of the grove, whose wants my fair supplies,
And nurtures like a child—my dwelling lies.

Verse 499. *And wanton glances emulate the dart.*] The eye darting arrows is an idea familiar to English poetry; as in these instances:

    Her eye darted contagious fire.   MILTON.
    Her eyes carried darts of fire,
    Feathered all with swift desire.
           GREENE'S "Never too late."
    I mote perceive how in her glancing sight
    Legions of loves with little wings did fly,
    Darting their deadly arrows fiery bright.
           SPENSER. Sonnet 16.
    And those love-darting eyes shall roll no more.
           POPE'S Elegy.

Verse 501. *The tall Mandára.*] The Coral-tree, Erythrina Indica.

Verse 506. *And nurtures like a child.*] Tender attachment to natural objects is one of the most pleasing features in the poetical compositions of the Hindus. It is very frequently expressed, and perhaps in few places with more beauty than in the drama of Sakontalá, where, upon departing from the bower of her foster-father, she bids adieu to the plants she had carefully tended, and the orphan fawn she had reared. The whole of this scene must be read

There is the fountain, emerald steps denote,
Where golden buds on stalks of coral float;   508
And for whose limpid waves the Swans forsake,
Pleased at thy sight, the mount-encircled lake.
Soft from the pool ascends a shelving ground,
Where shades devoted to delight abound;   512
Where the cærulean summit towers above
The golden circle of a plantain-grove:
Lamented haunts! which now in thee I view,
As glittering lightnings girt thy base of blue.   516

See where the clustering Mádhaví entwines,
And bright Kuruvaka the wreath confines;
Profuse, Aśoka sheds its radiant flower,
And budding Keśara adorns the bower;   520
These are my rivals; for the one would greet,
As I would willingly, my charmer's feet;

---

with pleasure; and may be classed with the departure of Goldsmith's village family from Auburn, and the farewell of Eve to the bowers of Paradise.

Verse 517. The Mádhaví entwines.] This Creeper (Giertnera racemosa, or Banisteria Bengalensis) is often alluded to by the Poets, for its superior elegance, and the beauty of its red blossoms.

Verse 518. Kuruvaka is the crimson Amaranth. The Sanskrit name is also applied to a blue species of Barleria.

Verse 519. Profuse, Aśoka sheds its radiant flower.] Jonesia Aśoka; speaking of which, Sir William Jones says, "The vegetable world scarcely exhibits a richer sight than an Aśoka tree in full bloom."

Verse 520. And budding Keśara.] A tree yielding a strong-smelling flower (Mimusops elengi).

And, with my fondness, would the other sip
The grateful nectar of her honeyed lip. 524

A golden column on a crystal base,
Begirt with jewels, rises o'er the place.
Here, when the evening twilight shades the skies,
The blue-necked Peacock to the summit flies, 528
And moves in graceful circles to the tone
My fair awakens from her tinkling zone.
These be thy guides—and faithfully preserve
The marks I give thee: or e'en more, observe, 532
Where painted emblems holy wealth design,
Kuvera's treasures—that abode is mine.

Verse 521. *These are my rivals, &c.*] These allusions refer to some particular notions of the Hindus respecting the Kèsara and Asoka, which plants are said to blossom upon being touched respectively by the face or foot of a female: the story is probably, originally poetical. [Stenzler od Raghuv. VIII, 61, and Kumáras. III, 26.]

Verse 528. *The blue-necked Peacock to the summit flies.*] The wild Peacock, although it lays its nest upon the ground, is said, by Captain Williamson, to roost constantly on the loftiest trees.

Verse 530. *My fair awakens from her tinkling zone.*] A girdle of small bells (क्षुद्रघण्टिका) is a favourite Hindu ornament; also silver circles at the ankles and wrists, which emit a ringing noise as the wearer moves.

Verse 534. *Kuvera's treasures.*]
   Thick with sparkling oriental gems
   The portal shone.——
         Paradise Lost, B. iii. 507.
For such Kuvera's nine treasures are sometimes supposed to be. Rámásrama (and Bharundikshita) commenting upon Amara [1, 71], thus enumerates them, from the Sabdárnava:

Haply its honours are not now to boast,
Dimmed by my fate, and in my exile lost. 536

पद्मो ऽक्षिया महापद्मः शङ्खो मकरकच्छपौ ।
मुकुन्दनन्दनीलाश्च खर्वश्च निधयो नव ॥

"The Padma, Mahápadma, Sankha, Makara, Kachhapa, Mukunda, Nanda, Nila, and Kharva, are the nine Nidhis." The Śabda Ratnávali also has the same reading. In Hemachandra [v. 133], and the Śabda Málá, कुन्द is substituted for नन्द. Nidhi (निधि) is the generic name; but how it should be rendered into English, I am not prepared to say. Mr. Colebrooke calls the particular Nidhis, 'auriferous gems'. See his translation of the Amara Kosha. Some of the words bear the meanings of precious or holy things: thus, Padma is the Lotus; Sankha the shell or conch. Again, some of them imply large numbers; thus, Padma is 10,000 millions, and Mahápadma is 100,000 millions, &c.; but all of them are not received in either the one or the other acceptation. We may translate almost all into things: thus, a lotus, a large lotus, a shell, a certain fish, a tortoise, a crest, a mathematical figure used by the Jainas. Nila refers only to colour; but Kharva, the ninth, means a dwarf. Mr. Kindereley, translating through the medium of the Tamul [probably from the Márkandeya Purána, c. 68.], has called eight of Kuvera's gems, the coral, pearl, cat's-eye, emerald, diamond, sapphire, ruby, and topaz. The ninth he leaves undetermined. In Dr. Hunter's Dictionary, I find one only of the nine in the Hindoostanee Language, نيلم or نيل Neelam or Neelmun, derived from नीलमणि 'a blue gem', and interpreted the Sapphire. पद्मराग Padma-colour, means a Ruby; and possibly the Padma may be the same: perhaps कच्छप. the tortoise, means tortoise-shell; and Makara may be an error for Maraka or Marakata, an Emerald, or it may imply the same stone from the green colour of a fish: these, however, are mere conjectures. Agreeably to the system of the Tántrikas, the Nidhis are personified, and upon certain occasions, as the worship of Lakshmi, the goddess of prosperity, &c., come in for a share of religious veneration. They have also their peculiar mantras, or mystical verses.

For when the sun withdraws his cheering rays,
Faint are the charms the Kamala displays.

To those loved scenes repaired, that awful size,
Like a young elephant, in haste disguise; 540
Lest terror seize my fair one, as thy form
Hangs o'er the hillock, and portends the storm.
Thence to the inner mansion bend thy sight,
Diffusing round a mild and quivering light; 544
As when, through evening shades, soft flashes play
Where the bright fire-fly wings his glittering way.

Verse 538. The Kamala is a name of the lotus.

Verse 546. Where the bright fire-fly wings his glittering way.] The fire-fly presents a very beautiful appearance, as its soft and twinkling light is contrasted with the deep shade of the bushes, in which it may be seen in great numbers during the wet season. The phænomenon is common to the East and the West Indies; and it may be amusing to see the effect produced by it on different persons and at different periods. Moore, meeting with it in America, writes some elegant stanzas on the subject; and adds to the lightness of his verse the solidity of prose in the authority of this note: —"The lively and varying illumination with which these fire-flies light up the woods at night gives quite an idea of enchantment. Puis ces mouches se developpant de l'obscurité de ces arbres, et s'approchant de nous, nous les voyions sur les orangers voisins, qu'ils mettoient tout en feu, nous rendant la vue de leurs beaux fruits, que la nuit avoit ravie, &c.—L'Histoire Des Antilles." See Moore's Odes and Epistles. We have now to hear the description of a Traveller of 1673, the learned and very devout Johannes Fryer, M. D.

"The next day, at twelve o'clock at noon, we struck into our old road at Moorbar, from whence before we were misguided: we packed hence by five in the afternoon, and left our burnt wood on the

There, in the fane, a beauteous creature stands,
The first best work of the Creator's hands; 548

---

right-hand; but entered another, which made us better sport, deluding us with false flashes, that you would have thought the trees on a flame, and presently, as if untouched by fire, they retained their wonted verdure. The Coolies beheld the sight with horror and amazement, and were consulting to set me down and shift for themselves; whereof being informed, I cut two or three with my sword, and, by breathing a vein, let Shitan (the Devil) out, who was crept into their fancies; and led them, as they do a startling jade, to smell to what their wall-eyes represented amiss; where we found an host of flies, the subject both of our fear and wonder, which the sultry heat and moisture had generated into being, the certain prodromus of the ensuing rain, which followed us from the hills. This gave my thoughts the contemplation of that miraculous bush crowned with innocent flames that gave to Moses so pleasant and awful a prospect; the fire, that consumes every thing, seeming rather to dress than offend it."

Verse 548. *The first best work of the Creator's hands.*] Literally, the first creation of Brahmá: and 'first' may refer to time, or to degree: it most probably here means 'best.' So Milton, speaking of Eve:

> "Oh, Fairest of creation! last and best
> Of all God's works."——
>
> Paradise Lost, B. ix. 896.

We now enter upon perhaps the most pleasing part of this elegant little poem, the description of the Yaksha's wife. I may perhaps come under the denomination of those who, according to the illiberal and arrogant criticism of such a writer as a Mr. Pinkerton, prove, "That the climate of India, while it inflames the Imagination, impairs the judgment;" when, standing in very little awe of such a poetical censor, I advance an opinion, that we have few specimens, either in classical or modern poetry, of more genuine tenderness or delicate feeling.

Whose slender limbs inadequately bear
A full-orbed bosom, and a weight of care;
Whose teeth like pearls, whose lips like Bimbas
                        show,
And fawn-like eyes still tremble as they glow. 552

Lone as the widowed Chakravákí mourns,
Her faithful memory to her husband turns,

Verse 551. *Whose lips like Bimbas show.*] The Bimba (Bryonia grandis) bears a red fruit, to which the lip is very commonly compared.

Verse 552. The Chakraváki is the ruddy goose (Anas Casarca), more commonly known in India by the appellation Brahmany Duck or Goose. These birds are always observed to fly in pairs during the day, but are supposed to remain separate during the night. [Sakuntalá, ed. Williams, p. 129.] In the Hindoostanee Philology of Messrs. Gilchrist and Roebuck, an amusing account of the popular belief on this subject is thus given: "This bird, in the poetry of the "Hindus, is their turtledove, for constancy and connubial affection; "with the singular circumstance of the pair being doomed for ever "to nocturnal separation, for having offended one of the Hindu di- "vinities (Munis or Saints), whence,

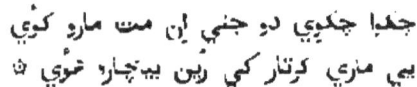

"Mark Heaven's decree, and man forbear
"To aim thy shafts, or puny thunder
"At these poor fowls, a hapless pair,
"Who pass the lonely nights asunder.

"If we believe popular tradition and assertions, the cause is so far "confirmed by the effect observable in the conduct of these birds to "the present day, who are said to occupy the opposite banks of a "water or stream regularly every evening, and exclaim the live-long "night to each other, thus:

And sad, and silent, shalt thou find my wife,
Half of my soul, and partner of my life,

چکوِي مَين آوِن؟ نِہيں نِہيں چکوا —
چلوا مَين آوِن؟ نِہيں نِہيں چلوِي

"Say, shall I come, my dear, to thee?
"Ah no, indeed, that cannot be.—
"But may I wing my love to you?
"Nay chuck, alas! this will not do."

Verse 556. Half of my soul, and partner of my life.] So MILTON:

Part of my soul, I seek thee; and thee claim,
My other half.—

जीवितं मे द्वितीयम्, "My second existence", are the words of the original; and the other expression, "my half", is not more uncommon in Sanskrit than in Western poetry. Thus these tender, and, as Mrs. Malaprop thinks, profane expressions of endearment seem to have obtained a very extensive circulation. 'My life', 'my soul', are common to most of the European languages; and the most frequent epithet by which a mistress is addressed in Persian or Hindoostanee, جی, is of a similar import. Amongst the Romans, 'vita' and 'anima' were used in the same manner, or even in the temperate warmth of friendship; as Horace calls Virgil:

Animæ dimidium meæ,
Half of my soul!

And Propertius, addressing his Mistress, calls her his Life:

Æratas rumpam, mea Vita, catenas.
I'll burst, my Life, the brazen chains.

We may suppose the Romans derived these pretty words from the Greeks; and indeed, as we learn from Juvenal, vi. 194, they were very fond of employing, though not in the most becoming manner, the original terms Ζωὴ καὶ ψυχή, the English translation of which has been given at some length by Mrs. Tighe, in her poem of Psyche; and, with some addition, by Lord Byron, in his Anglo-

Nipped by chill sorrow, as the flowers enfold
Their shrinking petals from the withering cold.
I view her now! Long weeping swells her eyes,
And those dear lips are dried by parching sighs. 560
Sad on her hand her pallid cheek declines,
And half unseen through veiling tresses shines;
As when a darkling night the moon enshrouds,
A few faint rays break straggling through the
          Clouds. 564

Now at thy sight I mark fresh sorrows flow,
And sacred sacrifice augments her woe.
I mark her now with Fancy's aid retrace
This wasted figure and this haggard face. 568

Greek song, the burthen of which is the old sentiment in a modern antique shape, or 'My Life, I love you', in the Ζωή μου, σᾶς ἀγαπῶ, of the Greek of the Morea.

Verse 566. *And sacred sacrifice augments her woe.*) Thus Laodamia to Protesilaus, in Ovid:

   Thura damus lacrymamque super.
  We offer incense up, and add our tears.

The Commentators, however, are not agreed how to interpret this passage in the original text, नियमाङ्कुशा nor the expression नियतति पुरे, "She falls before thee": they seem, however, to conceive it means, that the approach of the Cloud reminding her of its being the period at which absent husbands usually return home, she recollects that the return of her own lord is proscribed; and therefore either falls in a swoon, or with excess of affliction. The sacrifice is to be performed to render the gods propitious, or it is a sacrifice called वारुवति, usually performed by women at the beginning of the rainy season. Some interpret पुरे "In the city", not "Before, in front." (C. Schütz: "when thy glances fall on the city.")

Now from her favourite bird she seeks relief,
And tells the tuneful Sárika her grief;
Mourns o'er the feather'd prisoner's kindred fate,
And fondly questions of its absent mate.   572
In vain the lute for harmony is strung,
And round the robe-neglected shoulder slung;

Verse 570. The Sáriká (Grakula religiosa) is a small bird, better known by the name of Mainá. It is represented as a female, while the parrot is described as a male bird [See J. E. Hall in his edition of the Vásavadattá, p. 35]: and as these two have, in all Hindu tales, the faculty of human speech, they are constantly introduced, the one inveighing against the faults of the male sex, and the other exposing the defects of the female. They are thus represented in the fourth story of that entertaining collection, the Baitál Pachísí:

मैना बोली कि पुरुष बधर्मी पापी हत्यावान स्त्रीहत्ता करने वाले होते हैं । फिर सुनकर तोते ने कहा कि नारी भी हत्यावान झूठी बेवकूफ कानची हत्यारी होती है । ["The mainah said, 'Men are devoid of religion, sinful, treacherous and murderers of women.' The parrot having heard this replied, 'Woman is also deceitful, false, silly, avaricious and a murderess.'"]

Ladies have always been distinguished for maintaining pet animals; and the fancy seems to have been equally prevalent in the East and West, and in ancient or modern times. The Swallow of Lesbia, 'Passer deliciæ meæ puellæ', may rival the Sáriká of the wife of the Yaksha, and Bullfinch of Mrs. Throckmorton. See Cowper's Poems.

Verse 573. In vain the lute for harmony is strung.] The lute is here put for the Viná or Been, a stringed instrument of sacred origin, and high celebrity amongst the Hindus. In Bengal, however, players on this instrument are very rarely met with; and amongst the natives of this province the English fiddle is its substitute. In the Játras, or dramatic performances still current amongst them, I have seen the entrance of Nárada, the traditionary inventor of the

And faltering accents strive to catch in vain
Our race's old commemorative strain: 576
The falling tear, that from reflection springs,
Corrodes incessantly the silvery strings;
Recurring woe still pressing on the heart,
The skilful hand forgets its grateful art, 580
And, idly wandering, strikes no measured tone,
But wakes a sad wild warbling of its own.

At times, such solace animates her mind
As widowed wives in cheerless absence find: 584
She counts the flowers, now faded on the floor,
That graced with monthly piety the door.
Thence reckons up the period, since from home,
And far from her, I was compelled to roam; 588
And deeming, fond, my term of exile run,
Conceives my homeward journey is begun.

Víná, bearing in its stead a violin. The Víná is much the most harmonious and scientific of all the Hindu instruments of music. A description of it may be found in the First Volume of the Asiatic Researches.

Verse 574. "Robe-neglected" is here put for मलिनवसने, 'dirty clothes.' So Laodameia says:

Et quâ possum squalore tuos imitare labores, &c.
And with my squalid vesture ape thy toils.

Verse 576. Our race's old commemorative strain.] "The verse made in honour of my kindred": a circumstance that points out some affinity to the songs of the ancient minstrels and family bards.

Verse 586. That graced with monthly piety the door.] The Hindus pay a species of adoration to many inanimate objects. Amongst others, the door-way, or door-post, receives such homage as is rendered by hanging up a flower or a garland there once a month.

Lightened by tasks like these, the day proceeds;
But much I dread a bitterer night succeeds,　　592
When thou shalt view her on the earth's cold breast,
Or lonely couch of separation rest,
Disturbed by tears those pallid cheeks that burn,
And vision of her dearer half's return.　　596
Now seeking sleep, a husband to restore;
And waking now, his absence to deplore;
Deprived of slumber by returning woes,
Or mocked by idle phantoms of repose;　　600
Till her slight form, consumed by ceaseless pain,
Shews like the moon, fast hastening to its wane.
Crisp from the purifying wave, her hair
Conceals the charms, no more her pleasing care;　　604
And, with neglected nails, her fingers chase,
Fatigued, the tresses wandering o'er her face.

Firm winds the fillet, as it first was wove,
When fate relentless forced me from my love;　　608
And never flowery wreaths, nor costly pearls,
Must hope to decorate the fettered curls;
Loosed by no hand, until, the law divine
Accomplished, that delighted hand is mine.　　612

Verse 591. In this, and some of the following passages, considerable liberty has been taken with the order of the original.

Verse 607. Firm winds the fillet, as it first was wove.] The Veńi is a braid into which the long hair of the Hindustani women is collected, when they have lost their husbands. [So Sítá in Rámáy. V, 15, 21 (Madras ed.)] The dancing-girls also wear their hair in this manner.

Dull as the flower when clouds through æther sweep,
Not wholly waking, nor resigned to sleep,
Her heavy eyelids languidly unclose
To where the moon its silvery radiance throws 616
Mild through the chamber: once a welcome light;
Avoided now, and hateful to her sight.

Those charms that glittering ornaments oppress,
Those restless slumbers that proclaim distress, 620
That slender figure worn by grief severe,
Shall surely gain thy sympathizing tear.
For the soft breast is swift to overflow,
In moist compassion, at the claims of woe. 624

The same fond wife as when compelled to part,
Her love was mine, I still possess her heart.
Her well-known faith this confidence affords,
Nor vain conceit suggests unmeaning words. 628
No boaster I! and time shall quickly teach,
With observation joined, how just my speech.

O'er her left limbs shall glad pulsations play,
And signs auspicious indicate the way; 632

Verse 616. *To where the moon.*] The moon is supposed to be the reservoir of amrita or ambrosia, and to furnish the gods and manes with the supply. "It is replenished from the sun, during the fortnight of the increase. On the full moon, the gods adore that planet for one night; and for the first day, all of them, together with the Pitris and Rishis, drink one kalá or digit daily, until the ambrosia is exhausted." Váyu Puráńa.

Verse 631. *O'er her left limbs shall glad pulsations play.*] Palpitations in the left limbs, and a throbbing in the left eye, are here

And like the lotus trembling on the tide,
While its deep roots the sportive fish divide,
So tremulous throbs the eye's enchanting ball,
Loose o'er whose lids neglected tresses fall. 636

Soothed by expected bliss, should gentle sleep
O'er her soft limbs and frame exhausted creep,
Delay thy tidings, and suspend thy flight,
And watch in silent patience through the night. 640
Withhold thy thunders, lest the awful sound
Her slumber banish, and her dreams confound;
Where her fond arms, like winding shrubs, she flings
Around my neck, and to my bosom clings. 644

Behold her rising with the early morn,
Fair as the flower that opening buds adorn;
And strive to animate her drooping mind
With cooling rain-drops and refreshing wind; 648
Restrain thy lightnings, as her timid gaze
Shrinks from the bright intolerable blaze;

---

described as auspicious omens, when occurring in the female: In the male, the right side is the auspicious side, corresponding with the ideas of the Greeks, thus described by Potter:—

"The third sort of internal omens were the Παλμοὶ or Παλμικὰ σιωνίσματα, so called ἀπὸ τοῦ πάλλειν, 'from palpitating.' Such were the palpitations of the heart, the eye, or any of the muscles, called, in Latin, 'saltationes', and βόμβος, or 'a ringing in the ears', which in the right ear was a lucky omen: so also was the palpitation of the right eye, as Theocritus telleth us:

"Ἄλλεται ὀφθαλμός μοι ὁ δεξιός.
My right eye twinkles."

And murmuring softly, gentle sounds prepare,
With words like these to raise her from despair:— 652

' Oh, wife adored! whose lord still lives for thee,
' Behold his friend and messenger in me;
' Who now approach thy beauteous presence, fraught
' With many a tender and consoling thought! 656
' Such tasks are mine:—where absent lovers stray,
' I speed the wanderer lightly on his way;
' And with my thunders teach his lagging mind
' New hopes the braid of absence to unbind.' 660

As beauteous Maithili with glad surprise
Bent on the Son of air her opening eyes,
So my fair partner's pleased uplifted gaze
Thy friendly presence with delight surveys. 664
She smiles, she speaks, her misery foregoes,
And deep attention on thy words bestows;
For such dear tidings happiness impart,
Scarce less than mutual meeting to the heart. 668

Verse 660. 'The braid of absence' is the Veñi; see Note on verse 607.

Verse 661. Maithili is a name of Sitá, derived from Mithilá, the place of her nativity, and the modern Tirhut. The allusion relates to the discovery of her in Lanká, by Ráma's envoy, Hanoomán, the Monkey chief, said to be the son of the Wind. [Rámáy. V, 34.]

Verse 668. Scarce less than mutual meeting to the heart.] They have a proverb similar to this in the Hindustanee language, "A letter is half a meeting." The expression is common in the poetry of the Rekhta, and occurs thus in a Ghazal by Jirat:

کہتی قین کہ مکتوب بنی فی نصف ملاقات

Being, of years protracted, aid thy friend,
And with my words thine own suggestions blend!
Say thus: 'Thy lord o'er Ráma's mountain strays,
' Nor cares but those of absence blight his days. 672
' His only wish by me his friend to know,
' If he is blest with health, that thou art so:
' For still this fear especially must wait
' On every creature of our passing state. 676

' What though to distance driven by wrath divine,
' Imagination joins his form with thine.
' Such as I view, is his emaciate frame;
' Such his regrets; his scorching pangs the same; 680
' To every sigh of thine his sigh replies,
' And tears responsive trickle from his eyes.

' By thee unheard, by those bright eyes unseen,
' Since fate resists, and regions intervene, 684
' To me the message of his love consigned
' Pourtrays the sufferings of his constant mind.

It also exists in the Arabic language; and is thus given in one of the Exercises of Captain Lockett's Translation of the Mi'at Ámil, and the Sharah Mi'at Ámil, or an Arabic Grammar and Commentary:

المراسلات كم قيل نصف الملاقات

"Correspondence, they say, is half an interview."

Verse 675. For still this fear especially must wait.] It is to be recollected here, that even these heavenly Beings are of a perishable nature, and subject to the infirmities of existence. The whole are swept away at each Mahá-pralaya, or destruction of the Universe,

Which, like the baseless fabric of a vision,
Leaves not a wreck behind.

'Oh! were he present, fondly would he seek
'In secret whisper that inviting cheek;
'Woo thee in close approach, his words to hear,
'And breathe these tender accents in thine ear:'

" Goddess beloved! how vainly I explore
" The world, to trace the semblance I adore.
" Thy graceful form the flexile tendril shews,
" And like thy locks the peacock's plumage glows;
" Mild as thy cheeks, the moon's new beams appear,
" And those soft eyes adorn the timid deer;
" In rippling brooks thy curling brows I see,
" But only view combined these charms in thee.

Verse 695. *Mild as thy cheeks, the moon's new beams appear.*] Comparing a beautiful face to the moon has been supposed peculiar to Oriental Poets. Instances, however, may be found in English verse: perhaps that passage in Pope, where, speaking of an amiable female and the moon, he says, "Serene in virgin modesty she shines", may not be exactly in point, although the general idea is similar. Spenser, however, is sufficiently precise:

> Her spacious forehead, like the clearest moon,
> Whose full-grown orb begins now to be spent,
> Largely displayed in native silver shone,
> Giving wide room to beauty's regiment.

Verse 698. *But only view combined these charms in thee.*] This turn of the compliment, closely faithful to the original, conveys a high idea of the gallantry of a Hindu Bard, and as this gallantry cannot be the ten times repeated retail of romantic folly or chivalrous phrensy, it may be considered as the natural expression of unsophisticated tenderness. We have in these lines a complete description of beauty, agreeably to Hindu fancy; and I do not think the series of comparisons will much suffer by being contrasted with any similar series in classical or modern writers.

"E'en in these wilds our unrelenting fate
"Proscribes the union, love and art create: 700
"When, with the colours that the rock supplies,
"O'er the rude stone thy pictured beauties rise,
"Fain would I think, once more we fondly meet,
"And seek to fall in homage at thy feet;— 704
"In vain:—for envious tears my purpose blight,
"And veil the lovely image from my sight.

"Why should the god who wields the five-fold dart
"Direct his shafts at this afflicted heart; 708

Verse 701. *When, with the colours that the rock supplies.*] "Having painted you with mineral colours" (धातुरगैः), that is, according to the Commentators, with 'red chalk', &c. Our very limited acquaintance with the high land which is the scene of the Yaksha's exile prevents our specifying the mineral substances which he may be supposed to have employed. The expression in the text, however, is one of many circumstances that render it probable that the mountains which run across the northernmost part of the Peninsula are rich in the objects of mineralogical inquiry. We know that copper mines have been discovered in the eastern extremity of them, the ore of which is very productive. The Sálagrám stones, or Ammonites, are found in the Narmadá; and the several kinds of Makshikas, a class of ores not yet investigated, are usually called नर्दीज and तापीज, or 'River-born', and 'Tapti-born', in reference to their being found in the course of the Tapti river.

Verse 707. *Why should the god who wields the five-fold dart.*] Kámadeva, the Hindu Cupid, is represented as the Eros of the Greeks, armed with a bow and arrows. These weapons are of peculiar construction, and most poetically formed. The bow is of sugar-cane; the bow-string consists of a line of bees; and the arrows are tipped each with a separate flower. The weapons and application of the allegory will be best explained by a verse in Sir William Jones's Hymn to this deity:

" Nor spare to agonize an aching breast,
" By sultry suns and banishment oppressed?
" Oh, that these heavy hours would swiftly fly,
" And lead a happier fate, and milder sky! 712

" Believe me, dearest, that my doom severe
" Obtains from heavenly eyes the frequent tear;
" And where the spirits of these groves attend
" The pitying drops in pearly showers descend, 716
" As oft in sleep they mark my outstretched arms,
" That clasp in blissful dreams thy fancied charms,
" Play through the air, and fold in fond embrace
" Impassive matter and etherial space. 720

    He bends the luscious cane, and twists the string,
    With bees how sweet, but, ah! how keen their sting!
    He with five flowrets tips the ruthless darts,
    Which through five senses pierce enraptured hearts.
    Strong Chumpa, rich in odorous gold;
    Warm Arka, nursed in heavenly mould;
    Dry Nagesar, in silver smiling;
    Hot Kritlcum, our sense beguiling;
    And last, to kindle fierce the scorching flame,
    Love shaft, which gods bright Bela name.

In the Romaunt of the Rose there is something of a similar allegory: Cupid is armed with "ten brode arrows"; of which, "five were shaven well and dight", and of a nature to produce virtuous attachment; while the other five, "also black as fiend in hell", were 'Pride', 'Villaine', &c., and of pernicious properties.

    Verse 715. *And where the spirits of these groves attend.*] Sthali Devatás are, literally, 'the deities of the soil'; so completely has Hindu, like Grecian faith, peopled inanimate nature.

"Soft and delightful to my senses blows
"The breeze that southward wafts Himálaya's snows,
"And rich impregnated with gums divine,
"Exuding fragrant from the shattered pine, 724
"Diffuses sweets to all, but most to me;—
"Has it not touched? does it not breathe of thee?

"What are my tasks?—to speed the lagging night,
"And urge impatiently the rising light: 728
"The light returned, I sicken at the ray,
"And shun as eagerly the shining day:
"Vain are my labours in this lonely state;
"But fate proscribes, and we must bow to fate. 732

"Let then my firmness save thee from despair,
"Who trust myself, nor sink beneath my care:

Verse 733. Let then my firmness save thee from despair.] We are scarcely prepared for this sudden fortitude of the Yaksha; but it is not by any means unnatural. The task of consoling partners in affliction necessarily diverts the mind from its own distress.

Reference to the principle is very frequent in the writings of the Hindus. The Átma Bodha, or 'Knowledge of Spirit', a small treatise which contains the ethical part of the Vedanta philosophy, and which has been translated and published by Dr. Taylor, concludes with this stanza [v. 67]:—

दिग्देशकालाद्यनपेक्ष सर्वगम् । शीतादिदहिनसुखं निरञ्जनम् ॥
यः स्वात्मतीर्थं भजते विनिष्क्रियः । स सर्ववित्सर्वगतोऽमृतो भवेत् ॥

"He who has made the pilgrimage of his own spirit, a pilgrimage in which there is no concern respecting situation, place, or time; which is everywhere; in which neither cold nor heat are experienced; which bestows perpetual happiness and freedom from sor-

" Trust to futurity; for still we view
" The always wretched, always blest, are few: 736
" Life like a wheel's revolving orb turns round,
" Now whirled in air, now dragged along the ground.

" When from his serpent couch, that swims the deep,
" Sárangí rises from celestial sleep;   740

row; he is without action, knows all things, pervades all things, and obtains eternal beatitude." [C. Graul, Bibliotheca Tamulica. Lipsiae 1854, Vol. I, p. 195, agreeing with the Madras edition.]

A fine passage inculcating the same feeling occurs in Manu ch. viii. 84, where the legislator exhorts a witness to speak the truth:—

आत्मैव ह्यात्मनः साक्षी गतिरात्मा तथात्मनः ।
मा ऽवमंस्थाः स्वमात्मानं नृणां साक्षिणमुत्तमम् ॥

"The soul itself is its own witness; the soul itself is its own refuge: offend not thy conscious soul, the supreme internal witness of men." Sir WILLIAM JONES's Translation.

Verse 737.] Plutarch, in his 'Consolation to Apollonius', has a similar idea, in similar words:

Τροχοῦ [γὰρ] περιστείχοντος ἄλλοθ' ἡτέρα
Ἀψὶς ὑπερθε γίγνετ', ἄλλοθ' ἡτέρα.

The wheel of Life is ever on the round,
While one side's up, the other's on the ground.

Verse 740. The serpent couch is the great snake Ananta, upon which Vishńu, or, as he is here called, the Holder of the bow Sárnga (the horn-bow), reclines, during four months, from the 11th of Áshádha to the 11th of Kártik; or, as it has occurred in 1813 (the year in which the first edition was printed), from the 23d of June to the 26th of October. The sleep of Vishńu, during the four months of the periodical rains in Hindustan, seems to bear an emblematical relation to that season. It has been compared to the Egyptian Hieroglyphical account of the sleep of Horus, typical of the annual overflow of the Nile, by the late Mr. Paterson, in his Ingenious Essay on the Origin of the Hindu Religion. Asiatic Researches, vol. viii.

" When four more months, unmarked, have run their
course:
" To us all gloom—the curse has lost its force;
" The grief from separation born expires,
" And Autumn's nights reward our chaste desires.   744

" Once more I view thee, as mine eyes unclose,
" Laid by my side, and lulled by soft repose;
" And now I mark thee startle from thy sleep,
" Loose thy enfolding arms, and wake to weep: 748
" My anxious love long vainly seeks reply;
" Till, as the smile relumes that lucid eye,
" Thy arch avowal owns, that jealous fear
" Affrighted slumber, and aroused the tear.   752

" While thus, O goddess with the dark black eyes!
" My fond assurance confidence supplies,
" Let not the tales that idle tatlers bear,
" Subvert thy faith, nor teach thee to despair.   756
" True love no time nor distance can destroy;
" And, independent of all present joy,
" It grows in absence, as renewed delight,
" Some dear memorials, some loved lines excite."   760

Such, vast Dispenser of the dews of heaven!
Such is my suit, and such thy promise given:
Fearless, upon thy friendship I rely,
Nor ask that promise, nor expect reply.   764

Verse 764. *Nor ask that promise nor expect reply.*] We cannot help pausing here, to remark the ingenuity of the Poet in the con-

To thee the thirsty Chátakas complain;
Thy only answer is the falling rain:
And still such answer from the good proceeds,
Who grant our wishes, not in words, but deeds. 768

Thy task performed, consoled the mourner's mind,
Haste thy return these solitudes to find;
Soar from the mountain, whose exalted brow
The horns of Śiva's bull majestic plough, 772
And, hither speeding, to my sorrowing heart,
Shrunk like the bud at dawn, relief impart,
With welcome news my woes tumultuous still,
And all my wishes tenderly fulfil! 776
Then to whatever scenes invite thy way,
Waft thy rich stores, and grateful glooms convey;
And ne'er may destiny, like mine, divide
Thy brilliant spouse, the lightning, from thy side! 780

---

duct of his work. He sets out with excusing the apparent absurdity of the Yaksha's addressing himself to a Cloud as to a rational being, by introducing a pleasing and natural sentiment: see Verse 32. The Cloud has now received his charge; and something is expected by way of reply, expressive either of refusal or assent. To have given the Cloud any thing like the faculty of speech, would have been straining probability overmuch; and we see in the above lines with what neatness Kálidása has extricated himself from the dilemma.

Verse 773. Thus Ovid, in his Tristia:—
Prospera sic vobis maneat Fortuna, nec unquam,
Contacti simill sorte, rogetis opem.

So may on thee propitious fortune wait,
Nor may'st thou need such aid, nor mourn so sad a fate!

This said, he ceased:—the messenger of air
Conveyed to Alaká his wild despair.
The god of wealth, relenting, learnt his state;
And swift curtailed the limit of his fate, 784
Removed the curse, restored him to his wife,
And blest with ceaseless joy their everlasting life.

www.ingramcontent.com/pod-product-compliance
Lightning Source LLC
Chambersburg PA
CBHW022122290426
44112CB00008B/770